D0642716

THE SAMARITAN
STRATEGY

THE SAMARITAN STRATEGY

A New Agenda for Christian Activism

Colonel V. Doner

Wolgemuth & Hyatt, Publishers, Inc.
Brentwood, Tennessee

Unless otherwise noted, all Scripture quotations are from the
New International Version of the Bible, © 1973, 1978, International
Bible Society. Used by permission of Zondervan Bible Publishers.

Scripture quotations noted as TLB are taken from *The Living Bible*
(Wheaton, Illinois: Tyndale House, 1971) and are used by permission.

Scripture quotations noted as KJV are from the King James
Version of the Bible.

Wolgemuth & Hyatt, Publishers, Inc.
P.O. Box 1941, Brentwood, Tennessee 37027.

Printed in the United States of America.

Library of Congress Cataloging-in-Publication Data

Doner, Colonel V., 1948-
     The samaritan strategy: a new agenda for Christian activism /
     Colonel V. Doner   p.   cm.

Bibliography: p. 245
ISBN 0-943497-23-X : $13.95

     1. Christians—United States—Political activity.   2. Christian
     Right (Organization)   3. Conservatism—United States—
     History—20th century.   4. Church and social problems—
     United States—History—20th century.   I. Title.

BR526.D66   1988   322.4'4'0973—dc19   88-10627

For my Mother and Father

CONTENTS

ACKNOWLEDGMENTS

I am especially indebted to the patience of my bride Miriam who in the second year of our marriage not only supported my spending the time necessary to develop this manuscript but undertook a number of my ministry duties to free my time for writing. Her encouragement, research, and suggestions have been a tremendous help. Speaking of patience, Lorrie Cleveland who retyped this manuscript through five edits with amazing speed has genuinely proved her patience and her skill, and I am most grateful for her help.

I owe a special debt of gratitude to Ray Allen, chairman of the American Coalition for Life for his urging me to undertake this project and for his helpful comments on the manuscript. Gary Metz was invaluable in helping me conceptualize and refine much of the book's message, as well as providing strategic service in introducing me to some of the nation's finest editors and publishers. My editors, George Grant and Gretchen Passantino deserve recognition for their talent in graciously guiding the efforts of my first book.

I also owe a special thanks to Dick Key, Phil Sheldon, Victor and Sharon Porlier, and Bill Brister for their valuable suggestions and additions to the manuscript, and to Lisa Lavia and Jenni Hippenhammer for their cheerful labors.

And, of course, I am indebted to my two publishers, Robert Wolgemuth and Michael Hyatt for having the faith (or the courage) to publish this book.

PREFACE

In 1962, when I was almost thirteen years old, I read a small tract from an American missionary to South Vietnam who wrote about Communist soldiers invading mission compounds and driving chopsticks into the children's ears to break their eardrums so they would no longer hear their Christian teachers. At that moment I became filled with anger, indignation, and a resolve to resist with all my might such evil.

Without knowing it, I was embarking on a twenty-five year journey to restore justice, righteousness (conformity to God's principles), and mercy to our world. By the time I reached my fourteenth year, I had consumed over ten thousand pages of books and tracts on the "evils of Communism."

While Jerry Falwell was still preaching against Christians being involved in politics,[1] I was organizing Christian conservative youth chapters on high school campuses and had been featured in several newspaper articles.

Less than twenty years later, in 1978, I co-founded Christian Voice, a Washington D.C.-based political organization that *U.S. News & World Report* called "the vanguard" of the Christian Right. In the short span of just eight years (until April 1986 when my staff and I left Christian Voice to its new director) I watched the Christian Right launch itself high into orbit from a platform of enormous success and anticipation only to crash back to earth as a burnt out hulk.

I write this book not as an epitaph on the Christian Right gravestone but with hopes of its transformation into something different, more powerful, and more spiritually mature. As never before, our world needs the love, guidance, wisdom, and integrity that Christian leadership can provide. Millions are now crying out for God's answers to problems that man has failed to solve — war, poverty, exploitation, degeneracy, violence, disease, vanity, greed, selfishness, and all their myriad manifestations.

The Christian Church has an opportunity to lead. But first we must learn some lessons from the failure of those pioneers of the Christian Right who launched the first assault upon the apathy of the Church and the multiple tragedies bred by that apathy.

INTRODUCTION

Books are like letters. They are written to someone. Someone specific, not just anyone.

Who is it then that this book is addressed to? It is written to you, if you can identify with any of the following situations:

Overly Involved: You're burnt out. Trying to save the world on your own energy has left you depleted. Or maybe disillusioned. You've spent years as an activist. What good has it really done? What difference have all your efforts made in the long run? Aren't our nation and world in worse shape than when we began? You're concerned that the investment of your time and energy will not make a lasting difference. You fear you may be building on sand rather than rock.

Almost Involved: You've often felt that as a Christian you should be more involved in "social issues" or meeting the needs of others. But you weren't sure just how. The rigid agendas announced in a shrill voice by both the Christian Left and the Christian Right did not seem to represent a Christ-like approach to community involvement. So you backed off, but you still feel you should "be doing something."

The Searching: Your heart is after God. You're committed to learn to serve and obey Him. The question is, what does He really want you to do? And how? And where do you begin?

The Reformers: You have burning zeal to right social wrongs, to protect the innocent, to vanquish evil. You're heartsick over the lack of righteousness in our own land. There is so much to do. How are you to proceed in God's strength and wisdom and not your own? How can you really impact our community, our nation, and our world?

Never Involved: But you're curious. You wonder about the meaning of your life. Does God have a purpose for your life?

What is the Gospel all about anyway? What's all this talk about loving your neighbor, serving others, helping the helpless, the hapless, the homeless, the oppressed, the exploited? How does all this fit in with God's expectations of you?

If you identify with any of these situations, this book is written to you and for you.

In the last twenty-five years I have been through all of the stages I have just profiled. The last twenty years were spent as a full-time crusader for one cause or another. The last ten years as one of the leaders of the Christian Right.

Two years ago, after undreamed of success, I "dropped out." I was physically, emotionally, and spiritually drained. So was my senior staff. Within ninety days, we all left the organization and the movement we had committed so much of our life to.

I began to spend months seeking God's direction for my life, for our Church, our nation. I spent two years traveling the nation, meeting with our leaders who felt much the same as I — asking the question, where has the Christian Right, the Church, our nation, gone wrong?

I spent months on end searching the Scriptures — what did God really want His people to do? I was tired of no vision, my vision, or some other leader's vision. I wanted God's vision for my life, my Church, my nation, and my world.

From the many mistakes and offenses I've committed, from all the wrong turns and dead ends I've taken, I believe that God in His mercy has allowed my many failings to be used redemptively. If others, seeing God's vision, can avoid the many mistakes I and my colleagues made in the manner in which we pursued what we thought were Godly objectives, then this book will have accomplished its purpose.

The Samaritan Strategy is not just a different version of the same old tune, "How do Christians take over America?" While it does offer a new understanding of how we can restore justice and righteousness to our community and our world, it is much more. *The Samaritan Strategy* involves a way of life — our life — and it involves God's deepest purposes for our lives.

It is also an analysis of what went wrong with Christendom's latest agenda-oriented movement (the Christian Right) and, indeed, what goes wrong with most such movements, regardless of their theology or political slant.

But before we unfold the Samaritan Strategy, we will need to understand the state of "Christian activism today."

Chapters 1 and 2 chronicle the rise of the last wave of Christian activism, the Christian Right.

The path blazed by the Christian Right is critical to our understanding the challenges facing a reawakened Church. As the Evangelical Church slowly emerges from its eighty years of self-imposed exile from involvement with government, culture, and social needs, it will invariably get off to a number of false starts.

The Christian Right was not the first false start, and it will not be the last. But we can learn much from its mistakes.

Chapter 3 provides us with insight into why not only the Christian Right failed to accomplish its agenda, but also why so many well meaning movements fail.

The Christian Right failed in its mission because it was not perceived as Christ-like. The Christian Right, in demanding a society conformed to Godly moral behavior (righteousness) failed to emphasize an equally important need for social justice and mercy. Rather than seeing compassionate hearts motivated by love to solve the nation's problems, all too often the public saw only strong wills committed to fostering a particular moral/political agenda. Floundering without real direction or spiritual leadership and without a primary commitment to people's real needs first (and a political agenda second), the Christian Right was doomed to failure. Americans were searching for leaders that would put their needs first, not just the leaders' agenda first. They were looking for compassion, not just passion; love, not just logic. Learning from the mistakes of the Christian Right, we now have a rare opportunity to meet the needs of our generation.

Chapter 4 returns to the time of the American Civil War to understand the genesis of our Church's tragic commitment to noninvolvement and its avoidance of the great moral challenges of our day. It is not a pretty picture.

Chapter 5 offers a startling assessment of the needs and concerns of our generation. We investigate not the symptomatic problems like pornography and disrespect for authority and tradition but the underlying root causes. Rampant exploitation — in which we have all participated, both as perpetrator and victim —

has led to endemic alienation, particularly from our leaders. The result is a fearful people and a nation on the verge of total collapse.

It is clear that the American Church has lost its vision. So, in Chapter 6 we ask, what is God's vision for our communities, our world? And just as important, what attitude must guide our hearts if we are to honor God as we serve others in response to this vision?

In Chapter 7 we look to find out what part God expects us to play in bringing about His vision for our people. In the Good Samaritan, we will find our model.

In Chapter 8 we take a fresh approach to Christ's Lordship and the political process. We will offer a Biblical and carefully balanced approach to the process of governing.

Chapters 9 through 11 present a radically new agenda for Christians who would follow our Lord's mandate to serve others and make a difference. The problems are not new. The solutions are (at least to our modern day Church). AIDS, poverty, the elderly, exploitation, pornography, abortion, war, and oppression. What can we do? Can we balance justice with compassion, righteousness with love, political or Church activity with service? We can, and we must.

In Chapter 12 we see the necessity for developing new leaders to meet the pressing needs of our generation. Who will these leaders be? What qualities will they require? How will they lead? We will see that many of the answers will be found in "the Samaritan Strategy."

Chapter 13 answers the question, how do we begin? What do we do first . . . and how? How can we learn to balance self-effort with relying on God? How much does God expect us to do and how much will He do?

I write this book not as an epitaph on yesterday's Christian activism but as a recognition of its transformation into something different, more powerful, and more spiritually mature. Millions are now crying out for God's answers to problems that man has failed to solve—war, poverty, exploitation, degeneracy, violence, disease, vanity, greed, selfishness, and all their myriad manifestations. As never before, our world needs the love, guidance, wisdom and integrity that only a revitalized Christian leadership can provide.

I believe that in the parable of the Good Samaritan, God has given us the key to renewed vision, to revitalized leadership, and to a restored nation.

> On one occasion an expert in the law stood up to test Jesus. "Teacher," he asked, "what must I do to inherit eternal life?"
>
> "What is written in the Law?" He replied, "How do you read it?"
>
> He answered: "Love the Lord your God with all your heart and with all your soul and with all your strength and with all your mind"; and, "Love your neighbor as yourself."
>
> "You have answered correctly," Jesus replied. "Do this and you will live."
>
> But he wanted to justify himself, so he asked Jesus, "And who is my neighbor?"
>
> In reply Jesus said: "A man was going down from Jerusalem to Jericho, when he fell into the hands of robbers. They stripped him of his clothes, beat him and went away, leaving him half dead. A priest happened to be going down the same road, and when he saw the man, he passed by on the other side. So too, a Levite, when he came to the place and saw him, passed by on the other side. But a Samaritan, as he traveled, came where the man was; and when he saw him *he took pity on him.* He went to him and bandaged his wounds, pouring on oil and wine. Then he put the man on his own donkey, took him to an inn and took care of him. The next day he took out two silver coins and gave them to the innkeeper. *"Look after him."* he said, "and when I return, I will reimburse you for any extra expense you may have."
>
> "Which of these three do you think was a neighbor to the man who fell into the hands of robbers?"
>
> The expert in the law replied, "The one who had mercy on him."
>
> Jesus told him, *"Go and do likewise."* (Luke 10:25-37, italics added)

That is *the Samaritan Strategy. That* is the "new agenda for Christian activism."

THE RISE OF THE CHRISTIAN RIGHT

Have you ever been so outraged by something that our government or "the establishment" did or should have done and didn't that you thought to yourself, *if only I was running things, they would be different?*

Then have you wondered if it would ever be possible for you to actually influence or even redirect our government's policies? If you did, you probably dismissed such thoughts as fantasy. After all, most of us believe that like our vote, our voices don't really count.

Yet in the early eighties a relatively small movement of Christian men and women concerned with deteriorating morals and increasing national instability proved this time-worn cliché of political impotence to be unfounded. They were called the Christian Right. Despite their mistakes and the recent collapsing of their leadership, they effectively demonstrated that we as citizens still have the ability to make ourselves heard or to replace those who govern but cannot hear.

Such was the case in 1980 when a few organizations like *Christian Voice, Moral Majority,* and the *Religious Roundtable,* with limited funds and no more than twenty full-time political workers in their combined offices (press reports to the contrary were tremendously exaggerated) served as a catalyst to focus upon the built-up frustrations of millions of Christians.

The results were incredible, beginning with the election of a president committed to a new agenda. The news media reported:

> The impact of the *Religious Right* on Tuesday's election was even greater than anticipated, and yesterday President-elect Ronald Reagan said the message will not be ignored.

"I am going to be open to these people," Reagan said. "I'm not going to separate myself from the people who elected us and sent us there."

The *Religious Right*, once a major source of support for President Jimmy Carter, himself a "born-again" Southern Baptist, came out in numbers that shocked pollsters and politicians alike.

Millions of Evangelical Christians flocked to the polls, crucifying politicians who failed to conform to their definition of morality.

Pollsters say the Evangelicals — members of such groups as the *Moral Majority, Christian Voice, Religious Roundtable* and the *Californians for Biblical Morality* were most instrumental in defeating candidates who were viewed as liberal on the moral issues in the campaign.[1]

Obviously we had played a major role in defeating an incumbent president and in changing the decades-long liberal domination of the U.S. Senate.

Senator George McGovern, the shocked and just defeated leader of the Senate's liberal Democrats, warned that the Christian Right had "the potential to alter the course of American history."[2]

In 1984 this new influence in American politics was continuing to make itself felt. The Christian Right had been actively joined by most of the nation's TV ministers, giving us a perception of tremendous national strength. In recognition of our new-found potential, the Reagan campaign relied on us to secure the president's re-election and the Republican Party courted us aggressively. More media attention brought more money and therefore more effectiveness than ever before.

We suspected that we were well on the way to realizing the rosy future that was depicted in a four-hundred-page survey on American opinion published by the Connecticut Mutual Life Insurance Company in 1981. It predicted:

This report identifies a cohesive and powerful group of Americans, approximately 45 million strong, as "intensely religious," and demonstrates that religious Americans are likely to vote often and to become highly involved in their local communities. As a consequence, the effect of this group is spreading across the nation. These Americans have been able to inject religious and moral issues directly into political discourse, extending their influence far beyond that which their numerical strength alone would suggest.

Our findings suggest that the increasing impact of religion on our social and political institutions may be only the beginning of a trend that could change the face of America.[3]

Yet even as we counted our most recent victories, our death knell was being sounded.

Is the Christian Right Dead?

As early as 1984, a conservative thinker and theologian, Richard Neuhaus, observed, "the religious new right as an identifiable movement may have peaked."[4]

By mid-1987 Cal Thomas, former vice-president of the Moral Majority, in his nationally syndicated newspaper column, pronounced the Christian Right to be dead.

It should be obvious to the thoughtful observer that the Christian Right went off track, missing its potential destination of re-directing America to a better future. Sidetracked by misreading vital spiritual signals, the movement derailed, resulting in the total breakdown of its once powerful locomotive — the coalition of national TV ministers and political organizations that pulled the Christian Right train.

But what about the rest of the train? All the passenger cars filled with hundreds of thousands of pastors, concerned mothers, local activists, businessmen, bright-eyed, energetic college students, all committed to helping America return to God's standard of justice, mercy, and righteousness. I believe that they (along with a few of the engineers who abandoned the locomotive before it self-destructed) will benefit immensely from the lessons the Christian Right's shortcomings have taught us.

There is no doubt that the Christian Right helped to change the course of history. There is no question that the Christian Right was the catalyst for launching a new wave of Evangelical action, a new expression of concern, a new extension of our mandate to be "salt and light."

The questions that we must face now is where do we go from here? How do we clarify what God wants us to do as individuals, and how do we collectively work together to accomplish God's larger purposes for our lives and our world?

In other words, what is God's vision for us as a generation of Americans entering the last and most critical decade of this century? And how do we fulfill our mandate without repeating the mistakes of the pioneers of the Christian Right? These questions and the many implications they have for our lives are the focus of this book.

It is my deep desire to share with you the mistakes we made in trying to build a better world for our children. It is my heart's prayer to be used of God to stimulate you to reconsider your obligation before God to participate fully in a new vision of love and service to mankind.

We can only find true joy, real self-expression, and ultimate fulfillment when we synchronize ourselves with God's plan for our lives. "For we are God's workmanship, created in Christ Jesus to do good works, which God prepared in advance for us to do" (Ephesians 2:20 NIV). But before we begin our exciting journey to build meaningful lives, in obedience to our Lord's command to provide healing for our nation, we need to learn a little history about the rise and fall of the Christian Right.

The Rise of the Christian Right

The advent of the Christian Right was one of the major spiritual and political developments of the 1980s, as theologian Richard Neuhaus stated in his book *The Naked Public Square*:

> In the eighth decade of this century a new thing happened that portends, I believe, major changes in American religion and politics. The new thing was the religious new right.[5]

Following Ronald Reagan's landslide election in 1980, an anti-Christian Right group called Americans United for Separation of Church and State issued a year-end report that concluded:

> The emergence of the Evangelical Christian political movement was the most significant Church-state development of 1980. . . . The rise of the fundamentalist political groups like Moral Majority and Christian Voice has provoked more public debate on the proper relationship of religion and government

than any issue in several years. The phenomenon clearly was the premier Church-state issue of 1980.[6]

It was not new for Christians to be involved in politics. After all, the entire civil rights movement was led by clergymen. To a great, extent the anti-Vietnam War peace movement was aided and abetted, if not led, by elements of the liberal Protestant and Catholic hierarchies.

But what was new was that Christians were getting involved from a conservative perspective, rather than from the traditional liberal perspective with which twentieth-century Christians were expected to identify (i.e., the National Council of Churches, noted for supporting any number of liberal causes). As liberal critic Erling Jorstad observed in his book *The Politics of Moralism*:

> As the call for repentance and revival mounted throughout 1980, one astounding feature came to dominate the movement. The leaders and supporters were largely from the Evangelical and fundamentalist wings of American Protestantism, with some conservative Jews, Protestants, and Catholics alongside. So unexpected to the professional political observers was the entrance of this bloc that they did not know quite what to make of it.[7]

The Big News

The Christian Right was also "the big news story" of the early eighties because the media made it big news. Many Christian Right organizations were to some degree a creation of the media. The news media made our organizations look much larger and stronger than we actually were. It was true that the Christian Right, a spontaneous, localized grassroots movement consisting of tens of thousands of volunteers, was viable and growing; but the media consistently gave the few national Christian Right organizations credit for larger budgets, more members, and more "muscle" than actually existed. Memberships and financial strengths were routinely inflated by both the media and the Christian Right organizations themselves.

But the media needed a good story in 1980 and the emergence of the Christian Right seemed to be as good as any. The media did not understand the Christian Right. They did not understand Evangelicals. What was this new animal? I remember a number of times being interviewed by liberal New York network reporters who had no idea what an Evangelical Christian was. Their nearest conception of a Christian was a Catholic priest. When the media found out that there were forty to sixty million Evangelicals, they were even more curious, if not downright intimidated.

So the involvement of Christians in right-wing politics became big news! Would we unseat Jimmy Carter? Would we take over the United States Congress? Would we dominate the government *à la* the Ayatolla in Iran? What was going on here? Nobody seemed to really know, but the news media had decided to focus its attention on our efforts. In the process the massive publicity helped us mobilize tens of thousands, perhaps hundreds of thousands of volunteers and dollars.

The media coverage was so intense that I remember traveling to a small town in Iowa to speak to a few dozen people and there before me were Japanese and Swedish television network crews filming the event to broadcast "back home." It was not unusual for us to have all three networks calling my office on any one day demanding interviews, statements, information, etc.

What Was the Christian Right?

Before going further, I should give my definition of what the words *Christian Right* meant in common usage. The term *Christian Right* developed from the hybrid of two distinctives, *Christian* and *Right*. Members of the Christian faith took a "right-wing" political position or actively supported rightist causes. The term *right* by itself carries no particular moral meaning as in "right" or "wrong." In current political jargon, "leftist" usually refers to anyone who is liberal, i.e., left of center, such as Ted Kennedy or Walter Mondale, or "far left," which would be members of the Socialist or Communist party or their sympathizers. Rightists are those right of center, ranging from conservatives like Ronald Reagan and Barry Goldwater to "far right" libertarians like the late Ayn Rand who believe in little or no government at all.

Both conservatives and liberals espouse a similar goal, developing a just and humane society where people can live in peace. Secular liberals tend to believe that man is perfectible in and of himself. They believe the government, as the instrument of man, can solve most or all social problems, given enough time and money. Therefore, they rely heavily upon government programs, "big government" welfare expenditures, behavioral or environmental modification, and all of the latest psychological and sociological theories for the perfection of man. Karl Marx was the "ultimate" leftist as he proposed a Communist utopia where there would be no exploitation of the workers and no injustice.

Conservatives tend to be more cynical (they would say "realistic") in their approach, more leery of the fallen side of human nature. They do not believe that, left to their own devices, men will usually do what is right. They tend to suspect that most men are prone to malfeasance if not downright evil. Therefore, they want to keep government limited in its scope and power so that men do not accumulate too much power to do evil. Their answer for most social ills, rather than turning to an all-powerful government, is to rely on free enterprise systems to create jobs and affluence and to allow people the freedom to solve their own problems.

How the Christian Right Began

So now that we know what the term *Christian Right* meant, the next question, is how did it begin? What gave rise to the Christian Right? As Neuhaus observed,

> To be precise, it did not just happen in the late seventies; it had been happening long before that, or perhaps it is better to say that it had been building for a long time, getting ready to happen. In any case, with a suddenness that shocked most observers, it came to public attention in the year prior to the 1980 elections.[8]

Christian Right political activity had been building since the early sixties but received a massive boost in the late seventies. Christians were beginning to awaken to what Francis Schaeffer termed "post-Christian America." Sleepy Churches were rudely awakened to a "new" America, one in which government, media, and the educational elite were no longer practicing a policy of "benevolent neglect." Rather than taking a neutral or even generally supportive stance toward a Christian society, the "establishment," spurred on by a secular humanistic ethic and aggressive antagonists like the American Civil Liberties Union (ACLU), had clearly moved into an adversarial position against the Church. As the *New York Times* reported on February 19, 1980:

> Polls and interviews with Evangelicals make it clear that they believe their moral and spiritual values are no longer reflected in public policy. In the past they were largely confident that the country was "Christian" and that government generally did act on their concern for such matters as family life and religion in the schools; they now say they feel like outsiders who must fight the forces of "secular humanism" and atheism on such issues as abortion.

"Evangelicals suddenly found themselves standing almost alone on the front line of socio-political conflict, defending what had once automatically been assumed to be general American values," Dr. Harold O. J. Brown, a professor of theology at Trinity Evangelical Divinity School in Deerfield, Illinois, wrote recently.[9]

The founders of the Christian Right correctly observed that an increasingly secularized society was systematically attacking Christian values. This attack was most noticeably reflected in a change of the nation's law-base legalizing pornography, homosexuality, abortion, and the general liberalizing of restraints against sexual promiscuity. The attack also took form directly against the Church, the Christian school movement, and the home-schooling movement. It found its way into the Supreme Court, goaded by the ACLU and other humanistic advocates, and succeeded in taking God out of school and ruling against other Judeo-Christian values.

As Erling Jorstad observed in *The Politics of Moralism*:

> During those years the Supreme Court handed down several major decisions which helped increase Evangelical/fundamentalist frustration over the direction of American life. In 1973 the court greatly expanded the kinds of legal abortions allowed; it upheld busing of school children to achieve racial balance; it continued to prohibit religious exercises, such as Bible reading and prayer in public schools. It gave extensive flexibility to publishers and movie producers, who responded with what many thought were pornographic materials. Efforts by Congressmen to over-

ride these decisions by constitutional amendments were either bottled up in committees or defeated on the floor.[10]

Christians woke up to a post-Christian America that had grown away from Christian values and, in fact, had ardently opposed many of the values Christians held dear. Clearly, it was time to regain control.

What Were the Christian Right's
Fundamental Assumptions?

Part of the problem is that the Christian Right was never able to articulate a coherent philosophy of government or even a "platform" of ideas. This inability to project a clearly defined vision was one of the main reasons for the collapse of the Christian Right. Devoid of any systematic philosophy, the Christian Right's basic goal was to return America to a more "Godly society," which had vague similarities to either the 1950s or the 1850s, depending on with whom you talked. The Christian Right suggested it wanted to establish a sense of national righteousness (conforming men to God's laws). This desire found expression in attempting to correct a number of social ills that were variously perceived as threatening family, religion, national defense, personal safety, and the like.

Pollster Lou Harris, certainly no Christian Rightist, in his book *Inside America* described the ideological right, which we in the Christian Right were aligned with, this way:

> The coterie of issues that drew the ideological right together ranged from foreign policy objectives such as a huge buildup of arms to face the worldwide menace of Communism, a liberation of Central America from the clutches of Castro in Cuba and the Sandinistan government in Nicaragua, ridding Africa of Communist incursions as in Angola and Ethiopia . . . to domestic priorities such as outlawing abortion, defeating the Equal Rights Amendment, doing away with sex education in the schools and access to birth control for teenagers, introducing prayer into the schools, banning evolution from the school curriculum, allowing parents to take their children out of school to educate them in accordance with a new moral dictum, outlawing pornography, opposing all efforts to control the

sale and ownership of guns, barring homosexuals from any jobs in the public sector and especially in the schools, and ending all busing to achieve racial balance.[11]

All in all, not a bad description. But many people wanted to know what the goals of the Christian Right were *apart from the secular right*. These goals were never articulated because we never quite figured out what they were. We took it a "step at a time" and figured the first goal should be both electing men and women to Congress who would reflect Christian value systems and electing a conservative president. Eventually the goal would be to return America to a "strong nation" (morally, militarily, and economically) that would seek to export freedom and free enterprise to the rest of the world and would stop the expansion of the Soviet Union's colonial empire. Domestically, the Christian Right sought to return America to a "pre-1960s" set of moral and legal standards, i.e., outlawing abortion and pornography, returning prayer to school, etc. We generally envisioned a Church and business community unencumbered by government regulation, an America where citizens were free to pursue life, liberty, and happiness as guaranteed in the United States Constitution.

One last assumption that influenced our tone of urgency and "crisis" was that we believed time was running out and if we didn't "do something," no one else would. The world was in bad shape and only getting worse after generations of a slumbering Church. To make up for lost time we had to work extra hard, we thought, if we were to salvage the Republic from the gloom and doom that seemed to be just around the corner. I might add that if one read the daily newspapers, it didn't take being paranoid to become concerned about the rate at which America was "free falling" toward social and moral disintegration.

T W O

CHANGING HISTORY

What did the Christian Right actually accomplish? *Christianity Today* credited the Christian Right with helping to bring Ronald Reagan's pro-Christian and moral agenda into being. Even Lou Harris admitted,

> Ronald Reagan was the first president in modern times who appeared to be committed to the new theology of the right; a Church-based coalition determined to bring a new moral order to politics, then to government, then into such private institutions as the press and TV and, finally, into the daily lives of people themselves.[1]

Numerous polls and studies conducted after the 1980 presidential election indicated that white Evangelicals, particularly in the Southern states, deserted Carter by the millions, giving Ronald Reagan seven of the ten percentage points by which he won.

In a little-noted post-election analysis, Harris said that the key to the election rested in the hands of the twenty-eight percent of the white voters who are "followers of the so-called moral majority TV preachers." He also noted,

> Most specifically, it was their efforts which largely turned around the white Baptist vote in the South. Jimmy Carter won the white Baptist vote in 1976 by 56 to 43 percent against Gerald Ford. This time he lost the white Baptists by a 56 to 34 percent margin. The white followers of the TV Evangelical preachers gave Ronald Reagan two-thirds of his ten-point margin in the election.[2]

Through the efforts of the Christian Right, Ronald Reagan had won an incredible two-thirds of the nation's white Evangelical vote that made up eighteen percent of the total votes cast in the 1980 presidential contest.[3]

That, of course, is precisely what we had planned when I and a few colleagues formed *Christians for Reagan*, the nation's first "Christian political action committee," (PAC) and in that year the nation's tenth largest PAC in terms of independent expenditures on behalf of a presidential candidate.

We distributed hundreds of tapes of evangelist George Otis's interview with Ronald Reagan to radio stations and Christian television stations. In the interview Reagan gave his testimony and described himself as born again. This was the first part of our strategy to demonstrate that while Carter was a self-described Christian, so too at least was candidate Reagan.

Jimmy Carter's Achilles' Heel

The second part of our strategy was to show that Jimmy Carter was at the very least inconsistent in acting out his Christian faith when it came to government policy. One afternoon over lunch, my assistant, Sandra Ostby, said ABC network news was calling her daily to see if we were going to do any anti-Carter TV spots. Realizing that ABC was essentially offering us hundreds of thousands of dollars of free air time, I scratched out on the back of a napkin a short sixty-second commercial assailing Carter's stands on gay rights legislation, prayer in school, and abortion. Because I only had forty-eight hours to make ABC's deadline for its network news programs, I hired a local crew in our small town of Pacific Grove to show up at our old Victorian office building the next day.

I had Sandra sit on the porch and read from hastily prepared cue cards to tell how she as a Christian mother of four children could not possibly vote for Jimmy Carter because of his stands on moral issues. This commercial was combined with an even more controversial spot that utilized snippets of a gay rights march in San Francisco, followed by a picture of Jimmy Carter and the announcer mentioning the gay rights plank Carter had inserted in the Democratic party platform. It was simply too much for the president to bear.

Within a few days, during a national press conference, Carter attacked these "vicious" television commercials. This was a serious mistake on the president's part because it pushed an issue that would have been ignored, onto the front pages of every newspaper from our local *Monterrey Herald* to the *Washington Post*. The press not only reported Carter's direct attack, but also gave wide coverage to our charge regarding Carter's stand on the homosexual issue.

On Friday, October 31, only four days before the election, the nation's papers followed the lead of the *Washington Post*, which ran headlines that screamed "pro-Reagan TV spots depict President as gay rights advocate."

When it was all over, a tired and defeated Jimmy Carter acknowledged that the Christian Right "had a very profound effect" on his defeat.[4] The news media, certainly no friend of the Christian Right, summed up the elections as a major victory for the Christian Right.

Those Controversial "Report Cards"

Nineteen-eighty was also the first year we debuted the "individualized version" of our report card. Each "report card" was carefully crafted to demonstrate how a particular member of Congress had voted on four or five moral issues that we felt were of importance to the Christian community. The cards were printed on one side of a five-inch by seven-inch piece of paper and therefore were extremely inexpensive to reproduce. They simply stated how a congressman voted on a particular issue such as abortion, national defense, or a balanced budget. Each voter was then asked to contrast how he or she would have wanted his or her own congressman to vote. Contrary to some critics' charges, the report card never impugned a member of Congress's Christian commitment or moral integrity. It was simply a record of how they voted in Congress.

We were well aware, of course, that millions of Christians had no idea how their representatives in Congress vote (or even who they are!). It is difficult to have a truly representative Democracy if members of Congress know they don't have to accurately represent the people at home because the people at home never find out how they vote once they're in Washington. We expected that if Christians and conservative churches throughout a given congressional district were made aware of how their congressman had voted, it might make a difference. But we were in no way prepared for the dramatic impact that, in fact, our report cards had. Over thirty members of Congress, including the Senate's liberal leadership were consigned to early retirement, due in part to our report card effort. (Obviously President Reagan's unseating of Jimmy Carter and the impact of other conservative groups were extremely significant.)

The best example of our success was Senator John Culver of Iowa, one of the Senate's most liberal spokesmen, who had gone down in a blaze of defeat while complaining loudly about us awarding him a zero percent rating on the report cards we mass-distributed throughout Iowa. We had set up shop in the state and ABC network news was following me from pillar to post, recording every word for broadcast the following evening. It was not unusual for us to find television cameras from networks in Japan, Sweden, Germany, England, and Canada, that focused on what the media called a "classic battle" between liberals and the Christian Right.

Dan Rather, in a "60 Minutes" feature on the Iowa race, posed the question to me of why we were trying to defeat John Culver, who was regarded by his colleagues as "very bright and tenacious." My rather ungracious reply was that being bright and tenacious was not a recommendation in itself, because Joe Stalin, Adolph Hitler, Mao Tse-Tung, and the Ayatolla were also bright and tenacious. I said that what counted was Senator Culver being in step with the people of Iowa, which meant not voting for abortion, big government spending, or opposing prayer in school. While my statement was technically correct, I'm afraid it reflected a lack of balance and grace that was all too typical of myself and our movement.

Liberal hero U.S. Senator George McGovern, reflecting on his defeat, blamed "false information spread throughout South Dakota by Evangelicals."[5] Also surprising was the defeat of Indiana's John Brademas, the House Democratic Majority Whip who was the third-most powerful Democrat in Congress when he was defeated by John Hyler, a 27-year-old who had never run before for public office but who had dozens of churches in the district distributing our report cards.

This liberal "Waterloo" was fully reported by a shocked news media. *U. S. News & World Report* magazine recapped the election this way:

> Twenty-three of twenty-eight Congressmen defeated: with low ratings on two million moral-issues report cards distributed across the country. . . . The victims included not only McGovern, but also such Democratic senators as Birch Bayh in Indiana, John Culver of Iowa, Frank Church of Idaho, Gaylord Nelson of Wisconsin, and John Durkin of New Hampshire.[6]

The four hundred page survey on *American Values in the 80s,* published by the Connecticut Mutual Life Insurance Company concluded,

> It is widely accepted that political-religious groups . . . were a significant force in recent Congressional and Presidential elections.[7]

Of course, while I was pursuing these activities, both Ed McAteer of the Religious Roundtable and Jerry Falwell were very effective traveling to hundreds of cities throughout the country, stirring up the troops and attempting to get them organized into grassroots units. A major Religious Roundtable event was held in Dallas and featured Ronald Reagan speaking to over eighteen thousand ministers gathered from throughout the country. Organized by Ed McAteer and hosted by James Robison, this event was clearly pivotal in energizing the clergy on behalf of Ronald Reagan.

The Re-election of Ronald Reagan

In 1984, observers of Republican party politics had every reason to believe that the Reagan camp possessed a cocky assurance that their man was a shoo-in. He was a popular president who had won an historic 1980 landslide victory and faced a lackluster candidate in Walter Mondale.

But such was not the case. The presidential bid of fiery black leader, Jesse Jackson, had literally thrown the fear of God into the Republican strategists. Reagan's inner circle didn't fear that Jesse would win the Democratic nomination and go on to defeat the president through sheer charisma; but they were acutely sensitive to the very slim number of votes with which Reagan had won in the Southern states in 1980 compared with the huge numbers of unregistered blacks in those same states. Simple arithmetic pointed to the probability that if Jackson's campaign successfully registered record numbers of black voters to build his own support, and if these voters voted for the Democratic nominee in November, Reagan could easily lose his advantage in those states. Without those states Reagan could not win re-election.

The atmosphere I stepped into within the inner circles of the Reagan command stunned me. Rather than finding a supremely confident presidential campaign committee, I found a condition bordering on hysteria. The situation in the South looked glum. In many of the Southern states Reagan had carried in 1980 by only a few thousand votes, Jackson was registering ten times that many new black (Democratic) voters. In fact, the Reagan campaign staff was so nervous about Jackson, they were daily monitoring his progress.

The campaign staff was also convinced that their effort to re-elect the president was being sabotaged (unintentionally) by incompetence within the Republican party's national staff and by an overly cautious White House staff afraid for the president to be "too outspoken." It is hard to run for president, even for re-election, and not be outspoken! But the White House staff didn't want to "stir up the waters."

Ironically enough, it was the perceived threat of Jesse Jackson that forced the Reagan strategists to turn to the Christian community as the perfect counterbalance. Reagan strategists believed (with our coaching, of course) that there were equal numbers of unregistered white Evangelical Christians in those Southern states who could neatly offset any potential Democratic votes that the Jackson campaign signed up. To mobilize the Christian community on behalf of the committee to re-elect Reagan/Bush, the committee authorized the establishment of a *Christian Advisory Counsel* of a dozen key Christian leaders that was to meet bi-weekly at Reagan headquarters to plan strategy. I served as chairman of this task force. In fact, John Buchanan of the *People for the American Way*, cited my appointment in a nationally syndicated column complaining that there was an unhealthy connection between the Republican Party and the Christian Right.[8]

It was through this connection that we obtained a million dollar grant from Republican sources to fund the new *American Coalition for Traditional Values* (ACTV). In a full-page feature, *Newsweek* magazine reported: "The creation of ACTV signals a new era in American religion and politics."[9] With the newly acquired funds, ACTV (chaired by Dr. Tim LaHaye) sent out an impressive series of mailings to over 100,000 conservative churches. The mailings were followed up by a national telephone call from Ronald Reagan that linked together thousands of pastors to hear the president "personally" talking to them. The purpose of this unprecedented campaign was to get each Church to conduct a "voter registration Sunday" and to turn their members out to vote on election day.

Of course the ACTV campaign was only one aspect of a major all-out push by the Christian Right to re-elect their hero, Ronald Reagan.

In addition to ACTV's efforts, the Moral Majority busily organized volunteers in several key states and conducted an all-out organizational campaign in the state of North Carolina, where they had a full-time state director. Pat Robertson's *Freedom Council*, caught in the midst of a total staff changeover, "did virtually nothing on the 1984 campaign," according to one of its former national directors. But Pat himself used his daily TV show with tremendous effectiveness to politically educate and motivate his millions of viewers.

An important factor in the Christian Right's ability to communicate with the nation and even with its own troops was the news media's willingness to make Jerry Falwell the unquestioned spokesman for the Christian Right. In fact, the media soon began referring to the whole Christian Right as the Moral Majority, the name of Falwell's much smaller and less powerful political organization. But what Moral Majority lacked in terms of field organization, materials, or manpower, it more than made up for in its chief spokesman's access to the national media.

Falwell was on national TV talk shows and news programs such as "Meet the Press," or the front pages of the nation's newspapers almost daily. He was an unusual combination of politician and revivalist, of promoter and missionary, of TV star and country pastor. Some found him pompous, arrogant, and abrasive. Others found him sincere, forceful, and articulate. He relished the battle. He smiled his way through even the most difficult confrontations. He was the perfect spokesman for the Christian Right.

Stopping Mondale

The Christian Right (myself included) felt that, should Walter Mondale be elected, it would place the last nails in the "secular humanist" coffin being prepared for Christians in the United States. We devoted ourselves to making sure this scenario did not become a reality. Afterward many of us (again, including myself) were physically, financially, and emotionally depleted.

As our first tactic, I commissioned a series of TV commercials (much more sophisticated than our 1980 variety, but carrying essentially the same message) featuring Mondale's blatant pro-abortion and gay rights stances. As they had in 1980, all the network newscasts gave us "free access" to tens of millions of voters as they aired excerpts from our commercials. And, history repeating itself, Mondale, as Jimmy Carter had done in 1980, took to the front pages of the nation's press to assail Ronald Reagan for "embracing religious zealots."

Mondale's defensiveness only served to increase the magnitude of our attack. I rushed to production a national "television special" to promote voter registration and began hosting a daily radio commentary nationwide to help organize volunteer networks. We scored another "media hit" with the thirty-page *Presidential Biblical Scoreboard* magazine, which I co-published with its creator, David Balsinger.

It was the first time any publication portrayed both how all current federal officeholders voted as well as how their challengers stood on over a dozen moral issues. Mailed to over one hundred thousand churches, the *Scoreboard* immediately created a sensation. All three network news programs featured it, and Walter Mondale lashed out at the publication, claiming it made him appear "anti-family and un-Christian." I was particularly delighted to have earned Mondale's personal ire in both 1980 and 1984. *If he's attacking us, we must be having an impact,* I thought.

The Republican Convention

The Christian Right made its impact felt at the Republican convention in Dallas that August of 1984 in other ways beside the _Biblical Scoreboard_. TV evangelists Robison, Swaggart, and Falwell all addressed the GOP platform committee, giving the Christian Right's position on various issues from abortion to gay rights. I well remember the sense of excitement sitting in a room, helping them prepare their statements at the last moment before they walked out to the glare of the cameras, to have their comments broadcast by all three TV networks. In addition both Falwell and Robison were asked to give opening and closing prayers at the convention, broadcast to millions of Americans over every TV station.

The most telling indication of the Christian Right's significance was Ronald Reagan's incredible and highly controversial speech to the convention, in which he declared that the separation of Church and State had been an issue falsely constructed by liberals to keep conservative Christians out of the political arena. He encouraged us to take our rightful place within the governmental process. Not only was this a major encouragement to the armies of the Christian Right, but it served to underscore that the Republican and Democratic parties, with the help of the media and at the persistence of the Christian Right, had made the issues of abortion, prayer in school, and gay rights major campaign issues.

Ferraro's Folly

If ever a candidate was annointed to fan the flame of right-wing passion, it was Geraldine Ferraro, the feminist favorite and Walter Mondale's selection for his vice-presidential running mate. And it was the abortion issue on which she was most vulnerable. While Ms. Ferraro said that she personally opposed abortion, she took the position that she would not force her "faith" onto others and therefore would stand solidly for the pro-choice argument (pro-abortion) position. This statement got her in hot water with Catholic leaders like Cardinal John O'Connor of New York, who pointed out that if one did not bring their most intensely held spiritual and private beliefs to public office, then what did they bring? The only other position was to say that one would take a poll of the public on every issue and vote for whatever position fifty-one percent of the people took on any given issue.

Taking the cue from Cardinal O'Conner, following a speech by Ferraro in Scranton, Pennsylvania, local Roman Catholic Bishop James Timlin likened Ferraro's stand on abortion to saying "I'm personally opposed to slavery, but I don't care if the people down the street want to own slaves."[10]

Miss America vs. Geraldine

No one was sure on the Christian Right whether Ferraro was going to hurt or help Mondale, but I was determined to make sure that she wasn't going to help. It was my feeling that if enough Christians understood where Ms. Ferraro stood on the key issues of abortion, pornography, prayer in school, and the Equal Rights Amendment, they would vote against her. How could we reach enough Christian voters and educate them in time? The answer was to once again use television. But if we were to do television commercials exposing Ferraro's vacillation or contradictory statements on the issues, who would we select to deliver such a devastating exposé? Certainly it would look bad to have a man attacking Ms. Ferraro. This was George Bush's handicap during his infamous debate with her.

It would also not look good to have a female who had spent twenty years as a political operative attacking Ms. Ferraro. The one perfect selection seemed to be someone who held a position almost beyond reproach and seemed to represent all that was good and wholesome and honest about America, someone who would be attractive, gracious, and win the hearts of every viewer. That criteria sounded like a "Miss America," and that is exactly who I chose. I turned to my friend, Cheryl Prewitt, a Christian Gospel singer who had reigned as Miss America in 1980 and whom I knew shared my very strong feelings regarding President Reagan's re-election. Almost overnight I wrote and directed Cheryl in three commercials on which she was gracious enough to work well past "quitting time" so we could hold a national press conference within seventy-two hours.

The press conference featuring Cheryl's three commercials sponsored by our Christians-for-Reagan political action committee were a knockout success. Aired on all three major networks' prime-time evening news broadcasts, the word went out that Miss America had "taken on" Geraldine Ferraro over the moral issues of abortion, pornography, and prayer in school. The nation's press featured articles that began, "Fundamentalists led by a former Miss America unleashed an attack on Geraldine Ferraro with TV commercials questioning her integrity."[11]

The Texas Model

Probably the most effective role I was able to play in the 1984 congressional elections was the model my friend Ray Allen and I set up in the state of Texas beginning in 1982. In July of 1982, in the course of a six-week, non-stop speaking tour, I stopped in Texas long enough to organize a group of Christian activists. This later turned into a full-fledged effort to turn out the Christian vote for the fall election. The results were disappointing and we blamed it on the lack of adequate volunteer networks. We committed ourselves to setting up a "model" that would require a full-time staff gradually increasing from three to six people. This would demand my own presence in the state at least one week per month and would be geared toward networking with literally every Christian conservative active organization in every sizable town in Texas. The final goal would be to activate this network in the months preceding the election to do a massive voter registration and report card distribution drive. When election day came in 1984, the results were astounding.

Newspapers as far removed from Texas as the *Daily Oregonian* carried reports regarding our role in replacing four Congressmen considered to be "safe" from defeat.

On June 1, 1985, *The Dallas-Times Herald* reported:

The greatest impact the Religious Right claims occurred in Texas last year . . . an ultraconservative organization, distributed through churches nearly 2½ million copies of a "scorecard" rating candidates on social issues.

"There's no doubt," said Texas pollster and Democratic strategist George Shipley, "the Religious Right played a role in at least three of four Texas congressional races" in which Democratic incumbents were ousted by conservative Republicans.[12]

In fact, of the four House "safe" members we defeated, in two cases their immediate family members called our local office to lay the blame of defeat at our doorsteps. We were all too ready to receive the credit for one of the few bright spots in the 1984 Congressional elections. As the *Washington Post* summed up:

> Of the fifteen-seat Republican gain in the House in 1984, eight were in districts where conservative Christian activity was clearly an important part of the election, particularly in Texas, North Carolina, and Georgia. The Christian mobilization was critical to the reelection of Senator Jesse Helms (R-N.C.) and contributed substantially to the decisive victory of senator Phil Gramm (R-Texas).[13]

As Neuhaus observed:

> Given the alternatives thrown up by the electoral process, a minority becomes the politically effective majority when it is able to tip the balance in the direction it favors. And that is what the religious new right has been able to do with a frequency that is disconcerting to its opponents.[14]

Clearly, the Christian Right was well on its way to realizing its potential to reshape America as suggested in the Connecticut Mutual Life survey of American values:

> It is once again moral issues that have, via religion, vaulted to the forefront of the political dialogue, and suggests that this re-awakening of moral activism carries a special significance as the United Stated enters the eighties.[15]

Yet three short years later a chorus of voices, inside and outside of the Christian Right were writing its obituary.

In July of 1987, Christian Right author and attorney John Whitehead wrote:

> There is a discouragement or should I say a "smallness" in activist circles these days. Activism was once considered the wave of the future. Now few even use the term.

> Almost all the activists I began working with are now gone.[16]

After extensive polling, Lou Harris, in his mid-1987 released book *Inside America*, summed it up this way:

> In short, the Moral Majority cause has failed to become the wave of the future as we approach the last decade of the twentieth-century.
>
> After 10 years of piety and ideology, the American people have about had it with the approaches of political religious types.[17]

This assessment was particularly disturbing when contrasted against an earlier prophecy by Moral Majority leader Falwell that the early eighties were the "beginning of a decade of destiny to determine whether America really is a nation under God."[18]

We must ask ourselves what in the world happened to such a promising movement? We will discover some of the answers in Chapter 3.

THREE

WHY THE CHRISTIAN RIGHT FAILED

Going through my files, I discovered an August 1982 news-paper interview I had done, where I stated "the Christian Right will fade from the scene only after its objectives have been achieved."

At first I thought this formula did not fit the Christian Right at all, for, as Harris suggested, we had failed to secure the sort of fundamental and permanent changes we had sought.[1] But then Gary Metz, a Christian writer and publicist, pointed out that the Christian Right had in fact achieved its primary objective, the election of Ronald Reagan to eight years at the helm of the most powerful nation in the world.

At first I was stunned at what appeared to be such an over-simplification, yet it somehow rang true. The truth was that while the Christian Right's leadership had an agenda beyond Ronald Reagan, most of the "grassroots" did not. For them Ronald Reagan symbolized the all-American hero he had portrayed on the screen. The world was in his capable hands and, encouraged by his ever-confident smile, they could go back to sleep.

In 1980, the Connecticut Mutual survey pinpointed that

It is this special combination of political turmoil and economic decline that makes the swelling support for traditional values, as well as its spillover into direct political action, so compelling as a contemporary concern. Something unusual is happening.[2]

But Ronald Reagan brought with him a sense of both political and economic stability. He promised a return to conserva-tive, Christian, traditional values. Neuhaus's words, written halfway through the Reagan legacy in 1984, became prophetic:

As they began to feel more secure about their place in the new normality, the sense of resentment, and thus of belligerence, may decline. It is far from clear that the religious new right, as a politically mobilizable force, could survive such success.[3]

But by the fall of 1986, it was apparent that the Christian Right was failing to negotiate other serious political obstacles as well.

No sooner did the national Republican Party embrace Christians because it wanted their votes and volunteers, than it began to wonder about the honorability of its new suitor's intentions. What did these Christians really want? Would they be satisfied with Jimmy Carter's head or, once tasting power, would they also seek the heads of any GOP officials who did not agree to the complete Christian Right agenda?

The party hierarchy's worst fears were confirmed when Christians successfully took over state GOP organizations in Alaska and Minnesota. And there were rumblings in other states like Texas and California.

The GOP was clearly worried. They were willing to use Christians, but Christians "turning the tables" was not what the GOP strategists had in mind. And besides, the Christian Right didn't "fit in" with the normal Republican "country club culture." They were unworldly, simplistic, politically unsophisticated, narrow-minded, and real downers at the ever-present cocktail party. No one really understood what they believed. And what people don't understand, they inherently mistrust.

In 1980, and again in 1984, with the scent of the long savored victories inflaming their nostrils, the GOP overlooked these concerns. But they rediscovered their misgivings in 1986. Bolstered by an incumbent president who had achieved the biggest electoral victory in half a century, GOP leaders believed they could afford to be more "discriminating" in sharing their power. So, the GOP left the Christian political operators (like myself) high and dry and with empty coffers.

The *Star Wars,* set off among various TV superstars over the Jim Bakker/PTL scandal, was a severe shock to the Christian Right. Many of the TV stars dragged into this unseemly incident were leading lights of the Christian Right. Among my fellow board members of ACTV were Jim Bakker, Jimmy Swaggart, James Robison, Jerry Falwell, and Rex Humbard, all prominently mentioned by the media, night after night, in regard to the PTL controversy. Following the PTL bombshell were Congressional investigations and tons of media speculation on the abuses both real and imagined perpetrated by the largest of the "TV empires."

These Christian media titans were important to the Christian Right's success in more areas than just political activity. They were the major communication channels through which the Christian Right planned to funnel its social and moral agenda to activate the millions of Christians needed to support various legislative proposals.

No massive TV audience, no thousands of letters to Capitol Hill—no legislation! So, the Christian Right's two main political engines—alliances with the GOP and the electronic Church—both seemed to have sputtered out by mid-1987.

Still another problem was that within the Christian Right, leaders of each organization tried to appeal to all segments of the Christian or even the non-Christian community, but the rank and file membership often resisted their leaders' "open arms" approach. Local Moral Majority chairmen were often reluctant to work with anybody outside their independent Baptist circle which certainly excluded anybody with a charismatic flavor. Neuhaus insightfully described this dilemma:

> Leaders may proclaim their desire to integrate fundamentalist doctrine with more inclusive beliefs and ideals, but integration, whether racial or doctrinal, has not been the strong suit of fundamentalism. Moreover, in bidding for a larger constituency, such movements may alienate the constituency that is the primary base of support and vision. It is not easy to operate in two quite distinct orbits; the one composed of the truly saved and the other of those who can be recruited for the work that is to be done before the truly saved are taken off in Rapture. The impression made is that the movement is divided into first-class and second-class sections. And, as noted, the two classes tend to fall along the old lines of sacred and secular. Those directing polemical fire at "secular humanism" may themselves be suspected of assuming a secular disguise. Between secular human-

ism and secular religionism, so to speak, secular humanism at
least has the merit of seeming to be more straightforward. This
is yet a further instance in which the religious new right is crip-
pled and may be undone by internal conceptual confusions.[4]

Having said this, I must stress that I believe the Christian
Right's problems were much more fundamental than lack of interest due to a premature assumption of successfully resolving
the nation's problems, errors in political strategy, or the lack of a
cohesive agenda.

The Spiritual Flaws

There were serious spiritual flaws embedded in the foundation that I helped lay which caused the Christian Right's super-
structure to crumble. A strong foundation requires spiritual
alertness (an alertness easily dulled by the demands of the urgent
and the excitement of action), Scriptural accuracy (God's whole
plan is easily overlooked in the use of "selected truth"), and total
obedience (tough to do when it means death to self-will, self-
reliance, and ego needs!).

In doing what we thought right, I believe we were insensitive
to God's heart. In rushing helter-skelter to erect the framework
of our movement, I believe we overlooked vital spiritual principles. The primary reasons for the collapse of the Christian Right
as a cohesively structured movement were spiritual, not political
or tactical.

One deep-rooted and seldom, if ever, examined assumption
of the Christian Right was that the future of Christianity and
God's eternal plan for man was necessarily dependent upon and
proportionate to the fortunes of the United States. It was a reasonable assumption given America's historical role in missionary
activity and as a "defender of the faith," and one on which I had
based twenty-five years of my life's energy. It is also a premise
fraught with danger and easily distorted. It too readily leads to
the trap of defending America "right or wrong" (supporting the
status quo, as Francis Schaeffer observed).[5]

Certainly we are commanded to be good citizens, active in
our nation's affairs. As Christians we are commanded to be good
stewards of what God has given us, which certainly includes the

freedom we enjoy through our political and economic system. We are also exhorted to be "salt," acting to "preserve" the good elements of our society. We are to seek justice and righteousness, which will find many of us actively engaged in saving the lives of unborn babies, safeguarding the rights of women and children against sexual abuse and exploitation of all types, and helping to free the oppressed from Soviet-style totalitarianism.

So it was natural that we formed alliances with political movements like the conservative wing of the Republican Party that sought to keep America "strong and healthy."

Without knowing it, the Christian Right was attracted to the GOP just as strongly as northern Protestants were when they provided Republicans with a string of major electoral successes between 1860 and 1908, and for much the same reasons.

As historian James Reichley observed in his authoritative *Religion in American Public Life,*

> The Republican Party [of the late nineteenth-century] was above all the party of morality . . . the Republican Party strove to promote the concept of "right behavior" [including prohibition and Bible reading in school].[6]

Reichley also suggests of the same period:

> There is probably a natural affinity between the Protestant virtues of industry, sobriety, and family responsibility, and political support for the party of order.[7]

Reichley classifies the GOP as the "party of order," meaning its primary commitment to maintaining social order and the status quo as opposed to the more egalitarian ethos of the Democrats.

The problem is that since those running political parties and movements consistently prioritize their own goals above God's goals, when we tie ourselves too closely to their secular agenda, we may blind ourselves to what God wants to accomplish.

For instance, the Bible teaches that God disciplines nations that separate themselves from Him and then indulge in evil practices (for a dramatic picture of our current dilemma, read the eighth and twenty-eighth chapters of Deuteronomy). It is reasonable, therefore, to conclude that God may need to discipline America in order to humble her and return His children's attention and obedience to Himself (see 2 Chronicles 7:14).

If we unthinkingly support a "strong America" (militarily and economically), no matter how defiant of God she becomes, we may be working at cross purposes with God who may have ordained military or economic crisis as a way to bring us to our knees. It's interesting to note that America's three great revivals have all been preceded by severe economic instability.

Another danger of identifying too closely with secular power structures is that when our nation or political movements fail to stand for compassion, justice, mercy, and righteousness, we must not be prevented from speaking out due to a prior commitment of blind loyalty.

We must therefore exercise caution so that in trying to save our nation from the disciplining hand of God, we do not exalt our priorities over His. We must try to determine where God is going and flow with Him!

Lack of Vision

In the book of Proverbs we read, "where there is no vision, the people perish" (Proverbs 29:18 KJV) They also get burned out, confused, and scatter their energies in a hundred different directions.

What was the Christian Right actually for? What was our vision for the future? Yes, we were *for* stopping abortion, pornography, sexual degeneracy, big government, communism, and a host of other evils. We were *for* prayer in school and the rights of parents and churches to be free from government intrusion in ecclesiastical and family affairs. But these are single issues, not a cohesive platform or vision of what could be or even should be. And they are negative stands often made simply in reaction to the aggressive or adversarial positions of those not in agreement with Christian values.

Cal Thomas, in his obituary on the Christian Right observed,

> Evangelicals have contributed to their own political demise by failing to develop a unified social ethic. They have preferred to limit their agenda to the "gut issues" (abortion, school prayer, the family).

To many, it appeared that all the Christian Right had to offer was a negative/reactionary collage of "don'ts" rather than a comprehensive and constructive agenda of "do's." Worse yet, most Christians could not understand how all the issues connected to each other. If one was opposed to abortion and pornography, why should one also support Contras and Star Wars? Why should concern for protecting churches and Christian schools from government interference or regulation dictate allegiance to conservative or Republican political movements?

Compassion, Justice, and Righteousness

While it is possible for such a rationale to be thoughtfully developed through a Christian worldview, applying Biblical principles of compassion, justice, and righteousness to each issue, it was never fully developed by the activists of the Christian Right. Christian worldview thinkers and writers, like Schaeffer, Whitehead, and other scholars, were largely ignored by the major leaders of the Christian Right and their constituent Churches.

Without a clear Christian worldview, Christians were unable to act in unison behind a comprehensive and clearly understandable agenda. Each Christian Right issue on its own, with the possible exception of the pro-life issue, lacked the sense of life-changing or life-threatening urgency that compels volunteers to selflessly devote their energies on a long-term basis to see the battle through to a victorious conclusion.

And with its constituency divided among so many causes and projects, the Christian Right was unable to mobilize its forces in any unified manner except at election time. Even then, only the overwhelming importance and excitement of the presidential election year seemed to turn out the volunteers — at the expense of the crucial in between "off year" Congressional elections.

What happened, in fact, is that around each "single issue," i.e., abortion, pornography, etc., there developed a host of smaller organizations dedicated solely to eradicating that particular evil. Unfortunately, such organizations were for the most part too small to accomplish much on their own, too limited in scope and resources to cooperate in any effective way with Christian Right groups focused on other issues, and too compe-

titive for the limited supply of volunteers and money to cooperate with other groups focused on the same issue!

Turf battles, personality conflicts, and general mutual
animosity characterized many, though certainly not all, of the
Christian Right groups both locally and nationally. Once the
momentum of media attention and the consequent excitement
wound down, the volunteers upon which all movements are dependent "burned out" or simply moved on to the next issue or
cause that offered some momentary stimulation or meaning.

Effective action demands an integrated strategic use of resources (time, labor, and money) and the focused attention of all
participants. A movement that seeks to alter the course of the
world's mightiest and most complex nation, and accomplish this
redirection in the face of all out warfare from a powerfully en-
trenched opposition, had better be able to command complete
and total loyalty and selfless dedication and sacrifice for its objectives on the part of its supporters.

Single issues, even a whole pot full of them, will not
stimulate this necessary but rare level of commitment. What was
required was a vision of a better, greater, more just, and merciful
society to command such devotion. The Christian Right was
also incapable of finding a spiritually sound mandate for involvement. Without an orthodox and historically sound Christian doctrine that clearly demands all Christians be active in
some mode of service and "fruit bearing," the Christian Right's
battle was lost before it was begun. Without such a "nonoptional mandate" for Christian service, millions of Christians
would choose (and still do) to "opt out" by opting to emphasize
"personal growth," "peace," or "affluence," rather than "bearing
fruit" through service and self-sacrifice.

Fortunately, such a mandate does exist and will be dealt with
extensively as we progress.

The Need for Vision

An effectively communicated vision is the most powerful
method of transforming the world. The Marxists have proved
this. Various Communists who have converted to Christianity
have been appalled to find their old colleagues more committed
to their cause than Christians are to theirs.

Communist revolutionaries believe so fiercely in their cause they are ready to make any sacrifice for it, including your life or theirs. This is one reason they have been so successful in dominating so much of the world in just seventy years.

The Islamic religion represents another vision that its millions of adherents are willing, even anxious, to die for. The suicidal terrorist missions of various Islamic factions in the Middle East and the incredible casualties (over five hundred thousand dead by mid-1988) sustained by Iran in its "border war" with Iraq are instructive in demonstrating the power of vision to motivate men to make sacrifices, including the ultimate sacrifice of life itself.

John Stott, a leading Christian thinker, defines vision as "made up of compassion and indignation and a refusal to accept the unacceptable." He explains that vision first demands that we be compassionate — that we care about the well-being of people — God's creations, whom He loves and has commanded us to love as well. Next, vision demands indignation. We must become irate — angry with the injustice, the lack of mercy, or unGodly conduct that hurts others. But we must translate our anger into action. "To accept the unacceptable," says Stott, "is apathy. To not accept the intolerable forces us to set forth a vision of what could be."[8]

This concept of vision is what the Christian Right failed to understand. Without vision, there is no clear agenda. Without such an agenda there is no clear direction. Without direction, there is no effective mobilization of forces.

If the Christian Right's potpourri of goals was ever realized, what would our future look like? Would it look like the Kingdom of God? Would it look like the 1950s or the 1700s? Should the government be run by Christians or just be more friendly to Christian values? Should politicians enforce Christian values by law or just expound them by personal example and persuasion or perhaps a mix of these approaches? And how do we define Christian values?

What would a Christian conservative coalition in power really do about the economy, national defense, nuclear war, hunger, poverty, AIDS, etc.? No one seemed to know, or at least no one that could speak for any semblance of a unified Christian Right.

In meeting with other Christian Right leaders, including members of Congress, I often observed that our movement did not know where it was going, how to get there, or what to do if we ever did get there.

While the Christian Right's lack of vision—and we will suggest the outline for just such a vision in subsequent chapters—posed a serious obstacle to its ability to capture the imagination and energies of the vast majority of the Christian community, it was indicative of a much more fundamental flaw, one which I believe sums up the failure of the Christian Right, as well as so many other movements.

Whose Agenda?

I believe that what the Church and even the secular public noticed, whether consciously or unconsciously, was that the Christian Right did not appear to have a particularly strong Christian witness. That is to say, many of our more vocal spokesmen, including myself, seemed more interested in our own agenda than in Christ's.

Even the self-proclaimed atheist often respects Christ as a great "moral teacher" and has certain expectations of those who crusade in Christ's name. As "ambassadors of Christ," our actions are expected to be motivated by love and compassion as evidenced by our caring for the homeless and helpless, the poor in spirit and in fortune, the oppressed, the orphans, the widows, and in fact anyone in need—our neighbors.

When we do not visibly demonstrate a strong commitment to these priorities, we appear interested only in our own limited agenda. We are insensitive to real needs and individual sensitivities. When we do not act on Christ's agenda, we are acting on our own. And when we act on our own agenda, people do not perceive us as representing Christ, but ourselves. We are perceived, even if incorrectly so, as mere Pharisees, legalists, trying to impose our moral values, the letter of the law vs. the spirit of the law, rather than trying to serve the communities' needs.

As my Harvard-trained economist friend, Will Pilcher, says,

People intuitively know if you're grinding your own axe. If your own ego has not been crucified with Christ on the cross, then people see your ego, not Jesus' compassion, and they reject your efforts as self-serving or not rooted in deep concern for their own well being.[9]

The Lack of Compassion

Many Christian Right leaders, local pastors, and activists were motivated by a deep caring and concern for justice and righteousness, but it was not readily apparent to much of the Church and the public at large.

Christ sought to warn against this dilemma when He told us that people would recognize us as servants of God, empowered and directed by Christ, by our love for one another and by our unity. Unfortunately, the Christian Right displayed precious little of either. The absence of a tangible, personalized love for our fellow man was disconcertingly noticeable.

What proportion of our time and energy were we spending helping real people with real needs — the poor, the handicapped, the sick, the elderly, orphans, widows, the homeless, the abused, the disadvantaged, the persecuted?

To many, it did not appear that the Christian Right was legitimately concerned with these issues of compassion or even with the problems of real families struggling through the very trying problems of every day life. Because our message was not perceived as being firmly rooted in a foundation of love and compassion, we lacked the moral authority to command loyalty and we lacked the vision to attract zeal, energy, and sacrifice.

It was not enough for some national Christian Right ministries to add on what appeared to be "token" or "afterthought" compassion works (i.e., orphans, unwed mothers, etc.). Such efforts were perceived as too little, too late, and were often suspect as simply more public relations or fundraising tactics.

Primary Commitment

The public and the Church in particular had a right to know what our primary commitment was. Did our political agenda grow out of a self-sacrificing commitment to serving our community and helping our neighbors? Or did our commitment to compassion and service grow out of our political agenda as a politically expedient afterthought?

The public's perception of the answers to this legitimate and crucial question obviously flavored its reception of our overall message.

The fact of the matter is that when a Mother Teresa, who has devoted her life to serving others, speaks out for the unborn in opposition to the inhumanity of abortion, almost everyone listens. They may not agree, but they listen. She has earned their respect. They know she is truly concerned for others, that her "agenda" is to serve others, not just to foist her "morally superior" viewpoint on others less enlightened than she.

Now, how does this analogy compare when a TV evangelist expounds on the same subject? He is all too often viewed as raising millions of dollars—eighty to ninety percent of which goes to pay for the furtherance of his ministry, fundraising, TV time, and administration bills—for the perpetuation of his own ego-centered agenda or "empire." Knowing the many prominent TV evangelists I do, I know in some cases it is an unfair conclusion. Nevertheless, it is a conclusion held by most of the public and much of the Church. The same applies to Christian political spokesmen, activists, etc.

I think there are a number of other reasons, some more accurate than others, that contribute to the perception that the Christian Right did not truly care about people but rather about their own political agenda.

When confronted by human misery or misfortune, those rare souls who actually decide to "do something" usually fall into two categories. The larger and more obvious category are those who volunteer themselves to relieving the imminent manifestation of the problem. They volunteer to dish up food in a soup kitchen, counsel disadvantaged kids or pregnant mothers, visit the elderly, or even take short-term mission trips to help those in the Third World. Their efforts have immediate results, are highly visible, and personally rewarding.

The second category, in which I include myself, tends to be more conceptually ambitious and wants to deal with the root of the problem, rather than the immediate manifestation. We are highly indignant over a particular social evil and will be satisfied only when the root cause is remedied. Rather than a volunteer, this person tends to be a crusader. To help the homeless, the hungry, and the unemployed, we will work to redirect massive government funds or motivate the Church to give! To help orphans and the sick overseas we will seek to lobby the government for more foreign aid or organize a mass fundraising campaign at home. To help the oppressed we may organize citizens to demand that their Legislators support the world's Freedom Fighters! Against injustice and exploitation we may organize other citizens to pressure their Representatives into changing certain laws. If that doesn't work, we may organize the voters to change the Representatives who make the laws!

Of course, many liberals, as well as conservatives, fall into this category. While motivated by true compassion and indignation at injustice and evil, the results are not immediately obvious and motives may not be highly visible. Therefore, we should be careful when discerning motives. Appearances are not always what they seem.

Nevertheless, I think it also true in its self-proclaimed quest for national righteousness (conforming society to God's moral standards, for society's own benefit and for God's glory) the Christian Right overlooked God's equally important imperatives for justice and mercy for the oppressed, the poor, the less fortunate, and for our neighbors.

Christ's primary admonition to us was not to restore righteousness, but to love our fellow man, a theme we will more fully develop in Chapter 7. Out of that sense of compassion should flow our commitment to restoring righteousness to society, because a Godly nation provides for ideal conditions for peace and stability to raise families and nurture spiritual growth. In 1 Timothy 2:1-4, we are explicitly instructed to pray for good leaders in order to "lead a peaceful and quiet life in all Godliness" (1 Timothy 2:1-4).

How did the Christian Right lose this crucial balance between love, mercy, and justice on one hand, and righteousness on the other?

Unequally Yoked

Part of our problem was our alliance with the Secular Right, or the "New Right." Since the Christian Right did not have a political philosophy, it borrowed liberally from the Secular

Right. Since the Christian Right lacked political techniques, leaders, and thinkers, it leaned on those in the Secular Right. While I believe that the majority of those on the Secular Right were motivated by "good" reasons, they were not necessarily the "right" reasons. I believe it is good to oppose the breakdown of morality caused by legalized pornography, homosexuality, abortion, drug abuse, communism, government encroachments on the rights of churches and citizens, etc. I believe much of the Right opposed these evils for good reasons, i.e., to protect their own families' best interests, physically, emotionally, and economically. But when our focus is exclusively on our own families' well-being, we tend to forget about the needs of others or the different requirements of families less fortunate than our immediate socioeconomic group.

Many political conservatives do not recognize or understand that God is in control of all human events and, in the end, will reign victorious. They tend to be victims of a siege mentality. Their "survive the terrible odds at all costs" mentality often does not leave much room for love and compassion outside of immediate family and friends.

In Our Own Strength

Further, the Secular Right depends on its own strength—its own ability to make thing happen. Waiting on God and being sensitive to His leading is naturally unheard of. It should not stretch our imagination to understand how the Christian Right, faced with the nation's and world's urgent problems, could be absorbed easily by the Secular Right's emphasis on the urgent over the important, or how we could succumb to relying on our strengths and abilities to execute our plans, rather than waiting on God.

It is easy to forget God's promise to us, repeated in the Bible in hundreds of different illustrations:

> *With God* we will gain the victory and *He* will trample down our enemies. (Psalm 108:13, italics added)

FOUR

THE FAILURE
OF OUR CHURCHES

The Christian Right was doomed to failure without the active support of the nation's Evangelical Churches (supposedly home to over forty million "born again" Christians).

The Christian Right stood little chance of realizing its ambition of "reclaiming" the nation's government for traditional values, without the Church to provide an "endorsement" of the Christian Right's mission. Such an endorsement would by implication give the Christian Right's agenda "legitimacy" as an appropriate expression of Christian endeavor, without the Church's authority to help recruit and mobilize the hundreds of thousands of volunteers so desperately required by any crusade.

In our hearts we feared we would never obtain the support of the Church. In our numerous councils and strategy sessions, we debated the question: Should we attempt to "go around" the local pastors and organize their members without their permission (as the minions of the "electronic Church" had done and for which they were much resented), or should we attempt to work through the local Church?

What in fact happened is that different Christian Right leaders tried different approaches, and in the end most of us vacillated between the two approaches, switching to one when the other didn't produce results in the anticipated time frame.

Consequently, neither approach ever achieved demonstrable success. Surprisingly, most Evangelical pastors, including those with admittedly conservative political convictions, opposed "political involvement" either by commission or omission. Meaning that they either directly spoke against such activity or that they refused to actively encourage it.

After it became painfully obvious to me that the Church was at best going to be an extremely reluctant partner in our quest to pursue a higher standard of morality in our government and culture, I asked myself why?

It seemed so contradictory! The Church should be pushing us to get involved, not pouring cold water on our efforts! Clearly, something was very wrong. Were the many theologians and TV ministers wrong when they urged their followers to political and social action? Did local Churchmen and denominational leaders know something that I didn't?

With my ignorance of theology and Church history, I knew it certainly would have been easy for me to miss some central truth or doctrine forbidding or at least discouraging aggressive Church involvement in our culture. In my quest to find answers for these questions, I soon discovered why theologians tell us that a knowledge of Church history is so important: If we don't know how and why the Church developed its key doctrines and teachings throughout history, we cannot understand how our present day Church got to where it is.

In my studies (which I never before had time for as an "activist leader"), I quickly learned that the historical Christian Church and specifically the American Church, had been instrumental in affecting whatever governing system they found themselves within. Our Puritan forefathers believed their purpose was to establish a Christian nation resting on Godly laws. And most of the American Church acted on that belief until the turn of the century (1900-1920).

What happened? What terrible trauma took a Church, convinced of its destiny to "disciple the nations" (as Jesus instructed us to do in Matthew 28:19), and turned it into a bastion of aloofness, of apathy?

What strong forces or doctrines have paralyzed our modern-day Evangelical Church?

The Church suffered a loss of courage and paralysis of its will as it entered the twentieth century (scholars generally agree that the "Great Reversal" of our Churches dramatically retreating from social involvement took place from 1900 to 1930), but the undermining of the Evangelical Church's courage and its convictions began in the nineteenth century.

As early as the 1830s, the American Church began to show a distinct lack of courage, exemplified by its unwillingness to deal with the great evil of its time — slavery.

The Church's Lack of Courage

This so outraged Harriet Martineau that she wrote scornfully of the acquiescing clergy, who, "if they do not understand [Christianity's] principles, are unfit to be clergymen; and if they do, are unfit to be called Christians."[1]

The Church's pre-Civil War withdrawal from actively influencing political decisions is credited by some historians with playing a major role in provoking the Civil War in the first place. They hold that the Church, through its involvement, could have persuaded the government to outlaw slavery without the necessity of a terrible and tragic war that claimed over a half million American casualties.

One Church historian, who has painstakingly documented the fact that the Church's massive moral influence on business (i.e., plantation owners) and government could well have averted the greatest tragedy in American history, is C. C. Goen of Wesley Theological Seminary. In his book *Broken Churches, Broken Nation*, he tells us why our Churches (particularly in the South) chose to avoid involvement in the slavery issue.

> The real problem was the perception on the part of the Evangelicals that an anti-slavery Church would necessarily remain a very small Church. Slave-holders made it known that they would more readily "part with their Church privileges rather than with their slaves." The Churches persuaded themselves that their main mission was to "Christianize the nation" by multiplying converts, and their phenomenal success on this score seemed to justify the priority that placed "winning souls" above freeing slaves. But the soul-winning campaigns maintained their emotional momentum only by studious avoidance of all controversial issues. The Church's growth strategy depended on their not requiring converts to face the hard moral discipline demanded by Christian sensitivity to the evil of human bondage. So long as God seemed to smile on their zeal to bring in the unchurched, it was difficult to entertain any charge of fundamental wrongdoing. If slavery troubled a few sensitive spirits, its solution could still be delayed until a more convenient season.[2]

Could this "growth at any cost" attitude on the part of Churches be applied to many of our biggest Evangelical Churches today?

Could it be one reason why to our shame the Evangelical Church waited for five years after the *Roe v. Wade* decision that legalized abortion to get involved in defending the lives of babies, and even now only a small minority of our Churches are concerned with this dramatic evil?

Certainly this outlook can be applied to many of our Churches today, large or small! I have lost count of the times I have heard ministers and Church boards be quick to agree with our positions on various moral outrages ("of course, abortion, pornography, TV degeneracy and corrupt politicians are terrible") but who are unwilling to alienate any members or potential members by "pushing the point" or "making an issue" out of it.

During elections, my field staff reported that in state after state, pastors of Evangelical Churches could not bring themselves to encourage (or in some cases even allow) the distribution of our non-partisan "report cards" showing how local legislators had voted on moral issues. While these report cards did not ask anyone to vote one way or another, they obviously made a "pro-abortion" or "anti-prayer in school" legislator "look bad." The risk of potentially alienating Churchgoers (especially prominent ones) who happened to strongly identify with the political party of the offending candidate (or who were pro-choice themselves) was just too great a risk. Certainly it was as great a risk as pre-Civil War Churches faced if they forced congregations to come to grips with the moral dilemma of slavery.

Professor Goen sums up the pre-Civil War Church's lack of resolve and its tragic consequences in this thought-provoking statement that applies equally well to today's Church one hundred years later:

> It has been one of the lesser noticed tragedies of America's tragic era that the nation's moral and spiritual mentors were either unwilling or unable to exercise decisive leadership toward a more just and humane society. Committed to Church growth, swayed by sectional interest, and silent about racial prejudice, they could neither swim against the stream nor redirect its flow and so chose to protect their position by staying close to the main currents.[3]

Through their deliberate choice of expansion by evasion, the Churches fatefully undermined whatever anti-slavery witness they might have had by consistently applying Church discipline against slaveholding members.[4]

Look at the preceding paragraphs and replace the references to the evil of slavery with today's equivalents of abortion, moral degeneracy, economic or sexual exploitation, political oppression, lawlessness. Do you see a frighteningly accurate parallel with today's Evangelical Church?

Because of its mindboggling lack of moral courage, the American Church of today has avoided confronting the evils of 1.5 million legalized abortions annually; legalized exploitation and denigration of women and children through pornography; televised degeneracy, leading to increased rape, perversion, and sexual dysfunction in young people and married people; legitimization of homosexuality as an acceptable "alternative lifestyle," and, last but not least, the exploitation, enslavement and slaughter of Third World peoples from Mozambique to Ethiopia, Afghanistan to Angola, Nicaragua to Cuba, and the plight of homeless or starving millions around the world and around the block.

As I struggled to make sense of this travesty, I realized that our Church's noninvolvement and apathy are perfectly consistent with our wrong goals. If our Churches are motivated primarily by growth in members, finances, buildings, and community prestige, then settling on a course of "issue evasion" and nonconfrontation makes sense.

Many of our twentieth century Church empire builders have realized, as did their predecessors, that a Church committed to following Jesus and the prophets in their unremitting denunciations of social evil and their unrelenting concern for the poor and the oppressed would turn off many Christians who want to take, not give. These Christians want blessings, not sacrifice; joy, not duty; and peace, not work. They want to adjust their Sunday service schedules around Sunday brunch or sports events. Serious application of the Gospel to pressing community or global problems is much too disconcerting a topic for today's busy and self-absorbed Christians!

Many in today's Evangelical Church are committing idolatry as we place Church growth and prestige ahead of God's concerns for justice and righteousness, as we pursue ecclesiastical peace at the expense of the needy and suffering. It is the same sort of thinking that Jesus condemned in the religious leaders of His day, and for which God pronounced judgment on His people through the Old Testament prophets. No doubt this awareness is what motivated thousands of Evangelical leaders who gathered in 1974 in Lausanne, Switzerland, to review the status of world evangelization to declare: "We confess that we have sometimes pursued Church growth at the expense of Church depth. . . ."5

Quick Review of Recent Church History

To understand the weaknesses and blind spots in our Church today, we must gain some understanding of how we have arrived at our present unhappy predicament.

Richard Lovelace, Professor of Church History at Gordon-Conwell Seminary, points to seeds of destruction taking root in the American Church as early as the 1700s:

> ". . . piety begot prosperity, and the daughter had devoured the mother . . . covetousness leading to affluence to independence, followed by religious formalism leading to outright unbelief. From then on the people regarded the Church as a chaplaincy . . . while we spend our main energies pursuing success, or at least avoiding failure."6

Sounds all too familiar doesn't it?

Lovelace provides us with a vital key to understanding our present Church when he explains how the Church rationalized its avoidance of the slavery issue:

> Unfortunately, Southern Evangelical clergy and theologians lost their nerve, avoided challenging the economic concerns of the laity, and developed a doctrine now labeled heresy by their descendants: "the spirituality of the Church." This notion states that the Church should deal only with spiritual issues, and let political and social issues alone.7

Professor Goen tells how this "spiritualization" of the Church's role played out in the life of the believer:

Converts were taught to strive for mastery of their own lives; beyond that, they received no guidance on how their religious commitments could affect social roles that were defined by race, sex, or power. By casting morality in purely individualistic terms, therefore, Southern Evangelicals placed the institution of slavery beyond the reach of Christian social concern and their society beyond the pale of Christian action. Slavery was, in their insistent refrain, "purely a civil matter," and their refusal to confront it as a moral issue prevented them from ever learning the full extent of their moral responsibility in and for the whole society.[8]

Within a few decades after unilaterally disarming itself, the Church was left defenseless for the attack of the century: the onslaught of Freudian psychology (liberation from moral restraint), Darwinian evolution (invalidating the Biblical act of creation and the very nature and purpose of man), and Marxian sociology (anti-God as well as anti-capitalist).

In addition to an inability to defend itself against the challenge of the "modernists" (secular humanists and "Darwinists") with their denial of the Godly ordered world, the Church found itself being attacked from within.

Liberal theology, denying Biblical inerrancy and the "fundamentals of the faith," invaded American denominations from German theological schools of "higher criticism" and by the mid 1930s captured our major seminaries and denominations.

Confronted by such attacks, the fundamentalists took a last look around, ducked into their bunkers, and pulled the hatches shut behind them. They felt defeated by society's "liberated" worshipers of Darwin and Freud, who were sold on the ideas of relativism and immersed in sensuality and materialism. And even worse, liberalism had snatched the major denominations from the fold, too.

Within the bunker the "spiritual Church" adherents perfected a brand of "privatized, personalized" Christianity which established the basis for much of today's fundamentalist/Evangelical reticence to social action.

As Evangelical leader John Stott points out, a peculiar interpretation of dispensational pre-millennialism developed that "portrays the present evil world as beyond improvement or redemption, and predicts instead that it will deteriorate steadily until the coming of Jesus, who will then set up His millennial reign on earth. If the world is getting worse, and if only Jesus at His coming will put it right, there seems no point in trying to reform it meanwhile."[9]

Lovelace agrees that this interpretation taught "that the ruin of the Church and the decay of western society were a necessary prelude to the return of Jesus."[10]

The consequences of this view are all too obvious in America today. As Lovelace summarizes:

> The result has been that instead of ordering careers, families, businesses and governments around God's purposes, we have, at best, tried to talk about Jesus to others while investing our main energy in pursuing the same things as the world: survival, security and wealth.[11]

Any time fundamentalist leaders did emerge from their bunkers, they unleashed well-aimed (and usually well-deserved) attacks on the now-dominant liberal elements of the Church for replacing the "fundamentals" of faith and salvation with a "works-oriented" social gospel.

Why Fundamentalists Rejected Good Works

As so often happens in the midst of the heat of battle, the fundamentalists rejected "social action" and any doctrine of good works simply because that's what the liberals were preaching.

Tragically, in throwing the baby out with the bath water, the conservatives (Evangelicals) also lost their way, but in a different direction from their liberal opponents.

The Apostle Paul in Ephesians 2:8-10 teaches us how we are to balance faith and works. Salvation is by faith and faith alone. But once salvation is secured, it demonstrates itself through good works. Our redemption is more than a ticket to heaven, it is an obligation to actively serve.

> For it is by grace you have been saved, through faith and this is not from yourselves, it is the gift of God, not by works, so that no one can boast. For we are God's workmanship, created in Christ Jesus to do good works, which God prepared in advance for us to do (Ephesians 2:8-10).

The modernists forgot the first half of the formula, emphasizing works rather than salvation by faith, and fundamentalists reacted by disowning the second half because it was promoted by the modernists.

How devastating it has been to our Churches to have lost this balance! How often is the full truth, carefully balanced, preached in our Churches? How many born again Christians have a knowledge of what is expected of them in service, either to God or their fellow man?

I was brought up in a large "independent" Baptist Church, and I remember well the minister consistently pounding away relentlessly at the same message every Sunday — get saved or go to hell! While I'm sure this was a good message for the occasional unsaved person who drifted through our doors, it left those of us ensconced in our pews convinced that if we wanted to impact the world, the Church was entirely disinterested in anything but "get saved, go to heaven."

The Church, we were led to believe, had a two-fold purpose — to get people saved and to get those people to get other people saved. And then, of course, we were there to learn all our "don'ts:" don't do that, don't do this, etc.

If we were to learn any do's, if we wanted to help the poor, the oppressed, if we wanted to seek justice or mercy for all peoples, then we joined a secular cause: the Democratic Party or the Republican Party, or Marxism or the John Birch Society. What you did not become was a Christian activist.

Anticipating just such times as these, God through the Apostle James told us why our faith and our Churches lack power:

> In the same way, faith by itself, if it is not accompanied by action, is dead. . . . What good is it, my brothers, if a man claims to have faith but has no deeds? Can such faith save him? (James 2:17, 14)

During the generation spanning the 20s to the 50s, the American Evangelical Church fell into its own dark ages. As Stott comments: "But between the wars there was no Evangelical leader to articulate the providence and common grace of God as grounds for persevering hope. Historic Reformed Christianity was in eclipse."[12]

The important question we must now ask is, why does our current Church leadership refuse to be involved?

Evangelical Escapism

This is a complicated question that demands careful analysis. First, as just discussed, many of our Churches have been captured by a "theology of noninvolvement." While this "apathetic theology" would appear very alien to Church leaders over the last nineteen hundred years, it has been widely accepted since the early 1900s.

It is the reason that as Chuck Colson observed, "Christianity as a cultural force has less influence today than in perhaps the last 1500 years."[13]

Stott insightfully portrays the practical consequences of previous generations' "escapist" theology:

> Too many of us Evangelicals either have been, or maybe still are, irresponsible escapists. Fellowship with each other in the Church is more congenial than service in an apathetic and even hostile environment outside. Of course we make occasional evangelistic raids into enemy territory (that is our Evangelical specialty); but then we withdraw again, across the moat, into our Christian castle (the security of our own Evangelical fellowship), pull up the drawbridge, and even close our ears to the pleas of those who batter on the gate. As for social activity, we have tended to say that it is largely a waste of time in view of the imminent return of the Lord. After all, when the house is on fire, what is the point of hanging new curtains or rearranging the furniture? The only thing that we really should engage in is to rescue the perishing. Thus we have tried to salve our conscience with a bogus theology.[14]

The real tragedy of the "spiritual Church" concept is that it tends to reduce Christianity to a two-step process—get saved, go to heaven. This is like teaching an alphabet with only A and Z. What happens to all the steps in between (service, salt, light, works, mercy, compassion, standing in the gap, etc.)? Evangelical theologians like Carl Henry, Francis Schaeffer, R. C. Sproul, and John Stott agree that salvation is the first crucial step in our Christian commitment, not the last.

Schaeffer comments:

> Yet, having said this about the beginning of the Christian life,
> we must also realize that while the new birth is necessary as the
> beginning, it is only the beginning. We must not think that
> because we have accepted Christ as Savior and therefore are
> Christians, this is all there is in the Christian life. In one way
> physical birth is the most important part in our physical lives,
> because we are not alive in the external world until we have
> been born. In another way, however, it is the least important of
> all the aspects of our life, because it is only the beginning and
> then it is past. After we are born, the important thing is the liv-
> ing of our lives in all their relationships, possibilities, and capa-
> bilities. It is exactly the same with the new birth. In one way,
> the new birth is the most important thing in our spiritual lives,
> because we are not Christians until we have come this way. In
> another way, however, after one has become a Christian, it
> must be minimized, in that we should not always have our
> minds only on our new birth. The important thing after being
> born spiritually is to live. There is a new birth, and then there
> is the Christian life to be lived. This is the area of sanctification,
> from the time of the new birth, through this present life, until
> Jesus comes or until we die.[15]

In Philippians 2:12, the Apostle Paul tells us to: ". . . continue to work out our salvation with fear and trembling."

The *NIV Study Bible* footnote on this verse remarks, "Salvation is not merely a gift received once and for all; it expresses itself in an ongoing process in which the believer is strenuously involved."[16] Clearly, salvation is meant to be the beginning of a
new life of service, not the "end of the story."

Trivializing Salvation

The observations of theologians Stott and Neuhaus are en-
lightening here. Stott observes:

> There is a constant tendency in the Church to trivialize the na-
> ture of salvation, as if it meant no more than a self-reformation,
> or the forgiveness of our sins, or a personal passport to para-
> dise, or a private mystical experience without social or moral
> consequences.[17]

And Neuhaus:

> Within the Christian community there has been a great divide
> between those who understand salvation in essentially private
> or essentially public terms. In the privatized version, salva-
> tion is essentially a matter of my getting my soul into heaven,
> while the rest of the reality we call history can, quite literally,
> go to hell.[18]

What our modern day Evangelical Church has done is to
continue the mistakes that deprived our twentieth-century
Church of any spiritual authority or power.

In our quest for bigger and better evangelistic crusades we
have concentrated on how to get converts, not on what they're
supposed to be converted to or for. We have found that escape
(from worldly problems or the world itself) sells better than service (in confronting this world's problems), and that forgiveness
(for our lack of obedience) attracts more members than teaching
obedience (which is what Christ commanded us to be).

We have developed a Church that primarily stands for
escape, and offers forgiveness to those who don't wish to obey
or serve.

Why do our Churches seem to have a "natural tendency" to
trivialize salvation, to reduce Christ's message down to its foundation, forgetting about what we are to build upon that foundation? Why do we so studiously avoid the full truth and obligation
of our salvation? Why do we try to escape a deeper, fuller walk
with God?

Today's Church

Once again, the answer is fully consistent with the goals of
the majority of our Churches. A Church committed primarily to
growth cannot afford to upset the level of personal peace and
affluence its members have attained (or would like to). Most lay
leaders and Church members have made idols out of affluence
and the personal peace and quiet of leisure time needed to enjoy
it. A number of pastors have told me that they know of hundreds
of good pastors who sincerely yearn to challenge their congregations to greater spiritual heights or greater depth of commitment

and service but who are afraid that if they do, they will lose their Church, or a substantial portion of it.

After all, confronting hard issues face to face (the poor, sick, homeless, abortions, pornography, drugs, Soviet expansionism, and human rights abuses) is guaranteed to focus on unsettling realities.

These unpleasant "real life" problems are destructive to our sense of insulated personal peace and safety which most of us try to maintain at any price.

Unfortunately, the price we pay to escape from these unpleasant visions (and the sacrifice of time and effort on our part they invariably demand if we didn't block them out) is added to the misery of those we ignore. Our Church's silence and refusal to actively participate in our nation's governing processes and public debates has contributed to epidemic drug abuse by the young alienated from an uncaring society; the annual murder by abortion of 1.5 million babies; the tremendously increased levels of all forms of child abuse; the legitimization of homosexuality as an alternative lifestyle and the consequential spread of AIDS; the vast increase of the American homeless, including homeless families; the legalization of pornography and its consequent degradation of women and warped view of sex; increasing exploitation of people for commercial or personal gain; the slaughter, exploitation and enslavement of peoples in the Third World; and cultural acceptance of a precipitous decline in business and government ethics.

Our Need for Repentance

These are harsh charges, but true. We, today's American Christians, have helped to catapult our world toward self-destruction. The Gospel gives us all of the answers, but too often we've only offered the world more problems. Before we can rectify our wrongs, we must repent of our part in this tragedy. And repentance is the first step toward both personal and national restoration.

> If my people, who are called by my name, will humble themselves and pray and seek my face and turn from their wicked ways, then will I hear from heaven and will forgive their sin and heal their land. (2 Chronicles 7:14)

Repentance is also the key to a renewed mind, and only through a total change of our way of looking at the world around us (i.e., our convenience v. others' needs and God's will) will we ever be able to focus on doing God's will rather than our own.

If our modern Evangelical Church is not to fade into total irrelevance and be replaced by God with a Church willing to do His bidding, repentance faces all of us. Our proud ministers, proud buildings, proud congregations, all of us must humble ourselves. Humbling ourselves will come easier if we ask ourselves, have we cared? Have we carried God's heart? Have we tried to actively love our neighbors by caring for them? Have we seriously tried to find out, by reading our Bibles, what God expects of us? Or have we been too busy with our own agendas (personal, business, or religious), too worried about increasing or preserving our own well-being to worry about anyone else's?

Of course, not all pastors and Churches fall into the trap of compromise and irrelevancy. Certainly there are the every-day variety of reasons that keep good ministers from effectively involving their Churches. This past summer I was rocking on the porch with my 80-year-old father-in-law (who plays tennis daily and is in considerably better shape than I am) who was a much-beloved pastor for over fifty years. I asked him why weren't Evangelical ministers more involved in leading their congregations to serve with compassion, to fight injustice, to restore righteousness. He offered several practical problems faced by many pastors: lack of knowledge, lack of time, and lack of an effective ability to teach members how to be activists (apparently our seminaries do not offer courses on these subjects).

And there are other problems as well. Pastors facing a huge monthly mortgage payment on their new sanctuary will obviously tend toward a "keep everyone happy" approach. Mainline Churches may even face the loss of their property if they oppose denominational policy.

While these are perfectly understandable reasons, they are no longer acceptable ones in light of the demands that are made on us as we are challenged today as never before to meet the tremendous needs of our generation.

Fortunately, there are numerous indications that our Churches are breaking free of the blindness afflicting past generations.

One of those encouraging signs was the first article adapted by the delegates to the Lausanne World Evangelism Conference:

> We affirm our belief in the one-eternal God, Creator and Lord of the world, Father, Son and Holy Spirit, who governs all things according to the purpose of His will. He has been calling out from the world a people for Himself, and sending His witnesses, for the extension of His Kingdom, the building up of Christ's body, and the glory of His name. We confess with shame that we have often denied our calling and failed in our mission, by becoming conformed to the world or by withdrawing from it.[19]

FAILING TO MEET THE NEEDS OF OUR TIME

Any movement trying to redirect the nation's course must have as one of its primary goals that of convincing the populace that it is capable of leading them to a better, brighter future. Unfortunately, the Christian Right has squandered a golden opportunity to establish itself as an alternative source of leadership for the millions of Americans dissatisfied with our present state of confusion and stagnation.

At a time when America was looking for leaders with answers, courage, compassion, and integrity, the Christian Right failed to convince anyone — the Church, secular conservatives, or the traditionally value-oriented public — that we were the ones best suited to step into America's obvious leadership vacuum.

We in the Christian Right failed to provide real leadership because we did not understand the real problems that needed to be solved. Before a doctor can successfully prescribe a remedy for the patient's complaint, he must have an accurate diagnosis of what's wrong with the patient. The doctor must carefully examine the patient, listen to his list of complaints, and study his medical history. He must take time to really know the patient's symptoms *and* their underlying causes.

The Christian Right failed to provide remedies for people's problems, which is what leadership is all about, because we did not take the time to discover what was really bothering people. We were too absorbed by our own needs and agendas and too sure that we had one or two "cure-alls" that would heal any problem that came up.

We were like a doctor who refuses to see patients in person, saying that he doesn't have time to listen to their individual complaints; and anyway, he has developed his own miracle cure for everyone's problems. If they just take it their symptoms will disappear.

But we did not have a cure-all for society's problems, which we could have learned from a careful study of God's Word. In fact, we didn't even understand what the world's problems really were. Never taking time to discover the needs of our generation, it was impossible for us to meet them.

Of course, we were diligent in recording and categorizing the many symptoms of a nation and Church beset by serious moral decay and degradation. We knew we faced a patient with a potentially terminal illness. What we lacked was real insight into the cause of the illness. Our America does not need treatment for her painfully obvious symptoms of social breakdown as much as she needs radical therapy for the underlying causes of those symptoms.

What then, are the underlying causes of many of our nation's problems? What needs have these problems uniquely created within our generation? These are the needs that we are being called upon to meet.

Our Nationally Weakened Immune System

The AIDS virus is so deadly because it destroys one's immune system's ability to resist infections. With the immune system out of order, germs or viruses that would normally pose little or no problem, become fatal. In America our nation's "immune system" has been our citizens' commonly held Christian value system and our collective faith in the integrity of our system of government. Many scandalous outrages can take place in government or business, and our faith in the system keeps these "isolated viruses" from destroying the unity of the whole body. When we are displeased with the way things are going, we do not riot, assassinate, or turn to violence; we do not sanction violent revolutions, military coup d'états, or any disorderly replacement of offending leaders. In short, frustrations that might drive people in another country to radical or even violent acts to replace their leadership elites are not necessary in America because we have faith that, in the end, justice will prevail. At least we used to have that kind of faith.

Disease Called Alienation

A social/cultural virus called alienation threatens to destroy our national immune system. Without faith in our leaders and governmental processes, every isolated crisis can threaten our national well-being, or, added together, they can weaken our nation until it is too sick to carry on. Without a consensus on what values are to guide us and a large reservoir of goodwill toward each other, our national body politic is increasingly unable to repel effectively the many viruses now eating away at its very fiber.

According to a national poll conducted by Lou Harris in 1987, America is a shockingly alienated society. Our people are alienated as never before. "A substantial sixty percent of the adult population of the United States feel alienated from the power structure."[1] Harris provides some perspective on the stunning growth of alienation in America: In the period from 1966 through 1972, a majority of the American people did not feel alienated. Back in 1966 only twenty-nine percent felt that way.[2]

Just what, you ask, is alienation? I think a simple, but useful, definition is believing that you have no control over the decision makers or the decisions they make affecting your life — your voice doesn't count.

John Stott sums it up this way:

> . . . alienation is the feeling of economic and political powerlessness. The juggernauts of institutionalized power roll ruthlessly on their way, and the common man or woman cannot do anything to change their direction or speed, let alone stop them. We are nothing but spectators of a developing situation which we feel helpless to influence in any way. That is "alienation."[3]

To give added meaning to these definitions, the Harris poll also found that "fifty-five percent of the nation are convinced that the people running the country don't really care what happens to me."[4]

And even worse, sixty-six percent of the public feel that "most people with power try to take advantage of people like myself."[5]

What are some unmistakable signs of our generation's alienation? One of the most obvious is a precipitous decline in the level of confidence Americans have in their leaders.

Below is an easy-to-follow chart from Lou Harris's book *Inside America*. The chart clearly demonstrates that the level of confidence Americans have in their leaders is falling drastically.

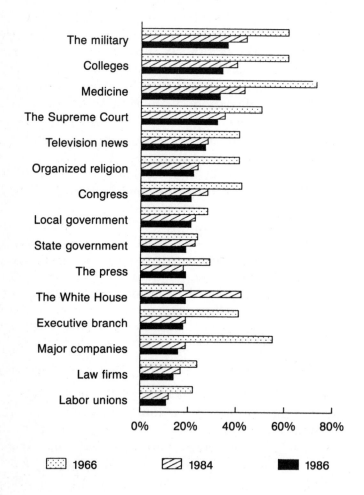

Figure 5.1

CITIZENS' LEVEL OF CONFIDENCE IN INSTITUTIONS

What the chart tells us is this:

> Bunched toward the middle of the pack are a host of leadership types: the U.S. Supreme court at thirty-two percent high confidence, those running television news at twenty-seven percent, and leaders of organized television news at twenty-seven percent, and leaders of organized religion at twenty-two percent. Again, all have fallen below their previous highs: the Supreme Court by twenty-two points, TV news by eighteen points, organized religion by twenty points, and the presidency by twelve points.[6]

> Lower still are three other groups of institutional leaders. Leaders of congress are currently at twenty-one percent high confidence, well down from their high of forty-two percent back in 1966.[7]

Harris observes, the situation is not improving:

> More significant than the standing of any one profession of leadership group is that all fell so far below the marks achieved in the 1960's and have not regained their prestige since.[8]

I might add, Americans' scandalous lack of voter participation, only thirty-six to fifty-five percent (voting averages from our last ten national elections), or about half of our potential voters, bother to exercise this hard-won right. This is a glaring example that many in our nation feel that their voices, their votes, simply don't count, so "why bother." In fact, our voting turnout is the world's lowest compared to twenty-eight other nations over the time period of 1969-1986.

And, of course, I could fill up a book with just the most obvious symptoms of alienation in our society. As George Reichley observed in his book *Religion in American Public Life*:

> During the 1970's divorce increased sixty-seven percent. Families headed by unwed mothers rose 356 percent. By the end of the decade, twenty-one percent of families with children under eighteen were headed by single parents. In 1979, seventeen percent of all children and fifty-five percent of black children were born out of wedlock. Recreational drug and pornography were readily available to all who could pay. Violent crime rose to an all-time high in 1980. A Gallup poll found one-third of Americans reporting a problem with alcoholism in their own families.[9]

The Harris poll also found that "great stress," a sign of alienation, is suffered daily by more than thirty percent of our population,[10] and that alcoholism, a prime mechanism for coping with stress and alienation, has its death grip on at least one member, if not two, in each of 28 million families.[11]

Drug abuse, the most extreme method of coping with alienation, is increasing its grip on our children, as well as adults. Calling drugs "a monster in our midst," Harris, in summing up his survey data, states:

> . . . four in ten teenagers regularly use marijuana, almost one in five use stimulants or uppers, one in nine use cocaine, one in twelve are using hallucinogens, one in twelve inhalants, one in fourteen illegal sedatives or downers, and one in seventeen illicit tranquilizers. Obviously, anyone might justifiably be frightened and even alarmed at the penetration of illicit drugs into the mainstream of American society. There is no guarantee of immunity for any family.[12]

American's increasing escape into pornography, sex and violence on TV and at the local theater, punk rock music, and increased acceptance of promiscuity are all signs of our alienation from once accepted Christian-based standards of social conduct.

Crime is on the rise, in part as a result of alienation from our nation's legal system. As both juvenile and white collar crimes expand at an alarming rate, it becomes frighteningly clear that the perpetrators of these crimes don't believe the laws forbidding these acts have any real moral authority.

Situational ethics and its "everything-is-relative" approach to life has also taken its toll, further alienating many Americans from our nation's historical mechanism for preserving social order — voluntary respect and observance of our Christian values and law.

Without voluntary observance of our laws, stemming from a community held faith and vision for America and trust in the integrity of our leaders who make and execute the laws, our nation will soon cease to function as a republic. We will open ourselves up to takeover by a harsh dictatorship, necessary to restore "respect" for law and order.

A friend of mine told me a story that illustrates my point. He is a businessman who makes frequent trips to Nigeria, one of

Africa's largest and most prosperous nations. Much to my surprise he said the Nigerians had adopted our own U.S. Constitution and Republican form of government as their own. Imagine my further surprise when he told me that the government, in an effort to enforce discipline upon an unruly populace, had resorted to force, utilizing a "war against undiscipline" campaign, including nightly executions of law breakers, broadcast over national TV.

The moral of the story? Without voluntary respect for a nation's moral codes exercised individually by each citizen, the most perfectly drawn constitution and laws are simply useless.

The Future

Unfortunately, the prognosis for reduced levels of alienation are, apart from God, not good. As our problems grow and become more complex and impossible for our government leaders to deal with (i.e., AIDS, terrorism, the Middle East, war, crushing national debt, balance of trade, etc.), people will be even more distrustful of and alienated from their leaders. As Christian standards continue to be cast aside, our ability to govern ourselves, to agree upon value systems and government policies, will be all but nonexistent.

Social scientists Eva Schindler-Rainman and Ronald L. Lippett, in their study on the need for more "volunteerism" to meet the needs of our generation, predicted:

> It is generally predicted that the explosion of expectations and demands for a better life will continue to generate distrust and competition, polarization and conflict between different segments of society. A continuing development of the cohesion and potency of the peer culture among the young will widen the gap between the generations. Youth's faith in the ability of the older generation to give guidance in coping with the present and the emerging future will continue to decline. Female confrontations of the male-dominated political and economic functions will intensify, as will the attack on the double standard in sexual mores. A coalition of all racial minorities is likely to confront the racial majority. The poor are developing an increasing sense of potency and outrage in their growing conflict with the affluent. The divisions between the radicals, the liberals, and

the conservatives in political life are becoming more sharp. In various areas of our economy, battle lines are being drawn between consumer groups and producers. Campuses are being increasingly disrupted by divisions between administrators, faculty, and students. New bases of conflict continue to emerge on the international scene. Issues of population pressure, food supply, industrialization, and territorial control will continue to create and aggravate conflict in the foreseeable future.[13]

And, finally, to underscore our unprecedented and perilous levels of alienation, pollster Harris sums up his findings with this note:

> The price that might be paid if the alienated ever became openly hostile could be enormous with overtones that would be traumatic. The trouble is that no one really knows what the *breaking point* might be for these literally millions of people. But when over 100 million adults say they feel alienated from the establishment leadership, a national condition exists that *cannot continue to be ignored* (italics added).[14]

The Christian Right Failed

The Christian Right needed to offer a remedy for our nation's growing hostility and alienation. We needed to offer God's vision for healing our people and for re-establishing a moral consensus based on Christian ethics. But because we did not have an accurate diagnosis of our patient, all we did was throw useless prescriptions at the various symptoms of the disease. The very phenomenon that gave rise to the success of the Christian Right was the one we misread.

In 1980, the Connecticut Mutual Life Insurance Company commissioned a major study called *American Values in the 80's: The Impact of Belief*. The study spent hundreds of pages documenting the rise of a new wave of Christian political activity. In its assessment of facts that created an atmosphere in which the Christian Right could grow, alienation and "disillusionment with leaders" were several of the prime culprits.

> Numerous articles and opinion polls have documented this widespread alienation from political institutions. Indeed, this survey demonstrates that there is a dramatic gap between lead-

ers and the public in a number of respects. They disagree strongly, for example, on moral, political and family issues. They are also dramatically different in terms of their level of religious commitment, their community involvement, and their attitudes toward work. Our diminished national self-confidence, however, takes on special foreboding in the context of a condition readily apparent as we enter the eighties: an economy in trouble. It is this special combination of political turmoil and economic decline that makes the swelling support for traditional values, as well as its spillover into direct political action, so compelling as a contemporary concern. Something unusual is happening.[15]

Fear Stalks the Land

Another underlying cause of our nation's cultural disintegration is fear. Fear of the future. Fear for our families. Fear of the unknown. As three Catholic scholars so forcefully described the fears that beset us in their book *Compassion*:

> Nuclear warheads and power plants, millions of hungry and dying people, torture chambers and immense cruelties, the increase in robberies, rapes, and twisted, sadistic plots, all give us the feeling of being surrounded by a mysterious network of powers that can destroy us any day or hour. The awareness that at any moment something could happen that could permanently destroy our life, health, or happiness, can fill us with an all-pervading sadness and fear.[16]

A government that was supposed to represent us and serve us has grown unresponsive and untouchable. Do you know anyone who has had to deal with any branch of government, other than perhaps local, and been treated efficiently and courteously as you would expect from someone who was serving you? I don't. In fact, every experience I have heard is a horror story of disinterested, unhelpful, and incompetent lifetime bureaucrats whose last thoughts are to serve you!

This process of bureaucratization and centralization destroys people's ability to mold, or even influence, the destiny of their lives or community. Without an ability to help direct, or even know about, the decision-making process of one's community, we become alienated. We feel isolated from those in positions of authority over *our* life. This lack of control over one's life leads to a pervasive sense of uneasiness that easily translates into fear.

Today, people are afraid, afraid because they know they don't have a vision, plan, or agenda to remedy successfully the challenges to our personal, economic, or national well-being. They also lack a consistent Christian worldview to adequately put these problems in their proper perspective. Worse yet, the terrible truth is dawning that no one else, not political, business, or religious leaders, has the answer either. Down deep, we know, or at least suspect, that it's the blind leading the blind. Our fear is not a big, screaming fear, but lots of little, nagging fears, fears that cause stress and loss of joy. Underneath these little fears lies a deep nagging fear too terrible to face, and yet increasingly difficult to suppress.

What happens if our leaders really do fail us (an increasing fear) and society continues to deteriorate (an ever increasing expectation) or the economy collapses, or World War III breaks out?

A *New York Times* poll taken in early 1988 provides us with an indication that these fears are becoming more pronounced:

> For the first time since Ronald Reagan became president in 1981, Americans generally do not believe that the nation's future will be better than its present or its past, according to the *New York Times — CBS News Poll.*
>
> The key reason for the difference between the overall national and personal future ratings seems to be that Americans still believe they can plan and regulate their own lives, even while the national economy and popular culture appear to be spinning our of control.
>
> The survey, which defined the past as five years ago and the future as five years ahead, found a continuation of Americans' historical optimism about their personal futures, an outlook apparently tied to confidence in their ability to control their own destiny. But it also found uneasiness about the outlook for their nation unmatched since the most troubled days of the Carter administration.[17]

Up to now, we've been talking about "generalized, non-specific" fear. Let's take a brief look at many of the specific fears that beset our generation. If we are sensitive to them, we can accurately diagnose their causes and prescribe their remedies. We must constantly remind ourselves that before we offer answers, we must understand the problems of our generation.

Specific Fears We Face

About our children: How can we protect our children from increasing immoral contamination from TV, peers, degenerate music, drugs, alcohol, humanistic public education, and the like?

It doesn't take paranoid parents, or even Christian parents, to be concerned with the 101 negative influences impacting our children at the close of the twentieth century. Scores of books are written on each one of these dangers, any one of which is enough in itself to destroy the innocence, joy, or traditional moral values we wish our children to retain.

About our families: How can we continue to provide for our families if politicians and Wall Street selfishness, incompetency, and short-sightedness wreck the economy through budget deficits, trade deficits, interest rates, inflation, national debt., etc.?

A careful reading of news magazines and newspapers reveals what Washington insiders like David Stockman, formerly Chief of the U.S. budget, have admitted publicly: "no one understands what is going on." One of Stockman's most shocking admissions was that no one in government, including himself, understood how much the government was spending or where it was spending it, let alone why!

While thousands of economists disagree with each other, unable to agree on a single course of action, the national debt expands geometrically, trade deficits are shocking, our annual federal deficit zooms out of sight, and the stock market shows signs of extreme frailty.

Most people suspect that someday, probably sooner than later, the bill is going to come due for our overextended private and government debt-financed lifestyles, and America as we know it will be over. For each of us, this is a frightening possibility.

About our neighborhoods: Are our families physically safe to walk the streets? Are they safe even in their own homes? Are they emotionally safe from the verbal abuse or lustful leer that is almost as damaging as a physical attack? Are they safe from the trauma of pain inflicted by their peers who are raised in unGodly, violent, and/or alienated environments?

It should not be surprising that, year-by-year, our families, towns, and cities grow steadily less safe, when we legalize all sorts of X-rated pornography that glorifies acts of sexual violence against women; when we consistently parole hardened, violent criminals because of overcrowded prisons or lenient judges; when we romanticize acts of theft or violence nightly on TV; and when our media and educational elites tell us that there are no moral absolutes.

About our nation: How will we handle the challenge of a more willful and perhaps militarily superior Soviet Union as it threatens to first penetrate and then dominate Asia (from Cambodia, Laos, and Vietnam to the Philippines and South Korea), the Middle East, Africa, and even our own backyard in the Americas? What does it all mean? An eventual choice between war or capitulation? And what about terrorism and Islamic turmoil in the Middle East? Is World War III brewing there?

The reason many of our youth desperately seek to drown themselves in "heavy metal" or "punk rock" music, drugs, and sex in an orgy of self-destruction is that they sense *there is no future*. Somehow, man will destroy the planet or civilization as we know it. Without hope for and in the future, all they are left with is disillusionment and hopelessness, expressed in their choice of escapes, their physical appearance, and their overall attitudes toward each other and life in general.

Looking for a Vision

If we add to all this the frightening suspicion that our leaders do not really have any viable plans, or even know how to create them, we have a society that is justifiably anxious, fearful, hostile, and hungry for answers. Yet, in a nation hungry, even starving for answers, the Christian Right failed to offer anything resembling a comprehensive solution for our problems.

The Christian Right prescribed treatment for symptoms, rather than for the underlying disease. This is like giving aspirin to a cancer patient. The pain may be lessened a bit, but the knowledge that the patient is going to die keeps him fearful, anxious, and alienated from those he turned to for healing.

Will stopping pornography, drugs, abortion, or other social evils solve our alienation and fear of the future? Of course not.

Everyone knows that if you solve one problem, there are ten more to take its place. People realize that our whole society is deteriorating, that there is no one to lead it, no consensus and no vision.

This also helps us understand why the Christian Right had such a difficult time attempting to energize people to a high level of activity on various single-issue causes. Most people thought, *so we win one issue, what good will it really do?*

To Sum Up

The Christian Right, in its hurry to stop the obvious deterioration of our nation, failed to devote the time to take stock of root causes. Men of action like to act, not analyze, and most recently the Church's strength has not been in analyzing social trends. Such a failure puts tactics before strategy, short-term goals before long-term objectives, and denies us any way to provide comprehensive answers to the very deep problems facing our generation.

The real problems facing us are not abortion, homosexuality, pornography, drugs, sex, and violence, communism, immorality, etc. These are the symptoms of much deeper problems of fear and alienation from God, from government, from each other. As our society becomes more alienated from both its leaders and its foundation, it increasingly turns to unhealthy forms of escape to bury its frustration.

Before we can offer solutions, we must learn to understand the underlying problems. We must feel the needs of those for whom we want to provide answers. This is the real challenge to meeting the needs of our generation. We will succeed only to the extent that we offer a vision that promises answers to people's fears in a way that gives them hope and confidence for the future.

As Christians we should know that God is the answer for man's alienation. God's love and compassion is the appropriate prescription for millions of hurting, alienated people. Our individual identity of who we are in God is essential to any true sense of personal security. Christian principals of honesty, integrity, and truthfulness in government are the remedy for a nation disillusioned with its leaders.

The Christian Right misunderstood our generation. Our generation is not *looking for single issues*, or busy projects. It is looking for real answers to fundamental problems. It is waiting for someone to point the way, from listlessness to purpose, from futility to hope, from despair to vision, from alienation to commitment, from fear and anxiety to the strength and courage of great convictions.

What are these convictions? To what purpose will they lead us? Is there a cause so challenging that in demanding our total commitment it will satisfy our personal longings for security and meaning as well as make our community and our world a better, safer place to live? We deal with this ultimate question in the next chapter.

SIX

A NEW VISION
FOR OUR TIME

America is a nation without vision. The Bible tells us that without vision the people "will perish" or will "cast off restraint," meaning fall apart. Losing their self-discipline and sense of direction and purpose, people become aimless, alienated and fearful.

Today, the vision that was America's throughout our history is gone, and our people are undeniably in the process of perishing—our culture dying, our national unity disintegrating. If it is vision we lack, we must ask some very basic questions. Just what is vision and why is it so important to us, to our families, to our nation?

What Is Vision

Vision provides moral energy or "fuel" for change; it gives direction for the present; and it acts as our guide for the future. Vision shows us a better life, the world that "could be," and inspires us to commit ourselves to the point of sacrifice to achieve it.

A common vision is necessary for building a Church or a nation. Author Goen describes the success of the early American Church:

> The Evangelical bodies that are the focus of this study quickly rose to cultural dominance mainly because they were all organizing the same basic impulse, sharing common convictions about purpose and destiny, and participating in the common task of creating a Christian republic.[1]

This vision provided the inspiration to build a nation we call our own:

Even though the churches were now separated from the state, the vision of a Christian social orders was as strong as ever. Evangelical Protestantism forged an impressive symbiosis with the ideals of democracy and freedom, seeing in the new nation a destiny-determining opportunity to shape an authentically Christian republic. "The true American union" would emerge out of democratic institutions whose chief sustaining power was the Evangelical enterprise.[2]

Vision also provides energy to conquer hostile nations. Unfortunately, one of the best examples of this is present day Marxism. How can such an evil as Soviet totalitarianism inspire such total devotion? Surely not from the track record of what Ronald Reagan refers to as the "evil empire":

> Twenty million Soviet peasants and Communist party members [were] murdered under Lenin and Stalin's bloodthirsty power purges [some of Stalin's more apparent atrocities are now being openly admitted as "enormous and unforgivable crimes" by the new Soviet leadership].[3]

> Fifty million Chinese peasants and intellectuals [were] murdered in "cleansing" and "agrarian reform" programs of Chairman Mao.[4]

> Millions more [were] dying in slave labor camps in the Soviet Union for unauthorized political or religious statements [read Solzhenitsyn's *Gulag Archipelago*], or rotting away for the same crimes in Cuba's dungeons.[5]

So, what is it that attract idealists, young and old, some even "religious" to such a despicable evil? It is a vision for a better world. Unfortunately the Marxist vision is one thousand percent different from the Soviet Communist reality.

Karl Marx, the founder of communism, in his *Communist Manifesto* published in 1848, called for a society free of exploitation and social injustice. Of course, Marx saw the merchant class, today's middle- and upper-economic classes, as the willfully evil exploiter of the working man. He saw the Church's role as one condoning this exploitation and protecting the "ruling classes." Thus, his many adherents today are committed to the total eradication of both religion (Marx said his goal was to dethrone God) and Capitalism (free enterprise).

Marxism seeks to perfect mankind and social systems by denying God and elevating man as the final authority and ultimate value. That such a secular-humanist system is doomed to failure is evident by the necessity of an Iron Curtain and Berlin Wall to keep the captives in, as opposed to an "open gate" to receive the millions who were expected to be attracted to the "workers paradise," as many American intellectuals used to refer to the Soviet Union.

But concerned, compassionate people and idealists in other countries, including our own, don't often get a glimpse of the inhuman face of true totalitarian communism. Instead they see the human face of a Marxist vision that offers seemingly hopeful answers to the injustice that the Church in its own countries has refused to confront. Obviously, vision is a powerful force in the lives of men and women. With it they can accomplish almost anything, and no sacrifice, even life itself, is too great if it furthers the vision's realization.

The Christian Right is living proof that without vision any movement is guaranteed to fail. When the Christian Right attempted to substitute isolated planks in place of a cohesive vision, we quickly discovered that one cannot mobilize an army with a disparate collage of single issues. Ninety percent of those we sought to mobilize viewed each issue separately. Finding none of them overwhelmingly compelling on their own merits, they took little or no action. Or, finding one all consuming issue, they concentrated on it to the exclusion of the other equally important issues. While most of the Christian Right's issues were of legitimate concern, most were not compelling enough to merit the devotion required to transform a society.

To make up for our lack of a vision compelling agenda, we were forced to rely upon emotion and fear to stimulate action. Every fundraising appeal letter virtually screamed that some terrible catastrophe would befall the reader or his family if the suggested action was not taken immediately. This sort of continued melodramatic overstatement was justly and roundly criticized as being hard-edged, irresponsible, negative, and reactionary.

Lacking a vision of our own, all we could do was react in a negative way to the vision or programs of those with non-Christian or anti-Christian visions and agendas. In this sense, we were guilty of being "reactionaries."

Vision for America

To answer the needs of our generation and to meet the challenge of the nineties demands that we regain God's vision for our nation. We don't need to create our own vision. We simply need to be obedient in carrying out God's vision. What, then, is God's vision for our society? What is God's supreme vision for man and his government? Psalm 72 portrays God's ideal government:

> He will judge your people in righteousness, your afflicted ones with justice. . . . He will defend the afflicted among the people and save the children of the needy; He will crush the oppressor. . . . For He will deliver the needy who cry out, the afflicted who have no one to help. He will take pity on the weak and the needy and save the needy from death. He will rescue them from oppression and violence, for precious is their blood in His sight. (Psalm 72:2)

And the Psalms also declare:

> The Lord loves righteousness and justice; the earth is full of His unfailing love. (Psalm 33:5)

> You love righteousness and hate wickedness; therefore God, your God, has set you above your companions by anointing you with the oil of joy. (Psalm 45:7)

> Righteousness and justice are the foundation of your throne; love and faithfulness go before you. (Psalm 89:14)

The *NIV Study Bible,* in its footnote on Psalm 72, declares that the "ideal concept" of government is founded upon the "sacred virtues" of "justice and righteousness."[6]

Proverbs 16:12 tells us that governments should be established upon righteousness. Isaiah 9:7 teaches us that Christ's government is built upon "justice and righteousness." What should our vision for America be? I suggest a society of justice, righteousness, mercy, and compassion. Let's examine each component to learn God's plan for reshaping our community and our nation.

In our modern use of language, the term righteousness has gotten a "bum rap." In its common usage, at least in the secular world, it implies a legalistic, cold-hearted, pharisaical, self-approval or self-righteousness. But that is not what it actually means. Perhaps because we have lost the true meaning of this vital concept we have also lost our ability to see God's vision for our nation.

Biblical Righteousness

The Biblical concept of righteousness is very simple: conforming to God's standard for human conduct, i.e., what pleases God in our personal character and in our nation. It is the carrying out of our duty of what "is right" toward both God and man.

The Hebrew word used throughout the Old Testament for righteousness, *tsedeq*, means "fairly, just, what is right." Webster defines righteousness "being in accord with what is just . . . free from wrong." "Just" in Webster's is defined as "what is morally or legally right." And "justice" is the administration of what is just.

In the King James Version of the Bible, the Greek word *dikaios* is repeatedly interpreted as "righteous" or "just," the two words being interchangeable. So, we can see that righteousness and justice are different sides of the same coin. True justice prevails when all people stand equal before a legal system rooted in God's righteousness.

God's Justice

God's sense of justice is not an abstract legal concept. It is a down-to-earth concern for people that they might be treated justly, compassionately, and rightly.

Hate evil, love good; maintain justice in the courts. (Amos 5:15)

. . . the living God is the God of justice as well as of justification.[7]

He upholds the cause of the oppressed and gives food to the hungry.

The Lord sets prisoners free,
    the Lord gives sight to the blind,
The Lord lifts up those who are bowed down,
    the Lord gives sight to the blind,
The Lord watches over the alien
    and sustains the fatherless and widow,
      but He frustrates the ways of the wicked. (Psalm 146:7)

Throughout the Bible, God clearly demanded both nations and individuals to live righteously and justly. Those who did not were justly judged, as were many of the nations in the Old Testament. Singled out for their injustices to other nations or to their own people, Israel was judged on the same basis.

In Isaiah 10:1-2, God pointedly condemns His own people, the Jews, for their unjust laws:

> Woe to those who make unjust laws, to those who issue oppressive decrees, to deprive the poor of their rights and withhold justice from the oppressed of My people, making widows their prey and robbing the fatherless.

God's disgust with injustice in the midst of His own children is made evident in Isaiah 1:21-23 and Isaiah 5:7:

> See how the faithful city has become a harlot! She once was full of justice; righteousness used to dwell in her—but now murderers! Your silver has become dross, your choice wine is diluted with water. Your rulers are rebels, companions of thieves; they all love bribes and chase after gifts. They do not defend the cause of the fatherless; the widow's case does not come before them.

> The vineyard of the Lord Almighty is the house of Israel, and the men of Judah are the garden of His delight. And He looked for justice, but saw bloodshed; for righteousness, but heard cries of distress.

It is abundantly clear from the Old Testament that God despises injustice and unrighteousness, and demands that we implement His principles to the fullest extent of our abilities.

How do these verses apply to us today? Have we elected (and re-elected) officials who make unjust laws? Do we seek justice, i.e., fair treatment for all people everywhere? Or do we ever think about other people's misfortunes? Or are we too busy, too distracted, too hard-hearted to even care? Have we acquiesced to a society that ignores the rights and needs of the poor in America or in the Third World nations that we influence? Have we assisted foreign governments in oppressing their people? Have we tolerated a society that willfully exploits women and children—economically, spiritually, and sexually?

Have our leaders lost their honesty and integrity? Have they rebelled against God's standards of justice and righteousness? And what about bloodshed? Does executing 4,400 babies a day in abortion clinics count?

Because of Israel's lack of justice and righteousness, God condemned their empty religiosity. Can He be any less pleased- with us today?

> I hate, I despise your religious feast; I cannot stand your as- semblies. Even though you bring me burnt offerings and grain offerings, I will not accept them. Though you bring choice fel- lowship and offerings, I will have no regard for them. Away with the noise of your songs! I will not listen to the music of your harps. But let justice roll on like a river, righteousness like a never-failing stream! (Amos 5:21-24)

God is calling us to account for our lives, our time, our use of His resources. How are we to obey His commands to see that justice and righteousness can flow unimpeded? Our first step must be to look in our own backyard to see what obstructions are holding back just and right treatment for all people.

The Failure of American Justice

Our justice is not just. Where is our protection for the inno- cent, the exploited, the oppressed, the abused, in this nation founded by Godly men and women for the establishment of jus- tice and righteousness? Tragically, we do not have to look far to find injustices perpetrated or allowed by the government we elect and quietly acquiesce to.

The Injustice of Exploitation

Certainly one of the greatest evils of our time is exploitation — taking from another for one's own gain or gratification. We have become so used to exploitation that it is now accepted as a nor- mal part of everyday life and, in many circles, even condoned as the way to "win," get what's yours, to look after "number one," and the like.

At home in America we exploit the poor by keeping them locked into a lifetime system of welfare handouts, destroying personal incentive, initiative, and self-respect. The one-way flow of dollars is controlled by politicians who demand and receive votes in return. (Realizing that welfare reform is a controversial subject, I will deal with it, and many of the other issues listed here at more length in subsequent chapters).

Around the globe, large American corporations aggressively exploit Third World nations by either taking unfair advantage of local labor or by keeping in power reprehensible dictatorships that safeguard a handsome return on American corporate investments. The latest example of this is Chevron Oil's shameless payment of hundreds of millions of dollars annually to the murderous Soviet puppet regime in Angola, Africa. The regime used its income to pay for over thirty thousand Cuban troops who in turn mercilessly suppressed the Angolan people. When challenged on its position, Chevron spokesmen argued that since their oil fields were under the protection of the Angolan government, it made sense to ante up a percentage of the profits. Besides, since Chevron is a multinational corporation, its interests did not necessarily coincide with American foreign policy, which opposes the Angolan regime. Chevron might have added that their policies also did not necessarily coincide with any concern for the lives of the downtrodden, oppressed, and beleaguered people of Angola.

Exploiting Ourselves

Not satisfied with exploiting others, we have turned inward, to exploit each other. To make money or gratify our lust, we exploit women by debasing them in pornography; and we exploit the readers, many of them children, by filling their minds with subconscious programming guaranteed to wreck any hopes of a moral, healthy sex life after marriage.

America's largest corporations give billions of consumers' dollars annually to Hollywood producers to turn out shows pandering to our worst instincts and society's lowest common denominator—abundant and graphic sex and violence. The consumer is exploited. He is actually victimized twice, once by paying for a product whose funds are used in a manner that degrades and deteriorates our whole culture, and the second time when the consumer or his children view the mind-rotting end result of what their money has produced.

Even the local phone company has joined in on one of the more obscene examples of exploiting those it supposedly serves. When the telephone monopolies were broken up and regional phone companies were forced to compete in the free market, it did not take them long to figure out that vast amounts of money could be made by leasing telephone lines to pornographers.

The Dial-A-Porn controversy has been the subject of numerous national TV shows and the focus of heated debate in Congress. Why? Because tens of thousands of children are running up their parents' phone bills, often in the thousands of dollars, to call a "976" number. Each day they are treated to recordings of lesbians "making love," or several women and men in an orgy — anal sex, oral sex and whatever else the sick mind of the day can produce. Each recording features the appropriate dosage of filthy words, graphic descriptions, moans, grunts, and screams. Besides corrupting untold thousands of young minds and bringing many parents to the brink of bankruptcy (ABC's "20/20" news program featured a father who was forced to work two full-time jobs to pay off his son's Dial-A-Porn charges). Dial-A-Porn has already demonstrated its more evil side effects.

In a $10 million dollar lawsuit, parents charged that their twelve-year-old son molested a four-year-old girl after listening to the suggestive recordings. In a rape trial the victim claimed that her assailant repeatedly called the Dial-A-Porn number to increase his stimulation as he attacked her.[8] What is our friendly local telephone company's response? Pacific Bell's plea was typical. They were "not responsible for the moral turpitude of their customers."[9] Of course, what they are responsible for is splitting the profits with their Dial-A-Porn clients for each minute of "976" billing that children, or adults, run up on their long distance bills.

All-in-all, their philosophy is very simple and very true to the new, selfish, and relativistic American ethic. Our local phone company is willing to do whatever they must to increase their profits. Exploitation is not even an issue.

Even baby food manufacturers happily defraud and exploit their customers as the following news story, reported from the *San Francisco Chronicle*, indicates:

"Beech-Nut Nutrition Corporation agreed yesterday to pay the government a $2 million fine and investigative costs stemming from a guilty plea to charges it sold phony apple juice," the Justice Department said. "The baby food manufacturer pleaded guilty to 215 felony counts for violating the Food, Drug and Cosmetic Act, admitting that it shipped phony apple juice between December 1981 and March 1983," the department said. "The company was marketing as pure apple juice a drink that was actually made from beet sugar, cane sugar syrup, corn syrup and other ingredients with little, if any, apple juice in the mixture," the government said.[10]

Exploitation has become so accepted that we do it to each other without thinking twice. We sell each other drugs. We take advantage of each other sexually and emotionally to gratify our own needs. We use deceitful business practices or wink at those who do.

More Abuse

Injustice includes a wide array of other, even more serious, abuses. Unfortunately, these abuses are becoming increasingly prevalent "in the land of the free and the home of the brave."

For the sake of the convenience of the mother, we are killing well over one million babies every year through abortion. One baby loses its life in the protective womb of its mother approximately every twenty seconds. God's reference to His people's becoming murderers in Isaiah 1:21 can be applied here!

One of the original pillars of our system of justice was that it effectively administered what was just. Criminals were punished, the innocent were set free. Today the reverse is often true. Vicious criminals are set free — most convicted rapists and child molesters spend little or no time in prison — while law-abiding citizens are arrested for having prayer meetings in their houses (zoning violations); and ministers are imprisoned for resisting state control of their Church schools.

No better example of the humanistic perversion of justice exists than the recent sentencing of Joan Andrews of Florida to five years in prison for unplugging abortion equipment, while the same judge on the same day sentenced two convicted murderers to only four years imprisonment![11]

Increasingly, American justice is characterized by criminals who laugh at the system, citizens who are harassed by it, and thousands of unscrupulous lawyers who make outrageous fees for suing everyone or everything for any and every conceivable reason. This dramatic failure of our legal system to dispense the very justice it purports to exemplify signals a primary breakdown in our claim to be a just nation.

Exporting Injustice

But that is not all. We cannot limit our discussion of justice to just what we dispense to our own citizens, because the United States as one of our world's two "superpowers" constantly dispenses "justice" abroad.

We were willing to sacrifice millions of American lives in World War I, World War II, Korea, and Vietnam primarily to provide for just resolutions against what we viewed as unjust aggressor's attacking innocent nations. The government of Japan bombed Pearl Harbor only after it was obvious we were planning to frustrate their Imperial designs. And just recently American troops freed the Caribbean Island nation of Grenada from a bloody coup orchestrated by Fidel Castro.

For decades we have attempted to export our democratic and humanitarian values to developing nations—including direct imposition of our values on often recalcitrant governments—but it seems that at least since Word War II, we have turned a blind eye to much injustice in the world. Even worse, in our attempt to pacify the territorial ambitions of competing superpowers or curry favor with some regionally strategic despot, we have often played an active role in enabling foreign powers to subjugate and enslave innocent peoples.

While it may not particularly bother our conscience (particularly since some readers may have no idea what I'm talking about), millions of souls (dead, imprisoned, or deprived of their freedoms) do not hold us blameless. And neither does God.

Justice and Righteousness Restored

Clearly, then, we can see that our nation is in need of an immediate restoration of justice and righteousness—what is morally right, fair, nonexploitative, and nonabusive—in our government's policies, both domestic and foreign. Such a restoration would go a long way toward offsetting the rampant alienation and disillusionment in our land.

The dilemma we face is, how are we to implement our vision of a just and moral nation? There seems to be much talk with very little progress in bringing this vision into reality.

Compassion: The Missing Key

Christ's compassion is the vital key we've been missing. The compassionate society, based on God's love and in obedience to Christ's commandments to love and care for our fellow man, is a good basis on which to begin returning justice, mercy, and righteousness to our land.

What is Christian compassion? Compassion means caring about what happens to others. It is empathizing, feeling their feelings, being sensitive and vulnerable enough to put yourself in their place of feeling. In their original Greek and Latin root words, *compassion* and *sympathy* both mean essentially the same: "to suffer with."

We all feel compassion when those in need come into our immediate view. A hurt family member, a friend in trouble, an injured animal, or a moving sermon can elicit our sympathy, even our involvement. But we must enlarge our focus beyond our own immediate circle of interest. If we don't, we will never sense the plight of the babies killed in our neighborhood's abortion clinic, the homeless woman on the corner, the anguish of the broken homes on our block, the child with AIDS in our school, or the Afghan child who, picking up a Russian "toy," has his hands blown off by a bomb.

Having vs. Being

There is a fundamental, but little understood, difference between having compassion and being compassionate. Having compassion implies that if, somehow, something gets our attention long enough or with enough impact, we may have a compassionate response. But it is on the outer edges of who and what we are. If we dig deep enough into our pocket as if for some change, we find a little compassion and sprinkle it on the object that has momentarily won our attention.

Of course, those folks who raise billions of dollars annually for various charitable causes know this is how we respond, and that is how they mold their appeals for aid through the mail or on television. But this is a long way from being compassionate, from having the welfare of others as a top priority, rather than our last priority.

Compassion, then, is a matter of degrees. How far are we able to extend ourselves outward from our own concerns and agendas? Whose agenda is primary in our minds, ours to help ourselves, or God's to help each other?

The Bible leaves no question as to what our position must be. In Luke 6:36 we are told to be compassionate just as God is compassionate. Philippians 2:1-4 tells us:

> If you have any encouragement from being united with Christ, if any comfort from His love, if any fellowship with the Spirit, if any tenderness and compassion, then make my joy complete by being like-minded, having the same love, being one in spirit and purpose.

The *NIV Study Bible* footnote to Philippians 2:1-4 observes: ". . . Christians are to have intense care and deep sympathy for each other."[12]

These verses and hundreds more like them indicate that God is deeply moved by human need, and so He instructs us to be as well.

> Therefore, as God's chosen people, holy and dearly loved, *clothe yourselves with compassion*, kindness, humility, gentleness and patience. (Colossians 3:12, italics added)

How do we increase our compassion? First we must begin by observing and thinking about, rather than blocking out, images and information that might be upsetting to us. If we continue to block out all "negative" images and news by concentrating only on our private world, we will soon be dead to life altogether. If we don't listen to the news, observing and reflecting upon the world's needs around us, we become small, uninformed, uninterested, uninteresting and unfeeling people. We are not good company. More importantly, we become totally incapable of reflecting God's love and compassion for our fellow man.

Some Examples

Perhaps some examples from my own life would be helpful.

When I was a boy of fourteen I read a tract from an American missionary (Tom Dooley, I believe) that described the brutal torture inflicted upon children by the Viet Cong in their strategy to intimidate people into submission through terror — the same sort of cold, calculated, total terror that the crazed colonel, portrayed by Marlon Brando, talks about in the Vietnam film classic *Apocalypse Now*.

When I read this small tract, I did not immediately dismiss it as something unpleasant or irrelevant to my life. I thought about it. I pictured the young children. I cried. I was filled with hurt and anger at the unspeakable evil of any power that tries to subjugate people through a philosophy that legitimizes terror as an appropriate weapon. The primary operating principle of Communist expansionism is its founder's, V. I. Lenin's, maxim that "the end justifies the means." As a teenager, the more I learned about such atrocities, of man's inhumanity to man, the deeper my resolve became to do something about it. Why? Because I felt the pain of the innocent victims, I could see the anguish on their faces, I could hear their pitiful cries for help and their moaning over loved ones.

When South Vietnam and Cambodia fell to the Communists in the mid-seventies, I was about twenty-five years of age and was involved in sending aid to refugees from war zones in Vietnam. When I heard the news, I was stunned. I had not expected a Republican president (Gerald Ford) to allow the Democratic Congress to cut off military aid to our Allies when they were surrounded by a savagely brutal and bloodthirsty army.

I went into my office, locked the door, and turned off the lights. I grieved the entire afternoon. Not because I supported the way America fought the war (which I did not), not because we had lost an ally or because the United States had suffered a humiliating defeat. I wept for the victims of the unspeakable atrocities I knew was to come.

And despite hysterical protests to the contrary by the antiwar movement and the liberals within the media and Congress, news reports over the next few days and years bore out the worst of my fears. When Saigon fell, hundreds of young women killed themselves rather than suffer violent rape and death at the hands of their "liberators." Brave soldiers fought to the last man to protect their families. Public officials blew their brains our while giving their flag a last salute. The lucky survivors were consigned to "re-education" prison and torture camps.

Of course, what happened in neighboring Cambodia made Saigon look like a fun day at Disneyland. Pol Pot, the Marxist "liberator" of Cambodia, massacred one-third of his entire nation's population after he seized power. This is reflected in the popular true-life film *The Killing Fields*. Several authors have confirmed that in their zeal to rid Cambodia of "pre-revolutionary holdover attitudes," Pol Pot's regime murdered anyone who had a college degree, worked for the previous government or even wore glasses (a sign of education in the old way). Their first act of liberation was to execute the entire Parliament and then force march the entire population of the capitol city of Phenom Phen, including every patient in every hospital, into "relocation areas" several hundred miles away. Of course, most died en route, or perished when they got to their new destinations, which were nothing but wild jungles.

A decade later, in 1985, a group of one hundred Christian Right leaders gathered in Washington, D.C., to view a twenty-minute video showing several black Africans being "necklaced." This is a practice popular with the black Marxist militants of the African National Congress (ANC), devoted to destroying the white government of South Africa through terrorizing any black leaders or black citizens who disagree with their methods or objectives. Victims have a rubber car tire placed around their neck that is then filled with gasoline and set on fire. People chant and cheer as the offending party burns to death.

I did not watch this video as a documentary about terrible or unbelievable things happening to people I did not know, in a country I'd never been to, and therefore didn't care about. I rose to my feet to demand that we as a group speak out against these atrocities. For the first time in my life I was unable to complete a speech (even a short one). My voice broke, and I could not go on. The pain I felt for those I had just seen martyred was too great to bear.

On perhaps a less dramatic but just as moving note, an experience occurred recently as my wife, Miriam, and I were driving through the countryside. On the side of the road was a large cemetery with a small hill in the middle. On the hill, next to a tombstone, sat a grandmotherly lady on the grass, all alone. How my heart went out to her. As I imagined her spending her days in loneliness, her sorrow and grieving for the lost "partner for life," tears coursed down my face. Today that particular vision still has the power to move me to tears.

I'm not suggesting that we be vulnerable to, or dwell on, every tragedy we see or hear about. In fact, the more sensitive you are, the more you have to be careful not to be overwhelmed, a problem I have been trying to balance for twenty-five years. I am saying that if we are to exercise compassion, we must begin with increasing our awareness and sensitivity to those in need, down the block, across town, in another state, or around the world.

Avoiding our Compassion

Tragically, our natural instincts are to avoid being compassionate. Most of us have enough problems of our own and don't wish to experience, even for a few seconds, the suffering of others. As the three scholars who wrote *Compassion* insightfully describe:

> One of the most tragic events of our time is that we know more than ever before about the pains and sufferings of the world and yet are less and less able to respond to them.[13]

> When the pains of the world are presented to people who are already overwhelmed by the problems in their small circle of family or friends, how can we hope for a creative response? What we can expect is the opposite of compassion: numbness and anger. Exposure to human misery often leads to psychic numbness. Our minds cannot tolerate being constantly reminded of things which interfere with what we are doing at the moment. When we have to open our store in the morning, go about our business, prepare our classes, or talk to our fellow workers, we cannot be filled with the collective misery of the world. If we let the full content of newscasts enter into our innermost selves, we would become so overwhelmed by the absurdities of existence that we would become paralyzed. If we try to absorb all that is reported by the paper, radio, or television, we would never get any work done. Our continued effectiveness requires a mental filtering system by which we can moderate the impact of the daily news.[14]

The central thought these scholars are expressing is that "bad news" distracts from our own needs, concerns, and agendas. And that is exactly the problem.

While the Bible gives us clear instruction to take care of our businesses and families, we are not told to do so by ignoring everything and everyone else. A fact unfortunately misunderstood by most Christians is our livelihoods are, in fact, part of God's calling for us: "Whatever you do, do it all for the glory of God" (1 Corinthians 10:31). At the very least our jobs or businesses should be viewed as something that sustains us so we can have the time and financial resources to help others. If God in His sovereignty prospers us financially, it is so we can fund the mercy works He calls His people to.

It is our total commitment to a "me" orientation, to selfish desire, to enjoy to the fullest whatever leisure time and activities our level of affluence, which we slave to maintain or increase, will allow, that hinders us from obedience to Christ in exercising compassion.

Increasing Our Compassion

So, now we must ask ourselves, how can we increase our compassion?

First, we need to pray that God will give us His compassionate heart, that we might see the world and other people with the same compassion God does. This is a prayer I've often prayed, and God has always been faithful to answer it. Of course, this is the sort of prayer that we know will be answered because we are obviously praying that the will of God be done in our lives.

Second, we must study the Bible. We call ourselves Christians because we are supposed to follow Christ, not just believe He exists. If we truly "believe in Him," then certainly we will follow His instructions to serve, to help. We will want to follow His example of allowing human needs to move Him to compassionate acts.

We must use our Bible concordances and search the Bible to see how God feels about justice and compassion for the poor, the oppressed, the orphans, and all those in need.

We must begin to allow God to renew our minds by cultivating a Christian worldview. We must not look at the world as

Christians wearing secular glasses and therefore seeing the world only the way non-Christians do. We must learn to see the world the way God does, for He expects this of us. When we view the world through God's standards of justice, righteousness, and compassion, we will be moved to action—to serve others.

Men like Francis Schaeffer and John Whitehead have provided us with a number of valuable books to get us started. I have recommended some of the best in the bibliography of this book. You need to buy them, study them, and reflect upon them.

Learning to Feel

Naturally, compassion does not exist in a void. The obvious needs of others act to bring out our compassion. So, we must begin to learn about the many needs around us. We need to allow God to unsettle us with a particular image that will release strong, motivating emotions within us. Only when we can feel with our emotions the pain of others will we be motivated to action, to sacrificing some of our precious energy, our valuable time, our scarce finances. "We have the mind of Christ and hold his feelings and purposes" (1 Corinthians 2:16, TLB).

God does not condone or ignore oppression, exploitation, violence, dishonesty, or immorality. Evil angers God (see Jeremiah 44:1-14).

Proverbs 8:13 instructs us that "to fear the Lord" (i.e., reverence for God and obedience to His commands and Lordship over our lives, our time, energy, and resources) "is to hate evil."

Throughout the Old Testament God literally wiped out nations because of their evil practices. His wrath and anger were stirred by things like child sacrifice, sexual abuses, and assorted other injustices.

God doesn't like these things any better today than He did then. The difference is that today, since we have received God's overwhelming power within us (see Ephesians 1:8-14, John 15:5-17, Philippians 2:13, 4:13), God expects us to feel His hurt, His anger, and to allow Him to use us to rectify the abuses and evils He brings to our attention.

When the New Testament describes multiple instances of Jesus' being "deeply moved" to compassion by the condition of those He looked upon, the Greek root word indicates that Jesus was moved by a compelling force from the deepest part of His body, from His "guts."

Testing Your Compassion

Developing compassion is like anything else. It takes a little practice. Perhaps it will be much easier for you than you think. Give yourself this "compassion test." Please read each example very slowly and think about it until a picture forms in your mind. Then ask yourself, would you feel moved to act if:

1. You thought someone was killing innocent babies in your neighborhood.
2. Your elderly neighbor was brokenhearted from loneliness.
3. You met an abandoned child, starved for love and positive affirmation.
4. You heard of a family out of work, unable to meet their food bills, being evicted.
5. An older or handicapped person explained to you that he had no place to live and would be forced to live and die on your corner sidewalk.
6. You heard of some orphans in your city who were growing sickly due to lack of nutrition.
7. You suspected local merchants were selling pornography that was bought by:
   a. thirteen-year-olds forming their view of sexuality
   b. married men "tired of just one sex partner"
   c. potential rapists or child molesters
8. You knew local politicians were passing laws to make it easier to get away with rape and other violent acts.
9. Your local Christian school was about to be closed by the government because sponsoring churches refused to obey bureaucratic orders.
10. Your local Congressman consistently voted to spend more than the government took in; refused to help those resisting Soviet wars of aggression; refused to consider the best interests of his country and your family.

The list could go on and on. You could add many more examples of those in need of mercy, love, care, compassion:

1. Victims of our sexual ethics
   a. AIDS victims
   b. Rape victims
   c. Divorce victims
   d. Sexually damaged or abused children
2. Victims of racism and "welfarism"
3. Victims of our materialistic, selfish, narcissistic society
   a. The unlovely
   b. The failed
   c. The poor, homeless
   d. The handicapped
   e. Unwanted children
   f. The forgotten elderly

Did any of these visions move your emotions? Did your adrenalin stir? If you felt motivated to intervene on any one of these situations, you are on your way to exercising compassion.

The absolutely crucial thing we must understand is that these thing *are* happening in our community — our town, city, or state. We must understand that caring for our neighbor is not limited to the person next door. Our neighbors are whoever we see, wherever we see them as Jesus clearly taught in His parable on the Good Samaritan, which we will talk more about in the next chapter.

What then is our vision for the future?

New Vision

Jesus Christ, as our example, told us to let our light — our expressing God's compassion, justice, and righteousness as through our actions — be an example to all mankind. He uses the illustration of a city of believers that would radiate God's light to all mankind. Such an example would inevitably attract others to God's justice and righteousness as a beacon of hope shining through the bleak darkness of man's exploitation of man.

You are the light of the world. A city on a hill cannot be hidden. Neither do people light a lamp and put it under a bowl. Instead they put it on its stand and it gives light to everyone in the house. In the same way, let your light shine before men, that they may see your good deeds and praise your Father in heaven. (Matthew 5:14-16)

Imagine how our neighborhoods and even our nation would change if forty million Evangelicals actually began to practice loving and caring for the needy. What an example it would be if we just practiced the Golden Rule of "doing unto others as you would have them do unto you."

Would the general public not follow our example as they saw the obvious benefit to society and to their own family? Would they not follow our lead to re-establish a just nation? Would they not select some of us to lead? Of course they would. It is precisely the way the early Christians in America molded our culture and built a government and civilization based on the motto, "In God We Trust."

That is why immediately before His parable on the city on a hill, Christ commanded us to be the "salt" or "preservative" that keeps our society together. But as Christ warned us in Matthew 5:13, when we as "salt" refuse to exercise our mandate to actively preserve God's vision for society, then we will be "trampled upon by men."

If we are willing to commit ourselves to action as the salt of our society by rebuilding the standards of justice and righteousness necessary for its preservation, our vision will once again appear as a city of light set upon a hill reaching out to all men and women searching for answers for fear, alienation, and confusion.

To Summarize

Our nation is perishing for lack of a vision to hold us together, to inspire us, to guide us, to give us something worthwhile to reach for—the "shining city on a hill."

If our nation is to avert its present course of self-destruction, of tearing itself apart, we must be united in our vision. As a first step, we need a symbol. The Greek root word for symbol means to *unite together*. Symbols draw us together and give us something to bind our otherwise divergent interests. Incidentally, semantically, the opposite to symbolic is the word *diabolic*. The Greek root word means "to tear apart," to disintegrate—exactly what America is now doing to itself. The name *Satan* is derived from this same Greek word *diabolos*.[15]

If our vision is a nation based on God's compassion, justice and righteousness, we need a symbol. A symbol that will represent what we should all be to each other. A symbol that clearly sets an example of how we must proceed if we are to implement our vision.

What better symbol than the Good Samaritan? We will develop this theme fully in the next chapter.

America's new vision must come from those inspired by God's eternal standards of justice and righteousness. We have seen that for justice and righteousness to be effectuated, they must spring from a Christ-like compassion. We have learned that if we will be obedient to follow Christ's instructions to act as salt and light in our neighborhood, this vision will begin to become reality.

Truly God has the answers for our generation's fears and alienation, and these answers should comprise our vision for a better world for all people. The question remains though, just how convinced are you about what, or how much, God really expects of you in regard to this vision?

SEVEN

WHAT DOES GOD WANT US TO DO?

We have seen that both the Church and the Christian Right have failed to understand and to meet the needs of our generation. We have failed to offer a dynamic and compassionate vision for our families, our neighborhoods, our nation—a vision of justice and righteousness for all citizens, empowered by God's loving compassion and implemented through obeying God in serving our neighbors.

Tragically, if God's vision for mankind was clearly presented from the pulpit in many of our Evangelical churches today, it would be met with a deafening silence. Most congregations would think it was a "nice vision," a vision that someone else would implement. No doubt a "Church vision committee" would be established and the usual small group of tired volunteers would be charged with implementing a few new service programs to represent the Church as a whole.

In other words, most Christians, upon seeing God's vision for man, upon hearing God's call to compassionate service, naturally assume that it is the job of the pastor, the elders, deacons or "activists" to implement—anyone but ourselves!

Service Is Not an Option

For the average Christian, who since the day of his conversion has never been taught anything different, service is clearly optional. We may choose to serve, or we may not, depending upon our schedule, level of talent or energy, or our general disposition.

Unfortunately, such Christians are in for a very rude awakening on Judgment Day, if not before. The Bible repeatedly teaches in the clearest and simplest terms that service is non-optional. The Bible does not present us with the luxury of choosing to be obedient "spiritual" Christians or disobedient "carnal" Christians. We are called upon to do our best to obey Christ if we love Him (John 14:24).

Of course, as we have seen, many shepherds have avoided confronting their flocks with this "hard message," afraid that some would stray to another "less demanding shepherd." Most of us would much rather just hear that God loves us and wants to bless us, as opposed to God requiring us in turn to love and bless others.

We have adopted a "hired gun" theology. We pay others like our pastor or TV ministers to fulfill our Christian obligations, so we can pursue our own self-interested agenda undisturbed. What is the purpose of a Christian life, your life? Just to "survive" and go to heaven? Or if you're very talented or very lucky, to "lead the good life" and then go to heaven? What is our life all about anyway? Does God have a specific plan just for your life?

If we are to implement the grand vision discussed in Chapter 6, we must mobilize the entire Church—every single Christian, not just a few activists. So we must ask ourselves, do we as Christians have a clear unequivocal, nonoptional mandate from God to serve others through social or political action?

Without such a mandate, as we in the Christian Right learned the hard way, it is impossible to mobilize the Church. Human nature being what it is, most people will always opt for "peace" or "escape" rather than involvement or confrontation. Most will let others do it, rather than expending their own precious time and energy.

So now we must discover once and for all whether God expects us to serve others or whether God's sole purpose for us is to get saved, get "spiritual" and to go heaven.

Loving Our Neighbors

What then does God really want us to do? Fortunately for us, it's no mystery, he tells us very clearly. It is to "love our neighbor" (see Matthew 22:39).

When the disciples asked Jesus what was the most important of all God's commandments, he answered:

Love the Lord your God with all your heart and with all your soul and with all your mind. This is the first and greatest commandment. And the second is like it: Love your neighbor as yourself. All the law and the Prophets hang on these two commandments. (Matthew 22:37-40)

Christ's commandment for us to love others became known as the "second greatest commandment."

And who are our neighbors? As Richard Lovelace states in *Renewal as a Way of Life,*

The love of neighbors then, is far more extensive than it first appears to be. In this century international telecasts make us neighbors of all the wretches of the earth.[1]

An active, expressive love for all men is one of the main commandments to us as Christians throughout the New Testament. "This is the message you heard from the beginning: we should love one another" (1 John 3:11).

- In I Corinthians 13:1-3 Paul tells us that all the other spiritual gifts are meaningless if we don't operate from love.

- James tells us love is the "royal, supreme law, the source of all governing man" (James 2:8).

- In Ephesians 5:1 the Apostle Paul says "Be imitators of God . . . walk in love."

- In John 13:34-35 Jesus commands us to "love one another . . . by this shall all men know that you're my disciples, if you love each other."

The tragedy of our Church is that Christ's command to "love our neighbor as ourselves" is one of the most misunderstood commands in the Bible, and that is a double travesty since Jesus makes it painfully clear that "there is no commandment greater."

When Jesus told us to love our neighbor, what was he talking about? Romantic love? Obviously not. What about some mysterious, indefinable, impractical form of abstract love, which is what most of us think he meant, if we think about it at all? Or was Christ teaching us an active love, demanding compassionate action, service and, yes, even sacrifice?

Love in Action

How can we "love" others when we aren't quite sure how we love ourselves? The answer is that love is action, not an idea. We love ourselves by caring for our own needs, and that is how we are to serve others. The famous Christian writer A. W. Tozer explained that love is a willingness to serve, to meet the needs of another:

> . . . emotional love surely was not in the mind of Christ when he told people to love God and each other. But the love that Jesus introduced is not the love of feeling; it is the love of willing, the willed tendency of the heart.[2]

In its commentary on 2 Peter 1:7, the *NIV Study Bible* defines love as an "outgoing, selfless attitude that leads one to sacrifice for the good of others."[3]

Could we convince our mate, our children, our parents that we loved them if we never took care of them, never helped them, never performed a helpful service for them? Of course not! After a short while our profession of "love" for them would be seen as a hollow charade at best and, at worst, a tool for selfish manipulation of others' feelings. Is it any wonder that the average person, when confronted with the stark contrast between Christians' professed love for all mankind and our shameful lack of service, sees us all as hypocrites?

The Lesson of the Good Samaritan

Is there a role model God has produced for us? Let's look at Luke 10 and try the Good Samaritan:

> On one occasion an expert in the law stood up to test Jesus. "Teacher," he asked, "what must I do to inherit eternal life?"
>
> "What is written in the Law?" he replied, "How do you read it?"
>
> He answered: "Love the Lord your God with all your heart and with all your soul and with all your strength and with all your mind"; and, "Love your neighbor as yourself."
>
> "You have answered correctly," Jesus replied. "Do this and you will live."

But he wanted to justify himself, so he asked Jesus, "And who is my neighbor?"

In reply Jesus said: "A man was going down from Jerusalem to Jericho, when he fell into the hands of robbers. They stripped him of his clothes, beat him and went away, leaving him half dead. A priest happened to be going down the same road, and when he saw the man, he passed by on the other side. So too, a Levite, when he came to the place and saw him, passed by on the other side. But a Samaritan, as he traveled, came where the man was; and when he saw him, he took pity on him. He went to him and bandaged his wounds, pouring on oil and wine. Then he put the man on his own donkey, took him to an inn and took care of him. The next day he took out two silver coins and gave them to the innkeeper. "Look after him," he said, "and when I return, I will reimburse you for any extra expense you may have."

"Which of these three do you think was a neighbor to the man who fell into the hands of robbers?"

The expert in the law replied, "The one who had mercy on him."

Jesus told him, "Go and do likewise."

Notice that Jesus was answering a question of supreme importance — how to obtain eternal life. His answer was not to attend Church more religiously or to abstain from some particular vice. His answer was to love God completely and to love our neighbors. The parable carefully demonstrates the importance of taking responsibility for those in need.

God is a God of action, and we are to be His physical instruments through which He acts. That is why Christ, at the end of His teaching on the Good Samaritan, commands us to "go and do likewise." We are to do what the Samaritan did and help those in need, those ignored or overlooked by others.

True Biblical love means being concerned and responsible for all God's creatures. True justice implemented in God's love will serve both rich and poor. Regardless of status, all people are in need of receiving God's love through us.

So that we cannot possibly miss our God-given purpose in life, Christ clearly outlines what He expects of us in the parable of the vine (see John 15:1-17). Christ explains we are to draw from His strength to produce fruit (results). What is the nature of the fruit we are to bear? "To love each other . . ." (verses 12 and 17).

Christ explains in verse 13 that this concept of love will require us to "lay down our life for our friends." Today, "laying down our life" may mean to sacrifice our energies, our money, our leisure, our time, our future, those things that make up our life. *The Living Bible* expresses Christ's teaching on the necessity of sacrificing our life this way:

> Then he said to all, "Anyone who wants to follow me must put aside his own desires and conveniences and carry his cross with him every day and *keep close to me*! Whoever loses his life for my sake will save it, but whoever insists on keeping his life will lose it." (Luke 9:23-24 TLB)

The striking and somewhat unsettling thing about Christ's teaching here is that if we insist on "keeping our own life," our own priorities and comforts, we will actually lose our life. Only when we voluntarily lose our life, to actively serve God and His priorities, do we truly gain spiritual life.

The Christian's Fruit

The parable of the vine teaches us that motivated by love, we should produce "fruit." So, we ask ourselves, what in the world is fruit? If we cannot understand what fruit means in our everyday work-a-day world, we will never be able to fulfill our call as Christians. We will never be able to be used of God to make His vision for our lives a reality; and consequently, we will never feel fulfilled or truly productive. Instead, we will feel incomplete, incompetent, and impotent, both as Christians and as individuals.

So what is fruit? It is the evidence of Christ's power, love, and compassion flowing through us, slowly changing us, and, among other things, leading us to have compassion on others and to serve them.

In the Bible, God has gone out of His way to repeat this crucial message.

> You my brothers, were called to be free. But do not use your freedom to indulge the sinful nature; rather, serve one another

in love. The entire law is summed up in a single command: "Love your neighbor as yourself." (Galatians 5:13-14)

And let us consider how we may spur one another on toward love and good deeds. (Hebrews 10:24)

In response to all He has done for us, let us outdo each other in being helpful and kind to each other and in doing good. (Hebrews 10:24 TLB)

Nobody should seek his own good, but the good of others. (1 Corinthians 10:24)

Producing Christ's "fruit" means that not only must we grow in Christian maturity and understanding, but, as the "mind of Christ" grows within us, it must flow out in a way that impacts those around us.

And we pray this in order that you may live a life worthy of the Lord and may please Him in every way: bearing fruit in every good work, growing in the knowledge of God. . . . (Colossians 1:10)

Our acts of service actually complete our faith, meaning that without service as the evidence of our faith, our Christian life will never mature, or be full and "complete."

Service is a mark of the maturing, serious Christian. One way to tell a spiritual adult from a spiritual child is that an adult produces more than they consume. They give more than they take. Much of the New Testament teaching is to help us become mature Christians. We are saved, but that cannot be the end of the story. Our salvation, which is through our faith in Jesus Christ and by God's grace, is also to be manifested by our actions.

You see that his faith and his actions were working together, and his faith was made complete by what he did. . . . You see that a person is justified by what he does and not by faith alone. (James 2:22, 24 TLB)

God is quite specific about what sort of service or fruit He has in mind for us:

> Is not this kind of fasting I have chosen: to loose the chains of
> injustice and untie the cords of the yoke, to set the oppressed
> free and break every yoke? Is it not to share your food with the
> hungry and to provide the poor wanderer with shelter — when
> you see him naked, to clothe him, and not to turn away from
> your own flesh and blood? . . . and if you spend yourselves in
> behalf of the hungry and satisfy the needs of the oppressed,
> then your light will rise in the darkness, and your might will be-
> come like the noonday. (Isaiah 58:6-7, 10)

> Religion that God our Father accepts as pure and faultless is
> this: to look after orphans and widows in their distress and to
> keep oneself from becoming polluted by the world. (James 1:27)

> Learn to do right! Seek justice, encourage the oppressed. De-
> fend the cause of the fatherless, plead the case of the widow.
> (Isaiah 1:17)

Because there is so much misunderstanding and confusion in
today's Church concerning fruit and service, it is important that
we recognize what fruit is not, as well as what it is. In other
words, we must know how to recognize the real thing and not be
fooled by its imitation.

Imitation Fruit

For too long we have tried to serve imitation fruit to a society
starving for real food. In the process we have largely become an
imitation Church producing imitation Christians whose imitation fruit is thrown back in their faces by a secular nation that
often can tell the difference between real and artificial fruit better
than we can. God clearly anticipated our tendency to produce
imitation fruit.

> If anyone has material possessions and sees his brother in need
> but has no pity on him, how can the love of God be in him?
> Dear children, let us not love with words or tongue but with ac-
> tions and in truth. (1 John 3:17-18)

> Do not merely listen to the word, and so deceive yourselves. Do
> what it says. (James 1:22)

Faith Is Not Fruit

Perhaps one of our most serious errors we have made as Evangelicals is to confuse faith with fruit. We believe in the tenets of the faith! And our faith is growing through more study, meetings, and prayer! So we think we are complete. Surely we need to do no more. This false notion, which has captured so many of our Churches, and thereby sidelined them to irrelevancy, is precisely the opposite of what the Bible teaches.

> What good is it, my brothers, if a man claims to have faith but has no deeds? Can such faith save him? Suppose a brother or sister is without clothes and daily food. If one of you says to him, "Go, I wish you well; keep warm and well fed," but does nothing about his physical needs, what good is it? In the same way, faith by itself, if it is not accompanied by action, is dead. . . . You foolish man, do you want evidence that faith without deeds is useless? (James 2:14-17, 20)

We know that faith in Jesus Christ as our personal Savior is our only door to salvation. But what our Creator is also trying to tell us, if only we will listen, is that all our claims to faith are rendered useless and foolish if they are not evidenced by action. Christ as Savior must also mean Christ as Lord. When Christ is Lord of all our life, our time, our energy, our wealth, we will evidence this by obeying His commands. We will produce fruit. We will follow Christ's example in serving others.

This is a difficult truth that we do not want to hear. But true "faith" or belief always manifests in action. We believe that if we did not respect the wishes of our mate or our employer, we would soon be in trouble. We act accordingly. At the same time, we profess to believe in God's work, we claim we have "faith," and yet we have no deeds to prove it.

> Let us not love with words or tongue but with actions and in truth. (1 John 3:18)

Bible scholar and professor of theology at Wheaton Graduate School, Lawrence Richards points out that our early New Testament Church fathers took a much stronger stand on service than we would ever dream of today.

In a sermon given in the first century, Clement argues that faith must issue in good works. One who serves God by keeping His laws will be saved, but one who transgresses Christ's commandments incurs eternal punishment. Nothing can save a person "if we shall not be found having holy and righteous works." This view is common in the apostolic fathers who lived in the late first and early second centuries.[4]

Why were our early Church Fathers so concerned about "righteous works"? Perhaps they, too, saw deeds as evidence of true faith, the difference between a purely mental assent, "decision for Christ," and a life-changing conversion.

Religious Acts Are Not Fruit

The most common trap we fall into is to think that our acts of personal piety or religious observance substitute for service. Our fundamentalist heritage has all too often been summed up in religious exclusions or slogans like "we don't smoke, dance, drink, chew, or go with people who do" to the exclusion of works of service. Unfortunately, in our zeal for personal piety, we have managed to miss God, because service cannot be replaced by religious exercises — special offerings, our sacrifices, fasting, or even prayer. Of course, service must be based on these things, but it cannot be substituted for by any one of them.

Proverbs 21:3 tells us that our pursuit of justice and righteousness is more important to God than the religious "sacrifices" that we may make as part of our normal Church routine.

> To do what is right and just is more acceptable to the Lord than sacrifice. (Proverbs 21:3)

In Isaiah 58:4, God clearly tells us we ". . . cannot fast as you do today and expect your voice to be heard on high." Why? Because God is looking for more than prayer and fasting. Isaiah tells us God is looking for acts of service as evidence of our sincerity and faith. In Isaiah 58:6 God says the form of fasting He favors is service: to establish justice, set the oppressed free, and provide for the poor and hungry. This is not to deny that God also favors fasting — because He does! What He wants us to avoid is "all form, no substance" or "all talk, no action." He requires us to be full integrated, mature Christians.

John Stott has an excellent comment on our tendency to substitute religious observances for obedience:

> Our God is often too small because He is too religious. We imagine that He is chiefly interested in religion, in religious buildings (Churches and chapels), religious activities (worship and ritual) and religious books (Bible and Prayer Books). Of course He is concerned about these things, but only if they are related to the whole of life. According to the Old Testament prophets and the teaching of Jesus, God is very critical of "religion," if by that is meant religious services divorced from real life, loving service, and the moral obedience of the heart.[5]

No wonder our nation, in looking for real fruit — vision, answers, compassion, and service — has rejected both the Christian Right and the Church.

Rather than choosing to be obedient to Christ's commands to "love our neighbor" and "lose our lives," rather than following the Bible's instructions to prove our faith through service, we chose to withdraw into personalized piety and individualized Christianity. Rather than offer ourselves as "living sacrifices" to serve our fellow man, and thereby to witness to him of God's love through our service and compassion, we chose the path of least resistance. We found it easier to declare ourselves "morally superior" because of our abstention from obvious physical vices, and we simply condemned to hell all those whom we were too lazy to help! Little wonder that so many Americans have turned their back on the Church, or those who, like the Christian Right, represented a "Christian agenda."

Feeling spiritually superior while "putting down sinners" was not the model that Christ set for us. It is, in fact, just the opposite, as Lovelace states:

> But Jesus' attacks on religious corruption and pretension are in strong contrast to His mercy and gentleness in dealing with forms of sin which are publicly disreputable. One of the things which aroused the hostility of orthodox onlookers was His public association with moral and religious outcasts. The self-centered religion of His critics invested its energy in building spiritual facades to appease their consciences or attract admiration. Jesus was concerned rather to minister to human need, and to go where there was a sense of sin instead of a false righteousness.[6]

In truth, it is the Church that turned its back on America as it chose personal pietism over witnessing through love, compassion, and service.

> This is my Father's glory, that you bear much fruit, showing yourselves to be my disciples. (John 15:8)

When the Christian Right attempted to convince the American public that we had their best interests at heart, they simply weren't buying. The public might not have clearly understood what Christians were really interested in, but they certainly suspected that we weren't interested in serving them. If proper actions are motivated by improper attitudes, our actions are wasted. If we are condescending, patronizing, prideful, or judgmental in our attitude, people will write us off. And they should. If we are to represent Christ, we must serve in love, compassion, and humility.

Personal Revelation

One of the Christian Right's main weaknesses was that we lacked a "nonoptional" mandate to demand that Christians serve. How many times I felt so inadequate standing behind a pulpit, imploring people to be involved, knowing that only a few would rise to the challenge. I knew something was missing. I knew that reciting the usual litany of abortion, pornography, and other "horror stories" was not enough to sustain people in a long-term commitment to restoring justice and righteousness in their community.

I knew that I needed a way to mobilize their time, energy, and devotion, not from any oratorical abilities, not from emotional manipulation, but from God touching their heart. I knew there must be a way to say, "Christ commands you to do this, there is no option." I knew all my logic, rationale, and arguments could be viewed for what they were—just one man's opinion.

One evening in April, 1985, I was on my knees praying in my hotel room before preaching in a major Washington, D.C., area church. I felt so empty, as if I had nothing really of value to share. That night even though my message was enthusiastically received, I vowed not to preach again until the Lord gave me His message in place of my logic.

I was to wait almost two years for that message. In March of 1987 I had holed up for a week in a small country inn situated on a bluff high above the stormy winter seas of the northern California wilderness coast. I was desperately seeking God, praying, searching the Scriptures, waiting on the Lord for direction.

And then in a quite phenomenal way, God began leading me to Scriptures, dozens, then hundreds, all on service. I didn't understand why at the time, but I spent five solid hours taking notes on what I read. Those notes later became the basis for a new vision birthed in my heart and for much of this book.

God honored the promise of one of my favorite Psalms (37:4): "Delight yourselves in the Lord and He will give you the desires of your heart." He was giving me the message that I had so desired since that night on my knees two years earlier.

Not only did He reveal forcefully His teaching on service to me, but I saw clearly that service was "nonoptional." Finally I had the "weapon" I so desired, the sword of truth to cut through the "Church's" apathy and willful neglect of its duty to insist that every Christian be active in some form of service — not necessarily political.

Service Is Non-Optional

The only options Christians have is not whether to serve our fellow man or not, but whether or not to obey Christ. We do have the option to be disobedient and to reap the consequences in our lives and our families. Jesus tells us in John 14:24 that "he who does not love Me will not obey My teaching." And in 1 John 5:1-3 we are told that if we truly love God and are a child of God, we will love all of God's children, and we will carry out God's commands, including His commands to care for others.

Service is nonoptional because we are commanded to serve, and we are commanded to be obedient to God's commands. In case we missed the message, Christ makes it clear in His parable of the vine where He tells us what to expect if we don't bear fruit: "He cuts off every branch in Me [Christ], that bears no fruit" (John 15:2).

Lest you think this is a harsh interpretation or an isolated example, "gentle Jesus" is even more explicit in His parable on the sheep and goats in Matthew 25. The implications of this parable are truly frightening for those to whom service is "an option." Quite clearly Christ tells us that those who do not serve the needy and oppressed are not serving Christ. In verse 45 Christ proclaims, ". . . whatever you did not do for one of the least of these, you did not do for me." He then warns us: "the consequence for this hardness of heart is they will go away to eternal punishment" (see verse 46).

Does Jesus really mean it? Will God really punish us? May I suggest that when one of the central messages of the Old and New Testaments is to love our fellow man, serve and care for others, and be obedient to God, by what right do we decide God doesn't mean business? In fact, John the Baptist in Luke 3:4-11 tells us that in preparing for Christ's kingship, we are to produce fruit, defined in verse 11 as helping others. In verse 9, John the Baptist issues a warning we cannot afford to neglect:

> . . . every tree that does not produce good fruit will be cut down and thrown into the fire.

God is not joking. If service wasn't imperative for us, it wouldn't be in the Bible, let alone repeated in almost every book! We choose to be disobedient at great risk to ourselves.

If you're still not convinced of God's judgment on those who do not produce His fruit, read the fifth chapter of Isaiah. It is, I'm afraid, an eerily accurate description of the condition our nation finds itself in today.

Created for Service

A good question for us to ask at this juncture is why is God so serious about us serving each other? The answer is very simple: it is what God created us to do. "For we are God's workmanship, created in Christ Jesus to do good works, which God prepared in advance for us to do" (Ephesians 2:10).

As Carl Henry observes in *The Christian Mindset in a Secular Society*:

> Scripture "thoroughly equips" the people of God "for every good work" (2 Timothy 3:17). The Christian priority is the need to know the revealed will of God which, along with other Biblically given imperatives, includes the divinely stipulated principles of social ethics.[7]

Foundationally, Christ died for our sins. But one of the results of His sacrifice and our consequent justification is our changed perspective toward service: ". . . who gave Himself for us to redeem us from all wickedness and to purify for Himself a people that are His very own, eager to do what is good" (Titus 2:14).

Word Meanings in the Old Testament comments on Romans 8:24, ". . . to what are we foreordained? Not to eternal salvation as is often claimed." The text says, "to be conformed to the image of His son."[8]

If we are being conformed in the image of Christ, doesn't that mean we need to be following His example in serving others? Paul writing in Romans 7:4 would seem to agree: "And now you are married, so to speak, to the one who rose from the dead so that you can produce good fruit, that is good deeds for God" (TLB).

Perhaps John Calvin, who along with Martin Luther was the driving force of the Protestant Reformation from which we derive our present day Protestant creeds, summed up best. Calvin believed that Christ has freed us from the bondage of sin so that we can be available to serve Him . . . and our neighbor.[9]

Now we must re-discover God's vision for service and commit ourselves to obeying His purpose for our lives. We must recapture the glory of the historic Christian Church from the days of the apostles through the nineteenth century, the Church that chose obedience over avoidance, service over neglect, involvement over apathy. As Stott observed:

> Motivated by love for human beings in need, the early Christians went everywhere preaching the Word of God, because nothing has such a humanizing influence as the Gospel. Later they founded schools, hospitals, and refuges for the outcast. Later still they abolished the slave trade and freed the slaves, and they improved the conditions of workers in mills and mines, and prisoners in gaols. They protected children from commercial exploitation in the factories of the West and from ritual prostitution in the temples of the East.[10]

In summary, we have a clear, nonoptional mandate to bear fruit by loving (caring for) our fellow man, and this means serving others.

What About Evangelism

Before continuing on, I need to address this issue lest I be accused of ignoring the "Great Commission" to disciple the nations. Precisely the opposite is true. First of all, those who are actively witnessing on behalf of Christ are obviously serving. Second, service is an extremely powerful form of witnessing, or of supplementing our witnessing: "Why are you helping me?" "Because of Christ." "I watch you help others, why do you do that?" "Because of Christ."

Christ said our good deeds would point people toward God:

> In the same way, let your light shine before men, that they may see your good deeds and praise your Father in heaven. (Matthew 5:16)

> This is to my Father's glory, that you bear much fruit, showing yourselves to be my disciples. (John 15:8)

If we really want others to see Christ in us so they will value our Christian experience and want to share in it, Christ tells us how:

> By this all men will know that you are my disciples, if you love one another. (John 13:35)

If God's purpose for His Church is to bear witness of His presence in the world, how are we to best do that? By telling interesting stories? By scaring people about eternal damnation? By selling passage to heaven? Or by demonstrating the presence of God in our lives through sacrificial service?

Service and evangelism should go hand in hand. That is why the delegates gathered at the International Congress on World Evangelism in Lausanne declared:

> . . . We express penitence both for our neglect and for having sometimes regarded evangelism and social concern as mutually exclusive.

> The results of evangelism include obedience to Christ, incorporation into His Church and responsible service in the world.

The salvation we claim should be transforming us in the totality of our personal and social responsibilities. Faith without works is dead.[11]

If our faith and our conversion experience is real, we will apply what we believe. Beliefs must have consequences, results, action! Real Christianity must translate into loving our fellow man through service and self-sacrifice as Christ commands.

But the goal of authentic spirituality is a life which escapes from the closed circle of spiritual self-indulgence, or even self-improvement, to become absorbed in the love of God and other persons. For the essence of spiritual renewal is "the love of God . . . poured out within our hearts through the Holy Spirit." (Romans 5:5 NASB)[12]

Now that we understand God has called us to serve, the question remains, does political involvement constitute service? We shall find out in the following chapter.

EIGHT

REASONS FOR POLITICAL INVOLVEMENT

We have seen that as Christians we have no option but to serve others with love and compassion; but is political activity an appropriate expression of Christ's mandate to serve? To answer this critical question, we should first look to the example that Christ and the early Church left for us.

"That settles it," some say, "Jesus wasn't involved in politics. He wasn't a Republican or Democrat. He didn't ask His followers to join a political movement."

But we must not rip Christ's actions out of the context of the time and world in which He lived and taught. What most Christians don't realize, because they don't read Biblical history, is that Christ took the ultimate political position of His day. He challenged the existing order and announced a new government—the Kingdom of God, with Himself as its Head.

The Jews were under the government of the Roman Empire and the Romans were content to let their subjects worship the god of their choice, as long as their god did not conflict with the ultimate god—the Roman state, embodied in Caesar.

The Romans themselves recognized a number of gods, representing various forces of nature. But the Roman Empire, which ruled the entire civilized earth during Christ's lifetime, believed that the ultimate god was the Roman state and the Roman Empire—the rulers of the universe!

While this notion may seem silly to us, it was deadly serious to good Romans. Refusing to worship the emperor was considered an act of atheism and treason, punishable by death. This is why the early Christians were persecuted so horribly by the Roman state, not because they believed in a different religion

(Rome recognized hundreds of different religions), but because they defied the authority of the state.

Since the Roman government combined its political power of governing with an official religion of emperor worship, to defy the state was both a political offense and a religious heresy. Christians were burned at the stake and eaten by wild animals for the crimes of treason and atheism. As Chuck Colson observed:

> During the early centuries, Christians were martyred not for religious reasons—after all, Rome was a land of man-gods. They were killed because they refused to worship the emperor; they would not put Caesar on the same level as Christ. The Roman government accordingly saw them as political subversives trying to overthrow the existing order.[1]

Christ As Revolutionary

When Christ stated that He, not Caesar, had been given all authority in heaven and earth by God, and that God's laws took precedence over Caesar's edicts, Christ challenged the political and spiritual authority of the world's government. He and His followers committed the ultimate rebellious political act: treasonous rebellion against the foundations of the state.

While Jesus proclaimed to render unto Caesar what is Caesar's, the Bible makes it clear that when man's law violates God's law, we are to disobey man's law, following God. How do you think the Roman Empire liked that? Christianity was beyond political. It was revolutionary.

To help us get a clear perspective on how Christ challenged the political system of His day, let's use a hypothetical modern day example.

Jerome Schwartz and his followers live in the USSR, an officially atheistic state where God is outlawed and where believers of any religion are often confined to mental wards. One day Jerome, a carpenter, announces to the Soviet high command that he is God, not the state. That he is "the way," not Marx or Lenin. And incidentally, he is going to tell all his followers to disobey Soviet law if it conflicts with his ten commandments.

How do you think he would be regarded? As just a peace-loving nonconformist? Or as a political revolutionary of the worst order?

We simply cannot escape the fact that Christ and the early Christians clearly opposed the political and religious values of their day. True, they did not get "involved in politics" because Rome was not a democracy and political involvement as we know it did not exist. What they did was even more extreme. As Acts 17:7 demonstrates, they proposed a higher law and a new King for whom they would sacrifice their lives. They unhesitatingly opposed the evils and misconceptions of the governing system.

The Gospel for the World

But didn't the early Church just "preach the Gospel," something that certainly doesn't sound very political?

Before jumping to any conclusions, we should discover what the word *Gospel* meant as it was used twenty centuries ago.

The ancient Romans of Christ's time used the Greek word "Gospel" to refer to Caesar Augustus' birth as the "Divine Savior King." It also referred to the King's speeches, decrees, and acts that were "Glad tidings which bring long hoped-for fulfillment to the world's longing for happiness and peace."[2]

As Bible teacher Monte Wilson points out:

After the ascension of Christ, the Apostles defied the Roman Empire and Augustus by declaring the Gospel of Christ. With this one phrase they said that Jesus, not Caesar, was the Divine Savior King and that He had ascended to the royal throne where He would usher in a new era of peace.[3]

The Romans comprehended this message more clearly than do many modern day Christians. They knew that what these first century believers had declared was that Jesus was establishing a rival government. The Christian Gospel is not merely "Jesus saves." Caesar would have had no problem with this message. No—the Gospel that brought persecution to the Apostles was that Jesus Christ, the Divine Savior King, God Incarnate, lived a sinless life, died as a substitute for sinners, rose again, and ascended to heaven where He now rules over time and eternity. In other words, "Jesus is the Sovereign Lord, His Word is Law, and His Kingdom will reign."[4]

The Roman Government understood that these men were throwing out a challenge to their presumed authority. The Jews realized that these Christians were telling them that if they wanted to continue to be a part of the "the Nation of God" then they had to bow to the resurrected King they had just crucified. Both saw Christianity as an enemy of their governmental systems; each realized it was a matter of "kill or be overthrown."[5]

Getting Involved Today

Jesus and the early Church challenged the political/religious system of their times. Yet the question remains, does God expect us to become involved in politics today?

First, let us define *political*. The term originates from the word *polis*, meaning the life or social interaction of people within a city. In our modern usage, politics is the practice of government in the civil realm, governing those aspects in the life of citizens that are not reserved for family or Church government. Politics involves influencing those who govern, or shape public policy through civil legislation.

If part of God's purpose for us is to minister to people's needs, does this not mean dealing with social problems? And what better way to deal with social problems than by influencing the government that governs all social relations! "It is God Himself who has made us what we are and given us new lives from Christ Jesus; and long ages ago He planned that we should spend these lives in helping others" (Ephesians 2:10 TLB).

As theologian Carl Henry observes:

> If the Church is to be faithful in matters of Biblical social ethics, then Christians cannot be silent when political movements support issues or take sides in ways contrary to Scriptural guidelines. Is the Christian witness only one of criticism and not of legitimating any alternatives? Christians are less than faithful to Christ's Lordship over all political concerns if they imply that no moral choices flow from Christ's Lordship in matters of political decision.[6]

How can we best implement God's compassion and love for the poor? What about taking care of the poor, the widows, the orphans? Should government play a direct role? Obviously policy will, at the very least, play an indirect role in terms of stimulating or stagnating the economy, which impacts the poor first, or in encouraging or discouraging Church and private/individual volunteerism.

What about God's command to liberate the oppressed? Aren't the greatest agents of oppression in the world government systems that are based on certain totalitarian and authoritarian philosophies of government? What could be a second cause of oppression, ruthless multinational corporations or greedy landowners in the Third World? Wouldn't an effective way of liberating the oppressed be to influence, modify, or replace those governments who either repress their people or who allow others to do so?

What about protecting the innocent? Can government policy play a role in protecting babies murdered through abortion? Can political involvement stop the oppression and exploitation of women and children through pornography? Can sex and violence on TV, and the resulting consequences of broken marriage, rapes, and women being viewed as sex objects be corrected through government regulation? Can our government's interpretation and enforcement of the Constitution play a role in either inhibiting or guaranteeing our freedom of religion?

Obviously, civil government can and does play a major role in all of these areas and many more.

Governments are in the business of governing people, deciding how they will be allowed to live (free or oppressed), how they will worship (freely or in persecution), and by what standard of morality will the laws be enforced (or imposed). Since God is concerned with people, He is obviously concerned with the sort of government people are subject to. That is why God, through His revealed Word, warns us:

A wicked ruler is as dangerous to the poor as a lion or bear attacking them. (Proverbs 28:15 TLB)

With good men in authority, the people rejoice; but with the wicked in power, they groan. (Proverbs 29:2 TLB)

When rulers are wicked, their people are too; but good men will live to see the tyrant's downfall. (Proverbs 29:16 TLB)

Where there is ignorance of God, the people run wild; but what a wonderful thing it is for a nation to know and keep His laws. (Proverbs 29:18 TLB)

In Romans 13:1-4 the Apostle Paul tells us that God established the institution of government for man's benefit. Biblical scholar Abraham Kuyper comments:

> . . . for a sinful humanity, without division of states, without law and government, and without ruling authority, would be a veritable hell on earth; or at least a repetition of that which existed on earth when God drowned the first degenerate race in the deluge.[7]

> The magistrate is an instrument of "common grace," to thwart all license and outrage and to shield the good against the evil. But He is more. Besides all this He is instituted by God as His servant, in order that he may preserve the glorious work of God, in the creation of humanity, from total destruction.[8]

As the International Delegates to Lausanne resolved in resolution number 13:

> it is the God appointed duty of every government to secure conditions of peace, justice, and liberty in which the Church may obey God.[9]

While the institution of government is ordained by God, God does not approve all governments. Obviously God did not approve of Hitler, Stalin, Idi Amin, or any other bloodthirsty dictatorship. To meet God's approval, governments must not violate His purposes for creating the institution of government — protecting the innocent, punishing the guilty, preserving peace, and respecting the rights of each citizen.

A Call to Action

Bob Dugan, public affairs director for the National Association of Evangelicals, points out the Biblical mandate in the NAE's call to political and social action entitled *The High Cost of Indifference*:

> The Bible tells us that government is ordained of God to provide temporal order and justice (see Deuteronomy 16:18-20), to settle conflicts, to restrain sinful tendencies, to correct lawbreakers and to promote the public good (see Exodus 18:13-26; Romans 13:3-5). God's desire is that governments also pro-

vide for the helpless and oppressed (see Deuteronomy 15:7-11; Isaiah 58:6-7, 10; Psalm 72:4, 12-14), avoid corruption and misuse of power (see Amos 8:4-6) and respect God's Lordship (see Acts 4:18-20).[10]

If governments persist in violating their God-given purpose of doing good for their people, they are illegitimate. Christians are duty bound to resist them when they oppose God's ordinances.

When civil rulers overstep their proper functions, the Christian is to obey God rather than man.[11]

As Professor Richard Foster concludes in his best-selling book *Money, Sex, & Power*:

All believers, but particularly those in democracies, are to call the state to its God-given function of justice for all people alike. We are to commend the state whenever it fulfills its calling and confront it when it fails.[12]

God also ordained government to provide for a peaceful environment conducive to our family's nurture, our spiritual growth, and conversion of others to Christianity. In 1 Timothy 2:1-4, we are specifically instructed to pray for God's wisdom and direction for our leaders so that "we may live peaceable and quiet lives in all godliness and holiness. This is good and pleases God our Savior, who wants all men to be saved and to come to a knowledge of the truth." That is why Dr. Norman Geisler, Professor of Systematic Theology at Dallas Theological Seminary, states that Christians have an "obligation to government to promote one that's good and just."[13]

Perhaps God's most important function for government to perform, as Colson suggests, is the dispensing of justice. God assigned the state the responsibility to order society by restraining evil and by establishing justice.[14]

As we have seen in previous chapters, God is unequivocally committed to justice, and ideally, governments should be His instrument for displaying His justice. Psalm 67:3-4 teaches us that the world's people will praise God as they see His just rule, as dispensed by Godly governments.

But for God to demonstrate His justice through government, He must work through Godly men and women in government. Several Proverbs amply demonstrate that this is so:

> When you remove corrupt men from the king's court, his reign will be just and fair. (Proverbs 25:5 TLB)

> Evil men don't understand the importance of justice, but those who follow the Lord are much concerned about it. (Proverbs 28:5 TLB)

> The good man knows the poor man's rights; the godless don't care. (Proverbs 29:7 TLB)

Clearly God is telling us that evil or Godless men in government will not be just and will not be concerned with the rights of the poor, the oppressed, or the other powerless victims of injustice.

We must have Godly men and women in positions of authority if we are to provide a peaceful, just, and moral order for people to live in. Those of us who are reluctant to get involved politically need to realize that if the moral people in this country don't take responsibility for the process of government, then the only people left to govern the nation will be the immoral, which is precisely what is happening. Furthermore, God judges a nation by its leaders, particularly in a democracy. Church history scholar Richard Lovelace comments:

> God deals with nations and peoples on the basis of their leaders, who in some mysterious way represent the people, express their mind and heart, and bring good or ill on the community by their actions. . . . In a democracy, there may be a connection between the spiritual center of gravity in a people and the kind of leaders they choose to follow.[15]

If we are to be obedient to God and defend those who can't defend themselves (see Proverbs 31:8), if we are to give fair judgment to the poor, the afflicted, the orphans, how can we possibly ignore the governmental process, which is responsible for the keeping of the peace, the administration of justice, and the legislation of morality? Clearly, we must make ourselves available to God to serve His purpose in the government or political process. To not do so, frustrates God's desire to provide for a just and peaceful society.

Keys to the Future

Authoritatively addressing this question, over two thousand Evangelical delegates who met in 1974 at the International Congress on World Evangelism went on record to encourage social and political action because they were "key" to reaching beyond immediate problems to long-term solutions:

> It [social action] looks beyond persons to structures, beyond the rehabilitation of prison inmates to the reform of the prison system, beyond improving factory conditions to securing a more participatory role for the workers, beyond caring for the poor to improving, and when necessary, transforming, the economic system [whatever it may be] and the political system [again, whatever it may be], until it facilitates their liberation from poverty and oppression.[16]

Although it may surprise us today, the fact that we Christians need to play a role in governing is not new. It is what the Church has practiced from apostolic times until the early part of the twentieth century when we gave up our Godly duties in exchange for ecclesiastical peace and safety from the real world.

The first Christians challenged the social, political, and religious order of their day. Not just by word, not just by civil disobedience, but also by positive, active contributions to their communities and cultures. One of the most interesting examples of this is the court system started by Christians. Since Christians were admonished by the apostles not to sue each other or settle their differences in secular courts, they looked to "Church courts" to settle disputes and dispense civil (not criminal) justice.

The citizens of Rome, unable to secure fair hearings in corrupt courts, began petitioning to have their cases arbitrated by Church leaders. Eventually Roman governors began to appoint the early Church bishops to positions as judges, because of their reputation for integrity. The traditional robes worn by modern judges are a symbol inherited from the bishops' robes worn by the first Christian judges in the Roman Empire.

Social and governmental participation did not end with the early Church. In fact, Christians have been increasingly active throughout the centuries, most notably in the last two centuries. In England, Christians like the great statesman William Wilberforce, led the fight to abolish slavery. Christians also abolished child labor abuses and fought hard to drastically reform insane asylums, prisons, and the intolerable working conditions of long hours and low wages prevalent in the Industrial Revolution.

Throughout the world, Christians established thousands of missions, orphanages, schools, hospitals, and medical clinics. They brought modern sanitation and literacy to millions in the Third World. Many of today's Third World leaders received their basic education at the hands of missionaries. Unfortunately, many went on to the "enlightened" secular universities of the West where they promptly became Marxists and atheists.

All of these reforms were brought about through "social action," much of it accomplished in the West by legislation.

Our Christian Heritage

In America, our great universities, hospitals, and primary mercy works were founded by Christians. From our very beginning as a nation, Christian political activists heavily influenced the formation of our American experiment in Republican democracy.

As Professor Mark Noll of Wheaton College recently noted:

Reformed [the theology growing out of the Protestant Reformation] attitudes toward life in the world have had an immense effect on American history. Calvinistic convictions about living all of life for the glory of God led to the remarkable experiment of seventeenth century New England where Puritans created the freest, most stable, and most democratic society then existing on earth. In the eighteenth century the Puritan passion for public justice provided, if not the specific ideology, at least much of the energy for the American Revolution and the creation of a new nation. During the nineteenth century, Protestantism fueled immense labors of Christianization and civilization — subduing a continent, democratizing a people, evangelizing at home through revival and abroad through missions, reforming practices, and surviving a civil war that ended with the prohibition of slavery.[17]

Professor Goen notes that Christian social action was a key to the stability of our new and volatile nation.

> The voluntary societies, as Lois Banner noted, "offered an attractive solution to what many statesmen in the early republic saw as three primary problems facing the new nation: first how to make the turbulent democratic element which had destroyed all previous democracies into respectable citizens; second, how to pursue benevolent and reform objectives without involving the dangerous power of the central state; and third, how to overcome the sectional divisions which threatened the unity of the nation." In a subsequent essay, Banner commented further on the social role of the societies as "workshops in republicanism." By bringing together in harmony people of diverse classes and sections, and providing stable organizations and a sense of community for a society in flux, they ensured that democracy would function effectively within the republican framework.

> The energies of these groups were amazing. By 1828 they had collected and distributed almost as much money as the federal government had spent on internal improvement.[18]

Goen also provides us with additional evidence of the deep, even foundational nature of Christian involvement in our nation's growth, from the observations of Francis J. Grund, an Austrian journalist who spent ten years in America researching for his landmark work *The Americans in their Moral, Social, and Political Relations* in 1837:

> "The religious habits of the American form not only the basis of their private and public morals, but have become so thoroughly interwoven with their whole course of legislation, that it would be impossible to change without affecting the whole course of their government." Carefully pacing his rhetoric, Grund continued: "Religion has been the basis of the most important American settlements; religion kept their little community together—religion assisted them in their revolutionary struggle; it was religion to which they appealed in defending their rights, and it was religion, in time, which taught them to prize their liberties. . . . It is to religion they have recourse whenever they wish to impress the popular feeling with anything relative to their country; and it is religion which assists them in all their

national undertakings. . . . Whatever is calculated to diminish its influence and practice, has a tendency to weaken the government, and is, consequently, opposed to the peace and welfare of the United States. It would have a direct tendency to lessen the respect for the law, to bring disorder into their public deliberations, and to retard the administration of justice."[19]

Author Rus Walton observes in his book *Biblical Principles,* our forefathers clearly understood that their role was to express and administer God's stewardship through government.

The Fundamental Orders of Connecticut (the first American Constitution, January 14, 1638) state:

. . . well-knowing that where a people are gathered together the Word of God requires that to maintain peace and union of such a people there should be an orderly and decent government established according to God. . . .

The Great Law of the Pennsylvania colony (April 25, 1682) states:

Whereas the glory of Almighty God and the good of mankind is the reason and the end of government, and therefore government itself is a venerable ordinance of God. . . .

And, again from Fundamental Orders of Connecticut, these words concerning personal responsibility to the Lord in the election of public officeholders and the enactment of civil laws state:

The privilege of election which belongs to the people, therefore, must not be exercised according to their humors, but according to the blessed will and law of God.

In other words, this: Because government belongs to God, government must be governed according to His laws.[20]

So, why *aren't* we involved? There must be some good reason, because when you think about it, our natural course should be for us to be involved in governing ourselves and our communities for our own protection if nothing else.

Even as a teenager I determined that if other people were making decisions that my loved ones and I would have to live or die by then I wanted to have something to say about the process. I guess I just didn't trust the "natural goodness" of our leaders to always be looking our for our best interests.

Something very unnatural must have persuaded us to stifle our natural instincts to help govern ourselves. Of course, the Church's opposition to involvement, which we discussed in Chapter 4 has no doubt plagued communities, whether through the political process or other avenues for volunteerism.

Modern Cop-Outs

But besides official Church apathy, we have also fallen prey to a few modern cop-outs. Let's briefly examine some of the current objections to Christian political involvement.

Perhaps our most popular (and therefore most dangerous) misconception is that "you can't legislate morality." This cliché is so smugly and consistently repeated that we have accepted its validity as part of universal law. As surely as "what goes up must come down," we believe you just can't legislate morality.

But wait a minute. What about laws against murder, theft, rape, incest, even lying (perjury) or cheating (fraud)? Isn't this legislating morality? Of course it is. All law simply codifies someone's moral values. The only question is, who's system of morality is legislated into law? Since Christians, after establishing the legal base at the founding of the nation, no longer believe they can legislate morality, or enforce existing laws, an interesting transition has taken place in the enforcement and interpretation of our laws, as well as the passage of new ones.

Crimes that our Christian-based law outlawed originally like abortion and pornography are now legal. Laws against murder and rape are enforced much more leniently than before. Violent murderers are often back on the streets within three to four years and rapists can be on the streets within six months. Meanwhile, laws are passed forbidding parents to spank their children or veto their abortions. New judicial interpretations allow courts to close down Christian schools and jail pastors for noncompliance with government regulations. Obviously those antagonistic to Christian values believe morality can be legalized. Too bad we don't!

The truth of the matter is that morality as found in man's heart cannot be legislated. We cannot by law force someone to stop "lusting or coveting in his heart." Only a change of heart, by accepting Jesus Christ as personal Savior, can accomplish that. The purpose of law is not to persuade people of the rightness of a moral position. The purpose of law is to punish the violation of a moral position. There are in our society many people who believe that drug use, rape, child abuse, and fraud are perfectly acceptable methods for their gratifications. The purpose of the law is not to restructure their internal moral order, for no man can do that. The purpose of law is to prevent them from violating our culture's rules for self-protection, which until recently were based upon God's sense of justice and righteousness.

No, we cannot change hearts through the passing or enforcement of legislation. But, yes, we can help assure that justice and righteousness for our people are rewarded or punished through the same mechanism. "When justice is done it brings joy to the righteous but terror to evildoers" (Proverbs 21:15).

Another objection to Christian political involvement is to say that politics is "dirty," full of manipulation, dishonesty, and untruthfulness. We shouldn't tarnish ourselves by being associated with such activities. Yet, if we are honest, we must admit that the Church also has those problems. So does the business world. Do we stop going to Church because of the disgrace that the Jim Bakkers bring us? Do we drop out of the business world because of the shady business reputations of some or of the revelation of massive and persistent fraudulent practices on Wall Street?

I find it strange that apathy is "clean" while involvement is "dirty." Rather than dirty our hands in the process of governing, we choose to allow abortion, pornography, unabated perversion, and moral deterioration to drown our communities and eventually our families. Now that's dirty!

Clearly, this objection is too insipid to devote any more thought to it.

Separation of Church and State

Another objection currently in vogue with our media, and with our educational and governmental elites is that the U.S. Constitution, more specifically the First Amendment of the Bill of Rights, forbids mixing religion and politics. This argument is anything but insipid. It is, in fact, outrageously absurd . . . and totally contrary to the truth.

What the First Amendment actually says is "Congress shall make no law respecting an establishment of religion, or prohibiting the free exercise thereof; or abridging the freedom of speech, or of the press, or the right of the people peaceably to assemble, and to petition the Government for a redress of grievances."[21]

Clearly, our founding fathers were not trying to keep religion, individual Christians, or even churches from political involvement; and if they were, they failed miserably from what we have just read about the last several centuries of American history. On the contrary, the framers of the Constitution were trying to keep politics out of *religion* by forbidding government to make an "establishment of religion," meaning to establish a government-founded state Church, such as the colonists had fled in Europe.

So, the First Amendment simply forbids the establishment of a government Church and actually guarantees us the free expression of religion, whether it's through the political arena or expression of religion or elsewhere. We can easily see that the true meaning of the First Amendment has been deliberately misconstrued by those who would ban us from the "public square."

Hitler and Goebels would have been proud of this "big lie technique" — the bigger, bolder, and more outrageous the lie, the more it will be believed!

Another objection still comes from those well-meaning hearty and increasingly isolated souls who still insist that the Bible doesn't sanction political involvement. While I think we have sufficiently addressed this question already in this chapter, I will add that I believe this is a deception from Satan to keep us from fulfilling the purposes of God to provide care, justice, and liberation to all people. It is a deception to frustrate our ability to serve God, to keep us from putting ourselves at His service to help govern our society. If God has ordained the institution of government, would He prefer evil men or good men to run it?

One last argument is that our leaders don't teach involvement. While this is unfortunately somewhat true, there are significant exceptions. Many of the nation's most significant or visible Evangelical leaders have spent hundreds of millions of dollars to convince Christians to get involved.

Highly respected theologians like Carl Henry, Francis Schaeffer, John Stott, and R. C. Sproul write volumes to theologically justify, even demand, the need for Christian involvement in the social arena. The leaders of some of our largest denominations, from the Southern Baptists to the Assemblies of God, joined with Tim LaHaye and myself on the board of the *American Coalition for Traditional Values* to mobilize Christians into the political process.

Dr. Billy Melvin—executive director of the National Association of Evangelicals, the nation's largest association of independent Evangelical Churches—has written:

> If we are to walk in Christ's steps, we also must love the world and do so in tangible ways. Our Lord met both the spiritual and social needs of those to whom He ministered. And that is what He expects of those who are called by His name in our day. To meet these needs will require an understanding of the theological considerations which mandate Christian engagement in the public order.[22]

Billy Graham stepped forward in 1980 to challenge Christians to take a more active role in the nation's political life:

> Instead of being a prophetic voice boldly declaring the clear Word of God to our secular society, we are instead tempted to become bland and innocuous, knowing that the world does not like prophets who challenge its cherished beliefs.
>
> Individual Evangelicals should be active in the political arena, and I am thankful for those who have sensed a special calling to politics.[23]

The Real Problem

While these "cop-outs" may hint at the reasons for our resistance to involvement, the real problem is "none of the above."

The real problem, as we explained in Chapter 4, is within our Churches, our pulpits, and within our own hearts. Church leaders have chosen to avoid politics, not because it is "dirty," but because it is a sure way to avoid laborious, unpleasant, and potentially divisive issues.

Opposing the local abortion clinic might cause some Church members to leave—so the babies continue to die. Leading a crusade against pornography or corrupt or dishonest government leaders requires too much "homework" and might lead to ridicule. Better to let the poison spread and the city rot. Helping the poor takes a lot of time, effort, and patience. It also makes many people uncomfortable. Let the government take care of them.

These attitudes are not only reflective of a sickly, weak, and disobedient Church, they are also an indication of our own resistance to Christ's Lordship over our lives, our actions, our time, our resources.

All those who teach Christ's Lordship agree that it must extend beyond just Jesus as Savior. He must be Lord over all of our life—our home life, our personal life, our business life, and our life in the social-political arena called our "city."

While I believe every Christian must be involved in the process of government, it may be only as an informed voter who votes intelligently and encourages others to do the same. Or perhaps to spend a few hours a week helping a worthwhile candidate every two years.

In order to insure that Christians have true representation in our government, there are some simple steps we can take.

1. Christians must pray daily for our country and its leaders. They must entreat God to send spiritual renewal to America.
2. They must be registered to vote.
3. They must be educated regarding where the candidates stand on moral issues.
4. They must help to select, elect, and actively support good men in public office.
5. They must vote on election day.

Obviously, full-time government service is only for a few, and political activism, demanding several hours a week, year-round, is not for everybody.

While we have shown in Chapter 7 that some sort of service to others is mandatory, it certainly does not have to be political service. But it may be. And at the very least we are obligated to be active citizens and informed voters.

As Billy Graham says,

> If America is to survive, we must elect more God-centered men
> and women to public office, individuals who will seek Divine
> Guidance in the affairs of state. Christians should get involved
> in good government. I would like to see every true believer in-
> volved in politics in some way, shape, or form.[24]

The most effective method of service might be a combination of a personalized one-to-one approach, along with working
toward structural political or social reform. If we wish to help
the poor or oppressed, let us do so directly by giving them a
helping hand today. But then let us address the long-term solutions to their misfortune by reforming social or government
policies for tomorrow.

Incidentally, I am not advocating more government policies,
regulations, or handouts as the answer. It may well be that the
government's policy should be to be less involved and to encourage more volunteerism, a subject we will deal with in the few
chapters that follow.

Service to our fellow man is a primary purpose for which
God has prepared us, and the process of governing—called politics—can play a vital role in allowing us to fulfill this calling. As
the delegates to Lausanne agreed,

> Evangelism and socio-political involvement are both part of
> our Christian duty.[25]

Now, let us see how God might use us in the many opportunities for service awaiting us in the nineties.

NINE

AN AGENDA
FOR THE 1990s

To meet the needs of our generation by implementing God's mandate to restore justice and righteousness to our society, we must be faithful to Christ's example of the Good Samaritan.

If our efforts to help those in need are motivated by Christian compassion, God can use us to heal our nation. As America looks to the body of Christ for healing and restoration, it will also find us bearing witness to His presence, His love, and His plan of redemption and salvation.

Whether we serve through the Church, through the community, or through political activism, we know we must reach out to those in need. We must make our life count. We will be held accountable for our fruit.

But where will you serve? And how?

There are literally thousands of opportunities for service through which we can express the justice and righteousness of God. Vital issues of concern are crying out for Christian vision, leadership, and service. When we intervene on behalf of the poor, God's compassion achieves concrete expression. When we turn our activism toward the family, God's concern for men, women, and children is forwarded through our actions. When we stand strong against aggressors and oppressors, we become light-bearers for God's justice and righteousness.

In this chapter and the two that follow we will explore some of the many opportunities for Christ-centered service by which Christians "put feet to the Gospel." How will you be involved in fighting poverty, standing for the family, and/or against aggression?

The Poor

God has not hidden His concern for the poor. When God's people in the Old Testament wondered why their prayers went unanswered and their fasting unnoticed, God gave them a very clear answer through His prophet Isaiah:

> No, the kind of fast I want is that you stop oppressing those who work for you and treat them fairly and give them what they earn. I want you to share your food with the hungry and bring right into your own homes those who are helpless, poor, and destitute. Clothe those who are cold and don't hide from relatives who need your help. (Isaiah 58:6-7 TLB)

> Feed the hungry! Help those in trouble! Then your light will shine out from the darkness, and the darkness around you shall be as bright as day. And the Lord will guide you continually, and satisfy you with all good things, and keep you healthy too; and you will be like a well-watered garden, like an ever-flowing spring. (Isaiah 58:10-11 TLB)

Any new Christian seriously searching God's Word to discern God's priorities for his life can easily see God's repeated concern for the poor, the helpless, the homeless, the oppressed, the hungry. Cindy Rocker was one such new Christian. She tells us how she felt when she came to Christ:

> Since I had no Church background, the answer to this question of how I was going to live my life differently did not come readily. Determined to find some answers for myself, I began to study the Gospels. I reasoned that, if I now called myself a Christian, and if that meant that I was a follower of Christ, I was, therefore, going to use Him as role model and I should learn how He spent His life while on this planet. I felt that if I could know how he spent His time and what was important to Him, I would then have the answers I needed.

> As I studied, over and over I saw that the poor were very important to Jesus. Meeting their needs was very high on His priority list. When I looked in the Old Testament, I say that the poor are at the very heart of God. At that point, I decided that, if the poor were so important to Jesus, if He spent so much of His time ministering to their needs, and if He was

going to be my role model, then the poor should also be high on my list of priorities!

Finally, I had the answer I was looking for. My conversion would manifest itself in my life as I served God by ministering to the poor with the love of Jesus. I would ask God to make His love visible to the poor through me.[1]

Cindy had made a good start; she had discerned God's heart and then committed herself to service, much as the early Church did. Francis Schaeffer points out that much of the reason for Christianity spreading so quickly in the first century A.D. was that Christians practiced what they preached:

[In the early Church, there was] caring for each other in the whole spectrum of life—including the material things of life. The Book of Acts says, "so there was no needy person among them." It was not theoretical. In those early days of the Church, there was no needy person among them. This was their community—caring for each other in the whole of life, including the material needs. Not only the material needs, mind you, but including the material needs.

And did this only operate in their own local congregations?[2]

Schaeffer goes on to point out that such provision was not limited to just members of the local congregation but to those in far off places as well. Unfortunately, many churches have failed to provide the leadership God requires from them in this area. Rather than helping people in need, churches and Church leaders are often too ready to live off the "fat of the land."

Neglecting the Poor

Often times people who classify themselves as liberals tend to be more aware of the needs of the poor and helpless within the U.S. than do conservatives who tend to overlook domestic poverty. Most conservatives believe that everyone has an equal chance in America to be successful, and if they are not, it must be a reflection of their own lack of ambition—they choose to be poor.

As a conservative, I believe we have failed to properly consider the role that families play in preparing one to take advantage of our free economy. If a child is told by their parents that they face a world of open opportunity, that in America anyone can succeed, if they are encouraged by their parents and receive a decent education, then they indeed have a good chance of "making it."

But what about the hundreds of thousands of children raised by single mothers, functionally illiterate, who have never held a job, and whose own mother never held a job? These children are not raised to believe in an open universe of potential opportunities, but a closed and malevolent universe of zero opportunity.

As anyone who has observed children knows, a child's attitude and consequent action are most deeply affected by their parents. The fact is, the children of the inner city ghettos and the rural poor do require our help. Unfortunately, it is not the sort of help usually offered by the liberal establishment.

The liberals have also underestimated the role of the family in instilling values and supplying ongoing support and encouragement. The standard liberal answer to help the poor is to increase their dependence upon the government, which only increases their lack of hope. Government welfare checks do not increase confidence in one's ability to provide a stable income for a growing family. Social welfare programs are incapable of instilling the values and reasoning necessary to succeed outside of the welfare rolls.

Conservatives have tended to ignore the poor because we're too busy pursuing success in our own world. Liberals chose to "throw money" at the problem, ignoring the real need of these families. They discovered that spending money, especially other people's money, is easier than devoting one's self and time to meeting the needs of the poor.

Ignored by conservatives, victimized by liberal tokenism, the poor are in trouble. They need long-term commitment from compassionate people who will help them on a one-to-one basis. This is the historical job of the Church. Unfortunately, the Church has also been guilty of neglecting the needs of the poor — who can usually be found within one square mile of where we assemble to worship.

We have misinterpreted Jesus' statement "the poor will always be with you" as approval of an apathetic attitude toward their needs. In the light of Jesus' love for the poor and hurting, such an attitude is far from being Christ-like. It is, in fact, anti-Christ. What the Bible tells us is that since the poor will always be with us, we will always have an obligation to help them meet their needs.

In Ezekiel 34 God warns ministers of His Gospel not to forget about the poor in their midst:

> This is what the Sovereign Lord says: Woe to the shepherds of Israel who only take care of themselves! Should not shepherds take care of the flock? You eat the curds, clothe yourselves with the wool and slaughter the choice animals, but you do not take care of the flock. You have not strengthened the weak or healed the sick or bound up the injured. (Ezekiel 34:2b-4a)

A few verses later God makes clear the consequences of continued failure to care for the poor.

> Because My shepherds did not search for My flock but cared for themselves rather than for My flock, therefore, O shepherds, hear the word of the Lord: This is what the Sovereign Lord says: I am against the shepherds and will hold them accountable for My flock. I will remove them from tending the flock so that the shepherds can no longer feed themselves. (Ezekiel 34:8c-10b)

How many churches do you know that truly provide for the unemployed, the bankrupt, those without adequate food, clothing or medical attention within their own congregations, let alone their own neighborhoods? How many churches spend more on their parking lot than on the poor? How many congregations will authorize $10,000 for padded pews but not $1,000 for blankets for the homeless down the street?

I am continually chagrined to see how many of our Evangelical churches that appear to be loving, committed fellowships don't know or seem to care about those few families in their congregation who need a helping hand. Their attitude seems to be: this is America, somehow it will work out for them; meanwhile, I'm comfortable!

Until our churches look after the needs of our own neighborhoods specifically, thoroughly, and energetically, we will look very much like the shepherds in Ezekiel 34. We will certainly not be ready to minister to those in need in our communities and our nation.

Who Are the Poor?

This leads us to the questions, who are the poor, and how many of them are there?

> After all the trillions of dollars spent on welfare from 1965 to date, 14.4 percent of our population (33.7 million persons) still live below the poverty line ($10,990 for a family of four). In 1950, one-in-twelve Americans were below the poverty line; in 1979, it was one-in-nine; today, one-in-every-seven Americans is reported to be below the poverty line.[3]

Clearly something is wrong with America's approach to the poor if the percentage of poor among us is growing steadily higher.

Who are the poor? A majority are black and Hispanic, living in the inner cities or the rural South, mostly invisible to the gaze of the average Christian. Some of them are the five hundred or more "homeless" of which approximately a third are in nuclear family units, many of them white. They are those not only without jobs, but with little hope of obtaining them. Current government policy assumes that without welfare checks, millions would simply perish.

To understand why our government has spent over $200 billion a year since the mid-seventies to solve poverty and yet has failed, we need to understand the origin of America's social welfare policies.

Before the 1960s, these policies simply did not exist. The Church, the extended family, or various other private charitable organizations provided assistance on a localized level. Then the government began stepping in to fill the service void that had been growing steadily during this century. As the Church had entered the twentieth century in retreat from its duty to serve others, it didn't take long for the politicians to notice that there was a large and growing segment of the poor that no one — certainly not the Church — seemed to be helping.

Charles Murray, the brilliant black scholar in his epic examination of the "failure of American social policy from the 1950-1980" entitled *Losing Ground*, gives us an excellent insight into the evolution of our current governmental poverty/welfare programs. He tells us that John F. Kennedy launched the modern American welfare state with his special message to Congress in 1962:

> The goals of our public welfare program must be positive and constructive. . . . [The welfare program] must stress the integrity and preservation of the family unit. It must contribute to the attack on dependency, juvenile delinquency, family breakdown, illegitimacy, ill health, and disability. It must reduce the incidence of these problems, prevent their occurrence and recurrence, and strengthen and protect the vulnerable in a highly competitive world.[4]

Who could disagree with such a worthy goal, especially with its emphasis on preserving the family unit and attacking "dependency"? With the void left in providing for social need by the withdrawal of the Church, it seemed to be a reasonable, if not perfect, solution.

When Christians fail to carry out their God-given mandate to serve their neighbors, others will step in to fill the void. They will be non-Christians, committed to using other means, like big government, to create a better world apart from God. Often they are referred to as secular humanists.

How Welfare Developed

Unfortunately, by 1967 Kennedy's vision that government social policy should be formulated to "get people on their feet again" had been totally abandoned in favor of a "permanent income transference." Working-class paychecks would have enough funds deducted to permanently support the millions without paychecks. This was actually a mild form of Marxism. The mandatory confiscation of part of your wealth to be given to someone less wealthy, all of which is decided upon by government bureaucrats over which neither giver or receiver exercises any real influence.

What caused this major change in the direction of our welfare policies? Murray points out the acceptance by the American intellectual elite of a radical notion: poverty was not created by one's own lack of skill, training, or initiative, or even by temporary bad luck. The problem was "the system." It was racist, anti-black, anti-poor. Therefore it would do no good to lend the poor a helping hand, since the system was against them.

> Whether the Establishment view of the black condition in the last half of the 1960's was right or wrong is not the issue that concerns us. The fact that this view was so widely shared helped force the shift in assumptions about social welfare. White America owed black America; it had a conscience to clear.

> If society were to blame for the riots, if it were to blame for the economic and social discrepancies between white and blacks, if indeed it were to blame for poverty itself among all races, and if society's responsibility were not put right by enforcing a formalistic legal equality, then a social problem could hardly be constructed on grounds that simply guaranteed equality of opportunity. It must work toward equality of outcome. A "hand" was not enough.[5]

Murray relates how President Lyndon Johnson's "welfare czar," Joseph Califano, haplessly

> . . . had called reporters into his office to tell them that a government analysis had shown that only 50,000 persons, or one percent of the 7,300,000 people on welfare, were capable of being given skills and training to make them self-sufficient. The repudiation of the dream—the end of the dole once and for all— was complete.[6]

With LBJ's vision of a new, massive "war on poverty," his aides embarked on an ambitious strategy to overwhelm the problem with dollars, similar to their strategy to overwhelm the Viet Cong with half a million American soldiers.

Both programs, conceived on grandiose levels, and executed without proper forethought, planning, or competence, ended equally disastrously. In mid-1987 *Time* magazine reported,

> Since the mid-1960s, the U.S. has enacted the most sweeping civil rights laws in history, fought a costly war on poverty and

aggressively pursued affirmative action to increase opportunities for blacks. Millions of them, as a result, have escaped the ghetto to join the mainstream middle class. But to the consternation of scholars, officials and blacks themselves, a seemingly ineradicable black underclass has multiplied in inner-city neighborhoods plagued by a self-perpetuation pathology of joblessness, welfare dependency, crime, and teen-age illegitimacy.[7]

The number of "hits" scored compared to the amount of "firepower" employed by the war on poverty was alarmingly low. As Murray notes:

Overall, civilian social welfare costs increased by twenty times from 1950 to 1980, in constant dollars. During the same period, the United States population increased by half.[8]

Consider these shocking statistics compiled by former Reagan aide Rus Walton:

Since 1950, the number of persons receiving public assistance and social welfare payments has increased from 6 million to 18 million [in 1974] to more than 30 million [in 1984]. Aid to families with dependent children (AFDC) payments soared from $3.5 billion in 1960 to $16.1 billion in 1984; the amount spent on food stamps increased from $550 million to $10.7 billion. In 1983 [latest available data], all governments spent $455.8 billion for public assistance and social welfare; that represented thirty-nine percent of all government spending and fifteen percent of the GNP. In 1984, "welfare" expenditures accounted for some sixty-four percent of the federal budget.

With these billions of dollars being spent, it would not be unreasonable to expect positive results. But not only were they not positive, they were a horror story — for the increasingly beleaguered taxpayer, the poor, and the well-intentioned but ill-advised "social engineers" who structured America's ill-fated war on poverty.

Welfare's Tragic Results

Just what were the results? First, the number of poor began increasing. Since 1960, a substantial segment of the poor, particularly those viewed as hard-core, long-term poor with little hope for employment, has been single, black mothers with illegitimate children. In 1960 there were approximately 225,000 such illegitimate births. After twenty years of "social engineering," the number of illegitimate births skyrocketed to almost seven hundred thousand:

> If the trend line from 1950 to 1963 had remained unchanged, the black illegitimacy rate would have increased another 6.8 percentage points by 1980. Instead, the slope of the trend line suddenly steepened. The increase was not 6.8 percentage points, but nearly four times that: In 1980, 48 percent of live births among blacks were to single women, compared with 17 percent in 1950. The problem lay not just in the number of illegitimate births, but in who was having them: teenagers. In 1955 teenaged girls gave birth to nearly half a million babies (490,000). But of these half million, only about 70,000 of the mothers were unmarried. In the 1980, the number of children born to teenagers was not markedly greater than in 1955 — about 562,000. But the number of single young mothers — teenagers — had grown to 272,000.[9]

Worse yet, unemployment levels were skyrocketing for able black youth — the very people billions of dollars were being spent to help. Murray comments:

> Focusing on the age groups on which the federal jobs programs were focused not only fails to reveal improvement; it points to major losses. Something was happening to depress employment among young blacks.[10]

Murray's study then begins examining the "labor force population" (LFP) figures of those who were beneficiaries of the world's greatest poverty program. Unemployment figures include all those unemployed whether they wish to work or not. LFP measures those who, given a chance, will work. As Murray observes:

> The hard-core unemployed were not people who were being rebuffed by job interviewers, but people who had given up hope or ambition of becoming part of the labor force.

> Beginning in 1966, black male LFP started to fall substantially faster than white LFP. By 1972, a gap of 5.9 percentage points

had opened up between black males and white males. By 1976, the year the slide finally halted, the gap was 7.7 percentage points. To put it another way: from 1954 to 1965, the black reduction in LFP was 17 percent larger than for whites. From 1965 to 1976, it was 271 percent larger.[11]

Murray concluded,

> . . . we had never witnessed large-scale voluntary withdrawal from [or failure to enlist in] the labor market by able-bodies males.

> On the face of things, it would appear that large numbers of young black males stopped engaging in the fundamental process of seeking and holding jobs — at least, visible jobs in the above-ground economy.[12]

Murray then poses the obvious (and extremely important) question:

> How could it be that, despite the combination of economic growth and huge increases in expenditures on the poor, the number of poor stopped shrinking in the early 1970's and then began growing?[13]

What Went Wrong?

How Indeed? What in the world went wrong? Murray offered several reasons why the state failed to successfully fill the void that appeared when the Church decided to withdraw from the social arena:

> A government's social policy helps set the rules of the game — the stakes, the risks, the payoffs, the tradeoffs, and the strategies for making a living, raising a family, having fun, defining what "winning" and "success" mean. The more vulnerable a population and the fewer its independent resources, the more decisive the effect of the rules imposed from above. The most compelling explanation for the marked shift in the fortunes of the poor is that they continued to respond, as they always had, to the world as they found it, but that we — meaning the not-poor and un-disadvantaged — had changed the rules of their world. Not of our world, just of theirs. The first effect of the

new rules was to make it profitable for the poor to behave in the short-term in ways that were destructive in the long-term. Their second effect was to mask these long-term losses — to subsidize irretrievable mistakes. We tried to provide more for the poor and produced more poor instead. We tried to remove the barriers to escape from poverty, and inadvertently built a trap.[14]

And he provides some very specific reasons, which were rejected by the social reformers, and whose rejection insured that those who launched the war on poverty would meet their Waterloo:

Premise #1: People respond to incentives and disincentives. Sticks and carrots work.

Premise #2: People are not inherently hard working or moral. In the absence of countervailing influences, people will avoid work and be amoral.

Premise #3: People must be held responsible for their actions. Whether they are responsible in some ultimate philosophical or biochemical sense cannot be the issue if society is to function.[15]

. . . social policy since 1964 has ignored these premises and . . . has thereby created much of the mess we are in.[16]

What Murray is pointing to is that, in their ultimate wisdom, our "public servants," made it more attractive for poor people to stay on welfare than to work. As Milton Friedman, one of America's leading economists sagely observes, if you pay people to be poor, poor they will be!

Creating a Class of Permanent Poor

How exactly this was accomplished is a tragic story of good intentions wreaking havoc, particularly on minority families, which also explains the massive increase in illegitimate births.

Prior to 1970 AFDC welfare regulations prohibited welfare benefits paid to a mother if there was "a man in the house" capable of earning a living for the family. After 1970 this ruling was changed. A mother could receive a welfare check based on the number of children she was supporting as long as the man in the house did not have legal responsibility for the children; for example, was not their legal father.

This rule change not only encouraged men not to marry the women they lived with (since that would deprive her of welfare assistance), but it also encouraged women to have as many illegitimate children as possible to increase their welfare allotment. Murray points out:

> The bottom line is this: Harold can get married and work forty hours a week in a hot, tiresome job; or he can live with Phyllis and their baby without getting married, not work, and have more disposable income. From an economic point of view, getting married is dumb. From a noneconomic point of view, it involves him in a legal relationship that has no payoff for him. If he thinks he may sometime tire of Phyllis and fatherhood, the 1970 rules thus provide a further incentive for keeping the relationship off the books.[17]

Is Murray alone in blaming "welfare-state liberalism" for making minorities permanent wards of the state? He is not. Ironically, Murray is joined by a host of brilliant black scholars who are aggressively challenging and repudiating the philosophical underpinning of our society's approach to poverty.

Black thinkers, like Thomas Sowell of Stanford and economist Walter Williams,

> . . . place the blame on a welfare-state liberalism that has made all too many blacks permanent wards of the state. This dependency on the federal government, the argument goes, has effectively robbed the masses of blacks of the initiative and creativity to address their problems.[18]

As Christians we shouldn't be surprised that our secular government's answer to meeting people's needs has ended in failure. Any program is destined for failure when, rather than devoting the necessary compassion, care, and attention to the poor's real needs, it just uses money as a cure-all. As Murray has proved, this approach creates dependency, destroys initiative, self-esteem, and self-reliance, and eliminates any hope of improvement.

The truth is, no government can deal with the root problems of poverty. No massive, cold, impersonal, uncaring, inefficient bureaucracy can provide the compassion, empathy, long-term persistence, sacrifice, and wisdom needed to help the truly poor.

Only Christ, working through His Church, can make a truly positive impact on poverty. As Pope John Paul stated on his tour of the United States:

> No institution can by itself replace . . . human love or human initiative, when it is a question of dealing with the suffering of another.[19]

Solutions

Affecting Government Policy. As we have seen, when the Church gradually withdrew from its commitment to care for the poor, the government moved in. Instead of Christians tithing ten percent to the Church to take care of the poor through a Biblical model, we are now taxed thirty-three percent by our government to support a system that not only does not relieve poverty, but in fact keeps people mired in it, hopeless and helpless. Adding insult to injury, this system promotes immoral behavior that destroys family units and deprives women of truly supportive husbands and denies God's children the right to any semblance of a normal father.

As Murray observes,

> It is indeed possible that steps to relieve misery can create misery. The most troubling aspect of social policy toward the poor in late twentieth-century America is not how much it costs, but what it has bought.[20]

What can we do? First, we must take responsibility for the government's well-intentioned but destructive welfare policies. After all, it is our government. We elected our representatives to represent us, to express our will on how our tax dollars are used to restructure society. Obviously we cannot dismantle our huge bureaucracy overnight, although an intriguing case has been made by black economist Walter Williams, as surmised by columnist Tom Anderson:

> Economists have figured out that it costs about *three* dollars to deliver *one* dollar in public assistance to the poor. That means that only twenty-five cents out of every tax/deficit dollar spent on welfare gets to the poor; the other seventy-five cents stays in

the pipeline to fuel the bureaucracy. What if we, the taxpayers, through the federal government, were to give each individual $12,000 a year, and each family of four $20,000 a year—cash, in monthly grants? That would cost us $86.4 billion a year in direct payments to individuals, and $145.5 billion for the payments to the families of four. That's $231.9 billion a year.

You say we can't afford it? *Look at this*: we spent $642 billion a year on "the needy" in the nation. Figure it out. We could fire almost all of those 530,000 government welfare employees, give the poor a higher income, and have about $410 billion left over![21]

Changing Policies. Forward thinking black scholars are in fact calling for the dismantling of the entire system—before it collapses of its own weight and inefficiency. Murray proposes:

. . . scrapping the entire federal welfare and income-support structure for working-aged persons, including AFDC, Medicaid, Food Stamps, Unemployment Insurance, Worker's Compensation, subsidized housing, disability insurance, and the rest. It would leave the working-aged person with no recourse whatsoever except the job market, family members, friends, and public or private locally funded services.[22]

He surmises that such drastic action would give one no other choice but to be accountable for one's own life, to take responsibility for one's family, to stand on one's own feet:

Parents tend to become upset at the prospect of a daughter bringing home a baby that must be entirely supported on an already inadequate income. Some become so upset that they spend considerable parental energy avoiding such an eventuality. Potential fathers of such babies find themselves under more pressure not to cause such a problem or to help with its solution if it occurs. Adolescents who were not job-ready find they are job-ready after all. It turns out that they can work for low wages and accept the discipline of the workplace if the alternative is grim enough. After a few years, many—not all, but many—find that they have acquired salable skills, or that they are at the right place at the right time, or otherwise find that the original entry-level job has gradually been transformed into a secure job paying a decent wage. A few — not a lot, but a few — find that the process leads to affluence.

Perhaps the most rightful, deserved benefit goes to the much larger population of low-income families who have been doing things right all along and have been punished for it: the young man who has taken responsibility for his wife and child even though his friends with the same choice have called him a fool; the single mother who has worked full-time and forfeited her right to welfare for very little extra money; the parents who have set an example for their children even as the rules of the game have taught their children that the example is outmoded. For these millions of people, the instantaneous result is that no one makes fun of them any longer. The longer-term result will be that they regain the status that is properly theirs. They will not only be the bedrock upon which the community is founded [which they always have been], they will be recognized as such. The process whereby they regain their position is not magical, but a matter of logic.

When it becomes highly dysfunctional for a person to be dependent, status will accrue to being independent, and in fairly short order. Noneconomic rewards will once again reinforce the economic reward of being a good parent and provider.[23]

Murray concludes with:

For let me be quite clear: I am not suggesting that we dismantle income support for the working-aged to balance the budget or punish welfare cheats. I am hypothesizing, with the advantage of powerful collateral evidence, that the lives of large numbers of poor people would be radically changed for the better.[24]

Surprisingly, he is not alone in proposing such a dramatic resolution. Besides black scholars like Murray, Sowell, and Williams, there are more. William Wilson, a distinguished black scholar and chairman of the Sociology Department at the University of Chicago, in a major work, *The Truly Disadvantaged: The Inner City, the Underclass and Public Policy*, also proposes major changes in our present approach. He argues against welfare programs designed mainly for minorities, contending instead for programs for job training readily accessible to whites and blacks alike.[25]

In yet another major work and blast at liberal tradition, Harold Cruse, a black scholar at the University of Michigan, has written *Plural But Equal: Blacks and Minorities in American Plural Society.*

In this complex work, Cruse joins his colleagues Murray and Wilson in blitzkrieging the white liberal tendency to try to artificially manipulate the black community into bogus form of economic and social integration. Professor Cruse concludes that the result of this policy was that

> . . . successive generations of black youth would be born, evolve, hesitate, ponder, persevere, and flounder into the blind anonymity of deferred dreams and frustrated hope — without a functional philosophy for coping with American realities.[26]

What does all this tell us? I have presented these samples as evidence of a new current in the wind foretelling a major change for tens of millions of Americans — really, for all of us. With the best and brightest of black thinkers demanding an end to the government's creating a dependence among its people, with the ascendancy of conservatives at all levels of government, and with a federal deficit out of control (public assistance spending currently represents over thirty-nine percent of all government spending[27]), the handwriting is on the wall.

By mid-1988 Alan Greenspan, the chairman of the Federal Reserve Board and therefore the most powerful economist in the nation, was repeatedly calling for Congress to begin "cutting back" benefit programs — including social security. Observing that the current federal budget deficit was already unacceptable, he pointed out the government's welfare benefits were expected to rise dramatically in the twenty-first century unless large cuts were soon made.

So, some 33.7 million people who now live below the poverty line are going to have their public assistance funding seriously altered, or else the government will have to risk damaging the entire economy by both raising taxes and increasing government deficits even more. All the while those who are supposedly the beneficiaries of the public dole will continue to decay mentally, emotionally, physically, and spiritually.

What can we do as individuals to effect government policy? Obviously we must work hard to elect those who will fairly represent our beliefs; who will, with compassion and integrity, work to reform the system.

Making a Difference. But there is much more that each one of us can do. In fact, there is something that only we as Christians can do, and it is very vital. Without it, there can be no reforming of the current unacceptable system.

Murray observes that the major challenge of restructuring our currently "out of control" welfare system will be to help those who, for whatever reason, or period of time, simply cannot help themselves.[28]

Noting that the economic troubles of the majority of the poor stem from the lack of jobs, he suggests keeping intact our unemployment insurance system. But what about those million who have never been employed? Or have been unemployed longer than their "unemployment benefits" will cover?

Helping those Beyond Government Reach

It is primarily these people that the Church must reach out to. We must be their bridge from failure and despair to achievement, independence, and hope. It is our golden opportunity to obey Christ in loving our fellow man, in providing for the poor, the oppressed, the widow, the orphan, and the elderly. But we cannot afford to wait until the current welfare system is dismantled or has collapsed of its own weight. As Christians we must set the example. We need to demonstrate that private initiative, rooted in our Christian compassion and service, is capable of filling the gap if we expect government social planners to seriously look for alternative methods of helping the poor.

For the government to terminate overnight the programs those welfare-dependent beings are on would be both immoral and unrealistic. There must be a bridge between the current morass of unmet expectations and the bright new future envisioned by the scholars we have mentioned. We are that bridge.

What kind of things can we do, directly as individuals, that will help the poor?

Providing Work. For one thing, we can help them begin to work. We have seen that as a result of welfare's killing any work ethic, the breakdown of our educational system, and the lack of apprenticing programs, many of the unemployed are fast becoming unemployable. Thus, American businesses have exported hundreds of thousands of jobs (in textiles and manufacturing) to Asia or Central America because they can't find people who are culturally trained to work with concentration, consistency, and discipline and who will work for the sort of wages offered (since welfare often pays as much as these jobs).

Similarly, U.S. agriculture imports tens of thousands of workers from Central America and Mexico (and now even China) because they can't find farm labor domestically.

Clearly something is very wrong here. Would it not be better to fill all these jobs with Americans now on welfare? Workers would have a sense of pride, of earning their families' incomes, of self-worth, of making it. Welfare costs would be cut. The money paid foreign workers, which adds to our huge trade deficits, would be favorably reduced.

Discipling for Progress. But what is required is more than job training! It requires cultural modifications to prepare for employment. It requires apprenticeship. Are we willing to take the time required to find and then teach apprentices how to work by our side? Are we willing to train them in ethics and principals as well as skills?

The real question is, are we willing to make the requisite sacrifices to be obedient to Jesus and serve the poor? Can we afford once again to reinforce the stereotype of the Evangelical Church as more interested in the ease and comfort of our affluent lifestyle than in demonstrating God's reality by sharing His love and caring?

Already a number of Churches, from the smallest to the largest, are heeding God's call to serve the poor. A very significant and truly hopeful sign for the maturing and evolving of the Christian Right is that most of these churches are headed by pastors actively identified with the Christian Right.

Letting Our Light Shine. Earlier we discussed Cindy Rocker, who as a Christian, made the startling discovery that Christ had a deep concern for the poor. When she asked other Church members why they weren't helping the poor, they had the obvious answer; they didn't know any poor people. Cindy went out and found thousands of migrant workers surrounding her town that desperately needed help. First she started a "Sponsor A Family Program" where Church families brought food, gifts, clothing and the message of Christ's love to needy families during the Christmas season. Next, she opened a thrift store so the poor could buy necessities at low-low prices with all merchandise donated and with proceeds funding other projects; a Christian preschool to teach English to migrant farm worker children; and a food bank supplied with donations from farmers and churches. Members of needy families worked in the store as payment for their food. [29]

In the state capital of Tallahassee, Florida, the four-hundred-member Christian Covenant Community Church led by Monte Wilson has reached out to the rural black families of Lamont, many of whom are headed by single welfare mothers and others barely scraping by as low-paid ranch workers. Church member Michael Buzby felt compassion for these people and arranged the donation of five acres of land. Michael then split his time between tree cutting (to earn enough to support his work with the poor) and providing food, tutoring, and spiritual counseling to the needy families of Lamont. In a short period of time, Michael's mission has been so successful that the Church is underwriting the cost to allow Michael to concentrate his full energies on serving the families of Lamont.

Within the city limits of Tallahassee, the Church is also starting a literacy class to reach out to the thousands of adults and young people who are functionally illiterate. Church leaders are distributing flyers to other churches and government agencies asking for their help in identifying potential program participants. The Church's senior pastor, Monte Wilson, believes people will be able to read simple chapters from the Bible within two to twelve weeks. (Incidentally, recent studies show that up to twenty million Americans are functionally illiterate—unable to fully comprehend a want ad in the local newspaper.)

Providing a Home. Church leaders at the five-hundred member Santa Rosa, California, Christian Church felt a burden for those who needed a Christian home. They bought an old Victorian home and cast a wide net, accepting everyone from stranded families traveling through, to local unwed mothers, to recent releases from the county jail, to single Church members in need of temporary quarters. Regular Bible studies are conducted and a good deal of healing happens just as the several dozen residents interact under the watchful eye of the all-volunteer, live-in staff. Each person on the staff works at full-time jobs, then counsels in the evenings and on weekends with other residents. The housing ministry's prime mover and full-time director, Reverend Sherman Brees, has completed a brief manual that provides suggestions for churches that desire to establish their own "ministry houses." As U.S. Senator Mark Hatfield has pointed out, if every Evangelical Church established a housing ministry, there would be a great reduction in the homeless and the welfare department caseloads. There would also be a lot more new Christians!

People that Care. The one-thousand member Shady Grove Church of Grand Prairie, Texas, pastored by Olen Griffing, an independent charismatic, ministers to the poor through their "People That Care" center. The center, located in a rented building seven minutes from their Church, collects food and clothing from Church members and purchases large quantities of low-cost food from the local Federal Food Bank. The staff, supervised by a full-time Church elder, helps Christians and non-Christians alike. Spiritual counseling as well as job counseling is offered (the Church offers classes to its members, training them to become counselors).

A Retreat for Healing. In Northfield, New Hampshire, Elizabeth and Samuel Baker sold their businesses, bought a two-hundred-year-old, forty-room farmhouse, and now run Zion Cornerstone Ministries—a home for the poor, the homeless, drug addicts, and unwed mothers. Residents work twelve hours a week to help operate the house and run the forty-acre farm. Mr. and Mrs. Baker give food, shelter, and religious guidance.[30]

Building for the Future. In Montgomery, Alabama, Millard Fuller sold his business and started Habitat for Humanity. Now 136 Habitat volunteer-affiliates around the country build or restore homes that are sold to poor families at cost with a twenty-year interest free mortgage. As mortgages are paid, revenues are used to build more houses.[31]

David Kitely's large Shiloh Christian Fellowship of Oakland, California, is meeting the tremendous emotional needs of the community through its model counseling center, manned by specially trained Church members. Listed in the yellow pages under counseling centers, the Shiloh Counseling Center does not charge any fees. Prospective counselees must fill out an application and a "consent to be counseled" legal form, and the Church carries insurance covering any "counseling malpractice" lawsuits. The center also refers people to specific clinics for drug or alcohol abuse, pregnancy counseling, wife or child abuse problems, and the like.

Glen Cole, a leading conservative political activist, heads up Sacramento, California's largest Evangelical Church, Capital Christian Center. His Church provides an unusually outstanding example of service to the poor. Their benevolence program provides for the public one week's supply of food for each family, gasoline allotments, even hot meals at local restaurants. Substantial financial aid can be provided for Church members behind on mortgage or rent payments.

The Church also maintains various feeding ministries for street people, and they maintain an active ministry to five hundred shut-ins in convalescent homes. The Church is highly active in political issues, especially abortion and pornography.

John Meares' two thousand member (and mostly black) Washington, D.C., congregation also provides loans to members to help them through difficult times. The public is encouraged to avail themselves of the Church's very successful emergency food bank.

Whether a street person is in need of food or a Church member of long standing is in need of an emergency loan, applicants for assistance are carefully counseled by Church deacons to understand how they arrived at their particular condition and what they can do to pull themselves out of it. The Church also offers extensive adult education and literacy programs, and tutors for younger students with learning problems. Church members have incorporated a separate organization, "Impact," to provide members with an effective channel for political action. Impact has already demonstrated its name by successfully reversing local ordinances unfavorable to Churches.

Jack Hayford's pastorate, the Church on the Way in Los Angeles's San Fernando Valley is known as not only the largest charismatic congregation in Los Angeles, but also as the "celebrity" Church, attended by many Christian performers like the Pat Boone family.

What the Church on the Way should be really noted for, however, is its outstanding service to the community. They sponsor a "Church of the street" in downtown LA (thirty minutes away) feeding and ministering to up to eight hundred people a day. They also provide food for those in need within their immediate community.

As outstanding examples of the sort of service that Christians must provide to the community if we are to help lead, the Church recently donated $25,000 to the city of Los Angeles for their homeless programs, and another $25,000 to World Opportunities to purchase a new food distribution truck. Not only has this Church "put their money where their mouth is." Eight out of ten board members of the local Salvation Army are from the Church on the Way. Obviously Jack Hayford's congregation is on the way for setting an example of leadership through service.

Another creative Christian response to overcoming poverty comes from the *Step* (Strategies to Elevate People) *Foundation*. *Step* was founded by a number of Christian Right activists like Arch Decker, the late Clint Murchison, and Mary Crowley, Holly Coors, Bunker Hunt, and Dee Jepsen. Long before many of us, they saw the need to "elevate" those in need.

Today the *Step Foundation* offers an excellent thirty-page manual detailing step-by-step how your Church can effectively involve itself in meeting the needs of your community. While I obviously can't reproduce the entire manual in this chapter, I have excerpted six brief points on what pastors can do compiled for *Step* by one of America's leading black pastors, Dr. E. V. Hill.

1. Preach about God's command to help the poor.
2. Inform congregations about the poor around them. Provide congregations with information and statistics about the poor through newsletters, audio-visual material, seminars, mission conferences on poverty, etc.
3. Organize your Church. Form task forces of people concerned about helping the poor.

4. Lead your Church in supporting those inner-city Churches, organizations, pastors, and lay leaders who are directly involved with the poor. Participate in meeting needs for volunteers, staff, funds, etc.

5. Use your influence in cooperation with others to effectuate change in customs and policies detrimental to the poor. Get involved in the community!

6. Exchange pulpits between suburban and inner city pastors.

7. Back or create special programs working for the good of the poor.

One of the most effective ways for a local Church to help the needy has been pioneered by Virgil Gulker, president of Love, Inc. Since 1981 Love, Inc., has launched over fifty local programs with eleven hundred participating churches. Dr. Gulker's strategy is to teach churches how to be "needs" resources centers. By learning to assess both legitimate needs in the community and the full potential of congregation members (by volunteering expert skills, time, etc.), Love, Inc., teaches churches to be "clearing houses" for the needs of their community.[32]

If we begin to visualize the plight of the poor and homeless, it will be easier to see why God is so concerned for them, and it will help motivate us to do something.

I recently read a heartbreaking story of a woman who had intentionally disguised herself as a street person to see what life was like. She reported to *People* magazine:

> Lund found that hope had died in most of her companions. Their conversation followed the themes of failure — fruitless job searches, broken relationships, lost children. "Not one of them wanted anything material when we talked about what we'd want if we had one wish — no sports car, no boat. They wished their family really loved them — if they could have one thing in the whole world, they wished they had the love of their family and a 9 to 5."[33]

Nothing could sum up the problem better than this statement by Kay McChesney, a sociologist who spent sixteen months studying homeless families in Los Angeles:

What we are dealing with is a collapse of moral leadership in this country. When you see a mother with a two-week-old baby and two toddlers walk three miles for a place to stay, then sleep on the steps of a Church because there's no room at the shelter, it's hard to remember that this is America, not Calcutta.[34]

Who will provide this moral leadership?

Accepting the Call

Will it be Christians, carrying out Christ's mandate to love our neighbors? Will it be Christians who follow Christ's instruction to teach all the nations about His love for them—demonstrated by our activity on their behalf? Will we learn to witness by not just preaching God's love but demonstrating it as well?

If we fail to meet this challenge, others will, as the *Los Angeles Times* reported on December 4, 1987:

> In an unprecedented editorial published simultaneously by their respective journals, the nation's doctors and lawyers have been urged to honor historic ethics tenets and greatly increase the amount of free services they provide to the poor.

> The editorial, appearing in today's *Journal of the American Medical Association* and *American Bar Association Journal*, urges each of the nation's 497,000 physicians and 675,000 attorney's to spend at least fifty hours a year providing uncompensated services to poor people.[35]

If we are truly to serve our communities, our motto must be: No one should suffer in need, abandoned or forgotten as long as the love of Christ dwells within us. And finally, we might be well-advised to meditate upon the consequences of our obedience or disobedience in helping the poor.

> If a man shuts his ears to the cry of the poor, he too will cry out and not be answered. (Proverbs 21:13)

> He who gives to the poor will lack nothing, but he who closes his eyes to them receives many curses. (Proverbs 28:27)

TEN

RESTORING RIGHTEOUSNESS

Nobody likes to be poor. And almost everybody would like to see poverty eradicated. Few blame the poor for being poor. If we think of poverty in terms of morality, it's usually that one is immoral if he could alleviate someone's suffering but doesn't choose to.

Yet there remains a number of social issues where our spiritual mandate is not so clearly understood. It seems easier for us to give a job to a needy person than to reach out in compassionate service to a homosexual or drug addict dying of AIDS.

Many Christians will rush to the aid of a family temporarily devastated by unemployment and sickness. Few Christians will extend God's loving forgiveness to a single woman with an "unplanned" pregnancy. Some of us who are quick to help young Christian leaders who have "star potential," but we're embarrassed by our lack of service to our own grandparents as their advancing age makes them more and more dependent on others.

We fill our minds with wholesome "family entertainment," but we avert our eyes and hurry past the adult bookstore downtown, unwilling to remind ourselves that pornography in America is an eight billion dollar a year industry, ruining the lives of our neighbors.

AIDS, abortion, the elderly, pornography—these are four issues crying out for God's compassion, justice, and righteousness. They are also four of the issues that we Christians have avoided far too long.

In this chapter we will see how these four issues threaten not only our values, but our very lives, and how we as the Church can become effective instruments of extending God's mercy and justice to our generation and our community.

AIDS

The Good Samaritan principle demands that we show compassion to all, even the unlovable and the unloved.[1]

AIDS is an unnatural death. Mostly its victims are people in the prime of their lives, from twenty to forty years old. Death from AIDS is a horrible, slow, painful death that is reaching epidemic proportions. The official statistics and projections for the growth of this epidemic are horrifying:

> "Based on the estimated five million to ten million already infected with the disease, the world can expect to see at least tenfold increases in the number of cases of the deadly disease within five years," says Jonathan Mann, World Health Organization Director of AIDS programs.[2]

A major *Newsweek* cover story blared this headline:

> FUTURE SHOCK: By 1991 an estimated five million Americans may be carrying the AIDS virus and every person who has the virus is capable of giving AIDS to someone else.[3]

Newsweek continued,

> The official projections for the next five years of the epidemic — 179,000 deaths and 270,000 cumulative cases of AIDS — have been widely publicized. What is less well known, but vitally important, is that those projections are almost certainly low. They do not include any estimates of ARC, or AIDS-Related Complex, a disease syndrome that is sometimes fatal in itself and almost invariably a precursor of AIDS; by most estimates, there are ten times as many cases of ARC as there are cases of AIDS.[4]

As we read about our neighbors who fall prey to this uncontrolled plague, we are reminded that we are all vulnerable. As Dr. James Curran, director of the Centers for Disease control stated, "This [AIDS] is a problem that all people need to be concerned about."[5]

Newsweek, in an earlier story, echoed Curran's concern:

Once dismissed as the "gay plague," the disease has become the number one public health menace. It could change history. Anyone who has the least ability to look into the future can already see the potential for this disease being much worse than anything this century has seen before.[6]

In early 1987 a *U.S. News & World Report* cover story ominously entitled, "AIDS: At the Dawn of Fear," reinforced, even added to, the previous level of concern:

> The disease of them is suddenly the disease of us . . . the number [of Americans now infected by AIDS] may be as high as four million. Conceivably all of these people could progress to the incurable disease; certainly a fourth to a half will. . . . All those who fall sick [i.e., one to two million] are doomed.[7]

James Miller, President Reagan's Director of the U.S. Office of Management and Budget (OMB), the man in charge of managing the budget of the U.S. government, states that in twenty years a significant portion of our society could be incapacitated. We could end up with two societies — those who have it and those who don't.[8] He put into words what many Americans were thinking, but didn't want to say.

AIDS is not going to disappear. On the contrary, in all likelihood, it will continue its devastation across a large cross section of our society:

> AIDS is one of the most difficult challenges ever faced by modern medicine: control of the disease may well be five to ten years away. . . . AIDS may well become the dominant social and political issue of the next decade — but it is first and foremost a crisis in public health, an epidemic that may be out of control.[9]

> With cases doubling every thirteen months, AIDS will soon take its place in the rogue's gallery of major world scourges. The death toll could be in the tens of millions.[10]

> Fact: The World Health Organization estimates that one hundred million people will test positive for AIDS in the next five to ten years.[11]

I recently talked with a scientist researching the AIDS epidemic. He confirmed that no vaccine is reasonably expected within the next five to ten years. He also explained that it is not possible to screen AIDS tainted blood from blood banks with one hundred percent efficiency because AIDS keeps altering its "appearance" and is therefore extremely difficult to track over the long stretch.

So, what will our response be to what very well may be the major threat to life at the end of the twentieth century? Will we follow the lead of some schools and churches and turn AIDS victims (including hemophiliac children) away to suffer in pain, misery, and loneliness? Or will we follow Christ's example and reach out to the dying and suffering?

Will we write off AIDS victims as deserving of their disease (if they're homosexual or drug addicts) and in our false piety confirm our neighbors' suspicions that Christians are cold-hearted and pharisaical? Or will we see in the devastation of AIDS an unprecedented opportunity for manifesting God's love and witnessing for Christ as we help the sick and dying?

As *Christianity Today* stated in a recent editorial,

> . . . this could be one of the Church's finest hours if it can show compassion and wisdom without compromising its beliefs.[12]

Practicing homosexuality is a sin strongly and unequivocally condemned by God (Romans 1:27; 1 Corinthians 6:4; 2 Peter 2:10; Jude 8). So is adultery and stealing and gluttony. And all are capable of being forgiven. The question we must face is, will we refuse to minister the Gospel to those who truly need it because their sin is so personally distasteful to us? The U.S. Surgeon General, C. Everett Koop, who is a Christian, in terming AIDS "the most vicious of infectious diseases in the history of this race" called for "compassion for people with AIDS."[13]

Reaching Out in Compassion

So, what can we do? What would Christ have His Church do?

A few churches have begun to set examples. The Catholic Diocese of New Orleans arranges shelter, food, and care for AIDS patients who have no one to turn to in their few remaining days.

The *Lutheran Witness* recently published this encouraging account of how several Lutheran pastors are meeting the challenge of AIDS:

> But the sickness and death resulting from AIDS: whether for a Christian or unbeliever, is agonizingly painful—not only because of terrible physical deterioration, but also because friends and even family, terrified of contagion, usually shun the victim. . . .
>
> . . . Frank Jacobsen, a retired pastor in San Francisco, visited his first AIDS victim six years ago. The patient's mother had called Jacobsen from out of state.
>
> "I took a Communion set," recounts Jacobsen. "The doctor told me that if I took the set into the room, I couldn't take it out. Every precaution was taken. I wore rubber gloves, a gown, a mask. I didn't know what approach to use. I asked him if he remembered the part of the prayer of confession, 'confess unto Thee all my sins and iniquities with which I have ever offended Thee.' I said, 'Let's say it together.' I could see tears in his eyes, and I asked, 'Do you really mean this?' He said, 'Yes.'
>
> "I visited with him many times and heard his confession and shared the Gospel. I conducted his funeral service. About fifty gay people came into the service, each one carrying a red rose. In my introduction, I told them the story of his complete repentance. I feel he died one of God's children."
>
> Jacobsen estimates that he has ministered to about twenty dying homosexual men. He says, "If we have a proper distinction between Law and Gospel, the Gospel really brings joy. I have seen some real hope and real joy after they know they are forgiven. They realize they are terminal, but it's like they are dying in peace. I have seen it."

How does Jacobsen view the AIDS epidemic? "The Lord has given to us an open door."

Rev. James Wessel of San Lorenzo, California, says the disease is "pathetic, debilitating. I've ministered to people in the hospital with AIDS, and I discover in them an openness, a realizing of their need for the Lord. I testify to them of God's love and power, His forgiveness in Jesus. I try to be caring, not condemnatory."[14]

At the fifteen thousand member Chapel Hill Harvester Church in Atlanta, Georgia, Church leaders started a ministry for homosexuals called "Challenge." Noting a number of homosexuals attending his Church, the senior minister preached about Christ's love rather than condemnation. Many homosexuals eventually responded by asking for counseling; thus the Church responded with the Challenge program. Challenge members (currently thirty-five of them) have witnessed Christ's liberating power from homosexuality and some have happily married. It is not uncommon for people to drive hundreds of miles to attend Challenge[14] meetings. As more churches follow the example of Chapel Hill, hopefully people in need won't have to drive from as far away as Tennessee or Florida!

We must follow in Christ's footsteps and extend His message to the unlovely, the disfigured, the unwanted. People with AIDS need care, friends, and the salvation message of Jesus Christ. We can't expect to find any more fertile ground for witnessing Christ's love, compassion, and salvation, leading to eternal life.

Furthermore, we must prepare our churches to deal with AIDS victims within our own congregations. I believe the editors of *Christianity Today* were correct when they predicted,

> Increasing numbers of churches are faced with the awful reality of learning how the body of Christ should respond to the physical and spiritual needs of stricken members. Yet all churches should be facing this possibility before AIDS enters their sanctuaries. And it will.[15]

The Elderly

Thousands of elderly people are spending their last years on earth alone, abandoned, old, frail, lonely, and deserted. After being vital, productive members of our society (perhaps even making significant contributions to society or raising "good kids"), one day their strength fails, and the next day they are removed from the role they cherished so much in the center of their families, their professions, and their communities. They are often consigned to understaffed human warehouses, where the personnel, if they have the heart, don't have the time or energy to give the love and attention deserved or required.

If we think about these people at all, it's usually in terms of "how terrible for their children to have deserted them — too bad for those old people!" But Christ tells us they're *our* responsibility — the widows, the poor, the helpless. In James 1:27 God tells us that what He accepts as a pure and effective demonstration of our Christian faith is looking after the orphans and widows, as well as keeping oneself free from worldly sin.

Notice that here the Bible places taking care of the widows on the same level with keeping ourselves free from sin. How many churches have you seen that share this same balance of concern? What I've noticed is that a lot of churches are very concerned with the "don'ts" of personal sin and very forgetful of the "do's" of serving others. James 1:27 needs to be stenciled on every Church bulletin until the message finally sinks in!

In Isaiah, chapter 1, God reprimands His people for their sin. He explains why He has allowed so many calamities to befall their once blessed nation. He is explaining why He doesn't honor their offerings or hear their prayers any longer. He admonishes them to "learn to do right" and to "plead the case of the widow."

What does God mean by that? Does He mean we should act like Perry Mason, pleading the case for widows in a court of some kind? No, God's message for us today is to put the highest priority on taking care of the needs of the widows and the elderly.

God reinforces this instruction in Isaiah 58. Isaiah tells us that God is not impressed with our prayers and even our fasting if it doesn't include physically helping the poor, the helpless, and the destitute — the elderly are usually afflicted by one, if not all three, of these things.

How would we feel if it was our parents or grandparents or, in a few decades, ourselves being forgotten in the midst of a world too busy to care? Let us remember to do unto others as we would have them do to us!

Can our churches muster the energy to adopt a retirement home or sanitarium, visiting and comforting the residents on a regular basis? Can our members put away for one evening every month their own worries, aches, and pains and overly busy personal agendas to help those in need? Can we pry ourselves away from the canned laughter of the TV to appreciate the real joy of some of God's creations as we spend time with them, listening to their stories?

In a recent cover story on the elderly, *Christianity Today* reported the experiences of one of two individuals currently ministering to the elderly:

> Pat Parker emphasizes the Church's responsibility to stay in touch. "I hear them saying, 'I gave my life to the Church. Was it worth it? Now when I expect some return, where is it?'" Janet Yancey, who runs an inner-city seniors program at Chicago's LaSalle Street Church, notes, "There's no bang for the bucks when you're working with older people. Some would say the best you can expect is that they're going to die. Young people have great potential. They're going to be missionaries. They'll earn money and pour it into our program. Old people are going to get crabbier and sicker. But God's command to me is not to put my money where there is a big bang. His command is to visit the homeless and the widow."[16]

Every Church should have a ministry to the elderly in their community. Every Bible school should make it mandatory for their students to spend consistent time comforting, counseling, or just providing companionship to the elderly for a few hours. Such time not only brightens the lives of the elderly, but serves as a more effective witness for God's love than many other things we might do.

Of course, many of our elderly need a good deal more than just companionship. Many of them (shut-ins) need food, medical assistance, or transportation.

Feeding the Elderly

Twelve years ago John Counts started the Living Word Outreach, a hot lunch ministry in Houston, Texas. John took the prophet Ezekiel seriously when he said that if you're going to be a shepherd, then take responsibility for feeding your flock (Ezekiel 34). Today John's flock has expanded to over forty thousand people in Houston alone.

John wanted to witness for Christ by sharing God's love and compassion with those on fixed incomes, so he visited the "Meals on Wheels" folks and the county welfare offices to obtain names of people who needed help and weren't getting it or needed additional help. John was successful in finding those who needed help, and they in turn have found someone to love, care for, and minister to them.

Other churches are also stepping out in faith as "God's feet and hands" to serve the elderly. Once again Southern California's Church on the Way provides us with an excellent example. The Church ministers to six different convalescent homes the Church has "adopted," bringing gifts, companionship, joy, and the loving witness of Christ. Some members actually adopt an elderly person, inviting him home for special occasions and holidays, and establishing an ongoing relationship.

Chuck Swindoll's First Evangelical Free Church of Fullerton, California, offers support groups for children of elderly dependent parents, telephone counseling for shut-ins, and outreach to local nursing homes. One day a week is set a side as a special event day for the elderly—a special luncheon, breakfast, day trip, and the like.

Chicago's LaSalle Street Church has a special ministry reaching out to elderly indigents who live isolated in single rooms in old boarding houses. Nationally, Presbyterian churches are seeking newly retired members to volunteer two years of full-time ministry to their older brothers and sisters.

Indeed, a hopeful trend in many churches is to have those retirees in the sixty-to-seventy-years-old bracket minister to their elders. My eighty-year-old father-in-law provides us with an example worthy of emulating. Living in a retirement community, he provides those without transportation his driving services to the airport, to downtown hospitals, stores, and medical offices. He often is on the go from 6:00 A.M. to midnight.

Abortion

Did you think that your Christian duty concerning abortion had been taken care of by the various well-known pro-life organizations already active? Well, it hasn't. None of us can ignore the plight of abortion victims when, worldwide, fifty-four million babies are killed through abortion and their fifty-four million mothers are forever scarred, physically, emotionally, and spiritually by these legal and supposedly safe procedures. If our Christian responsibility regarding abortion was fulfilled, abortion wouldn't be the number one method of birth control worldwide.[17]

In America today between 1.2 and 1.5 million babies a year are sacrificed on abortion tables to the distinctly American idols of convenience, career, and freedom from commitment. Or to put it another way, the lives of some human beings are prematurely terminated because they will interfere with the freedom of others. The person doing the termination has been taught to regard herself, her life, her freedom, and her convenience as the highest possible good. Self becomes an idol, worthy of the sacrifice of another life.

Since the Supreme Court legalized abortion in *Roe vs. Wade* (1973), fifteen times more babies have died than the total of all Americans killed in wars from 1776 to 1986. These infant victims are often cut to pieces or "burned" to death by a saline solution, the two most common types of abortion.

> In the early weeks of pregnancy, doctors perform abortions by inserting a sharp instrument or vacuum tube into the uterus through the cervix. The suction rips the child apart, sucking his remains into a jar. The majority of early abortions are done in this manner.
>
> The procedure most widely used during the second trimester of pregnancy [four to six months] is known as "dilation and evacuation." The abortionist dilates the woman's cervix and then uses forceps to clip apart the unborn child and remove the remains. Many babies are "terminated" though they are clearly human beings, with identifiable fingers, toes, eyes, ears, nose, etc.
>
> "Salting out" is another mid-term abortion technique in which a salt solution is injected into the womb. The developing child is slowly poisoned and hours later delivered dead.
>
> Evidence exists that the unborn child feels excruciating pain during this procedure. Yet some children have survived such abortions and emerged alive. Even then, the baby is usually left to die.[18]

Many of those who support abortions argue that a baby is not a fully developed person until it can think or even take care of itself. Until then, it is merely a "fetus" or protoplasm. This is the same rationale Hitler used to exterminate babies, the handicapped, and the elderly, who weren't "competent" to live. And it is an absurd argument as well. If a baby is a legal human being the second it is out of its mother's womb, what about the second before, the week before, or four months before? What about when the baby within its first few weeks begins developing distinctly human features? Where do we draw the line? The Bible indicates God recognizes us as human beings from the time of our conception:

> For You created my inmost being; You knit me together in my mother's womb. I praise You because I am fearfully and wonderfully made; Your works are wonderful, I know that full well. My frame was not hidden from You when I was made in the secret place. When I was woven together in the depths of the earth, Your eyes saw my unformed body. All the days ordained for me were written in Your book before one of them came to be. (Psalm 139:13-16)

As pointed out in *The High Cost of Indifference*:

> By the end of the first week of life, the new human being is a mass of different types of cells. By the end of the second week, these cells have become tissues. And by the end of the third week, organs have begun to form. In fact, human heartbeats have been detected as early as eighteen days after conception. By six weeks, measurable brain waves are sending impulses throughout the body, causing its tiny developing muscles to kick. The embryo now has all the internal organs of a mature adult.

> During the next four weeks, he will reach four inches in length. The baby grimaces, squints and frowns. He breathes amniotic fluid and will swallow more if the fluid is sweetened. He will stop swallowing if it is soured. After the sixteenth week, the baby will grow and develop at a rate that, if it continued throughout the remainder of pregnancy, the baby would weigh fourteen tons at birth![19]

It is during this stage of the first twelve weeks of prenatal life of the first trimester that approximately eighty-five percent of America's abortions are performed. By the end of the twelfth week the baby is, in fact, a "miniature person."[20]

Norman B. Bendroth points out that:

Dr. Micheline Matthews-Roth, of Harvard Medical School, concluded that "it is scientifically correct to say that an individual human life begins at conception, when egg and sperm join to form the zygote." Dr. Hymie Gordon, a geneticist at the Mayo Clinic, went so far as to say that he had never read of "anyone who has argued that life did not begin at conception."[21]

Pro-abortion forces were dealt a severe blow to their "unfeeling-protoplasmic-mass" theory in the early 1980s with the film *Silent Scream.* Employing the latest sonogram technology, the film showed a baby squirming in agony as the abortionist's cutting device entered the mother's womb and began to dissect it. The film was made all the more potent by the fact that it was produced by America's former leading abortionist, who had realized what he was doing and had become an ardent pro-lifer.

Fetal Experimentation

Even with a strongly anti-abortion president, the growing pro-life movement has been unable to secure legal protection for unborn children. While "pro-choice" (the choice to terminate a human being) and pro-life forces will remain locked in battle into the nineties, we face an even more horrible extension of the abortion horror—fetal experimentation.

No doubt many thought Malcolm Muggeridge, the brilliant English writer, had gone too far when he predicted we were at a crossroad:

> Either we go on with the process of shaping our own destiny without any reference to any higher being than Man, deciding ourselves how many children shall be born when and in what varieties, which lives are worth continuing and which should be put out, from whom spare parts—kidneys, hearts, genitals, brainboxes even—shall be taken and to whom allotted. Or we draw back, seeking to understand and fall in with our Creator's purpose for us rather than to pursue our own, in true humility praying, as the founder of our religion and our civilization taught us: Thy will be done. . . .[22]

But Muggeridge's predictions increasingly are confirmed by eerie developments like the following: Staff employees of a large hospital admitted they had collected more than $58,000 from commercial firms by selling the bodily organs of stillborn and premature babies, some from "late-term elective abortions." An Ohio medical research company tested the brains, hearts, and other organs of nearly one hundred fetuses as part of a $300,000 pesticide project for a company.

A notice from one university stated that a large collection of human embryos was needed for microscopic neurological stains required in a study. Even as early as 1972 an anesthetist at a leading women's hospital testified "it was repulsive to watch live fetuses being packed in ice while still moving and trying to breathe, then being rushed to a laboratory."

Medical World News reported June 8, 1973, on an experiment conducted at the University of Helsinki. There, babies born alive by Caesarean section had their heads cut off and were attached to a machine which pumped various chemicals through the babies' brains as part of an experiment to find out how blood circulated within the human brain.

In 1978 a twenty-eight-year-old engineer considered getting his wife pregnant so she could have an abortion for the sake of his deteriorating health. The man had lost the use of his kidneys and desperately needed a kidney transplant. Since he was an orphan, he had no known close relatives who could have been compatible donors. His wife volunteered to become pregnant and abort the baby after five or six months to have the kidneys from the baby transplanted into her husband. The surgeon decided not to go along with the surgery after a majority of the hospital's Board of Ethics expressed views that such an enterprise would be immoral (although such cases are now being viewed more favorably in many nations).

As I mentioned in the beginning of this discussion, the main rationale for abortion today is really convenience. It is tremendously inconvenient for the mother to have to carry a child for nine months and then raise it or find suitable adoptive parents. In our society, with its premium on absolute moral freedom, hedonism, self-fulfillment, freedom from commitments, and denial of responsibility for our sexual conduct, this rationale makes perfect sense. Why allow a pregnancy to interrupt a career? It is much easier to rationalize that the child is non-human and that therefore the abortion is a nonevent.

Meeting the Need

If we are to meet the needs of so many women, and even girls in our generation, the Church must repent of its complicity in this unprecedented genocide. Christians must seek God's forgiveness for standing by while we allowed pornography and all sorts of sexual messages transmitted through a multitude of media to legitimize promiscuity, which in turn helped create the massive increase of abortions. Our churches condemn promiscuity, but fail to act against it in a socially effective way. Then, when a girl gets pregnant, the Church, even her church, condemns her, rather than providing her with love and family support. When in desperation she turns to abortion to avoid the stigma of unwed motherhood, she is condemned for that, even while the Church itself refuses to lift a finger to outlaw abortion. The Church simply condemns each part of the dilemma — promiscuity, unwed motherhood, and abortion — while refusing to play a constructive, redemptive role in any part of the process.

Who will God hold most responsible for this American tragedy — a young teenager or illiterate welfare mother talked into an abortion, or God's elect meeting down the street who just didn't care enough about the problem to do anything?

Realizing that children and babies are God's creations, made in His likeness, the early Christians saved babies when pagan Romans routinely abandoned their unwanted offspring to die. So must we. We need to reform the adoption process and adopt these children ourselves. We need pregnancy counseling centers to counteract every abortion clinic. And we need to elect men and women to Congress who someday will end this blight on our nation.

Fortunately, more and more Christians and churches are meeting this challenge. Several national TV ministers have announced programs to establish counseling centers or homes for unwed mothers, following the example of hundreds of local Churches. Almost a million women each year are counseled in these centers, most of them choosing not to have an abortion.

In my hometown a few members of the Santa Rosa Christian Church were deeply touched by the plight of unwed mothers and unborn babies in their community. They organized a local pregnancy counseling center. Before too long they realized that with their center controlled by just one Church, they were limiting its potential growth and outreach. So, they did an unusual thing—they actually gave up control by inviting a broad-based board of concerned Christians from several churches to direct the center. With the increased feeling of mutual ownership, the center became financially independent and greatly expanded its outreach. Another encouraging example is cited by the authors of *Turning Point*:

> The origin of the Austin, Texas, Crisis Pregnancy Center is typical. Two women, following a Bible study in 1983, talked in a kitchen about establishing a counseling center. They called a meeting and set up a steering committee that assessed needs, raised funds, and hired a director.
>
> In its fourth year of operation, the Austin CPC was still almost entirely a volunteer operation. It had, though, a well-established budget, a record of a thousand clients served during 1986, and hundreds of stories of babies saved and women's lives turned around.[23]

While this example has been repeated in hundreds of communities, we still have a long way to go before we match the numbers of abortion clinics or Planned Parenthood abortion counseling centers.

You Can Help

What can we do? First, we can read and familiarize ourselves with the full scope of the genocide we are committing on the unborn. When God looked at His chosen people in the most Godly nation on earth centuries ago, He saw a lack of mercy and justice that included the shedding of innocent blood.

> See how the faithful city has become a harlot! She once was full of justice; righteousness used to dwell in her—but now murderers! (Isaiah 1:21)
>
> The vineyard of the Lord Almighty is the house of Israel, and the men of Judah are the garden of His delight. And He looked for justice, but saw bloodshed; for righteousness, but heard cries of distress. (Isaiah 5:7)

Can He feel any differently about America today? Incidentally, it may be instructive for you to read the rest of Isaiah to see what God does to discipline nations that turn away from His standards of justice and righteousness!

I also recommend you read *Death Before Birth* by Harold O. J. Brown. Dr. Brown, a Harvard graduate, is one of America's leading Christian thinkers and gives thoughtful treatment to both the history of and the future of abortion. He deals with Biblical questions, medical questions, as well as law and ethics. Of this book U.S. Surgeon General Everett Koop says, "almost flawless from the medical perspective and confronts . . . with a Biblical view and spiritual imperative that the reader can ignore only if he is prepared to disregard the Word of God."[24]

Who Is for Life? is a short collection of essays by leading theologians Francis Schaeffer and John Stott, Britain's foremost Christian writer Malcolm Muggeridge, and Mother Teresa. The authors are all the recommendation this excellent little book needs! Available from Crossway Books.

Arresting Abortion is edited by America's leading pro-life attorney and author, John Whitehead. Contributors include Franky Schaeffer, Dr. James Kennedy, and Joseph Scheidler. Covers many "how to's" for activists, ranging from passing legislation, to picketing abortion clinics, to counseling pregnant mothers. Available from Crossway Books. Also recommended: *The High Cost of Indifference,* which has an excellent chapter on abortion, edited by Richard Cizik; *Closed: 99 Ways to Stop Abortion* by leading pro-life activist Joseph Scheidler (Regenery Gateway), a book that draws sobering comparisons between Nazi genocide campaigns and today's abortions, also shocking data on fetal experimentation; *The Abortion Holocaust: Today's Final Solution* by William Brennan; *Window on the Future,* and *Handbook on Abortion,* both by the National Right to Life; and *Whatever Happened to the Human Race,* co-authored by theologian Francis Schaeffer and C. Everett Koop, the U.S. Surgeon General.

Of course, the most effective thing we can do is to find out what pro-life groups are already active in our community and ask how we can be of assistance. For more information of what you can do, I recommend you contact the Pro-Life Action League, 6369 N. Le Mai Avenue, Chicago IL 60676; the Christian Action Council, 701 W. Broad Street, Suite 405, Falls Church, VA 22046; or the National Right to Life Committee, 419 Seventh Street NW, Suite 402, Washington, D.C. 20004.

The American Coalition for Life, headed by my good friend Reverend Ray Allen. ACL provides a unique program of training volunteers to meet regularly with their congressman in Washington. ACL also provides a "legislative watch" update and other helpful newsletters. You may contact them at American Coalition for Life, P.O. Box 1895, Washington, D.C. 20013.

The Christian Action Council, America's largest Evangelical pro-life organization, lobbies in Washington, D.C., and will also advise you how to start or join a Crisis Pregnancy Center (CPC) program. Such centers are locally run and funded with the help of the local churches and the community in general. Services usually include free pregnancy testing; facts regarding pregnancy, abortion, and alternatives; housing with Christian families for homeless clients; childbirth classes; clothing and furnishings to accommodate both mother and baby; classes for single parents; information on breast feeding and nutrition; referrals for adoption; medical care, legal assistance, and other community services; and ongoing counseling and friendship.

Liberty Godparents have established homes for unwed mothers of all ages, in which they can live, attend school, and receive counseling. They also offer a full service adoption agency. Contact Liberty Godparents, Lynchburg, Virginia at (804) 847-6828.

Other organizations include Birth Right, 686 N. Broad Street, Woodbury, NJ 08096, with over three hundred and fifty chapters offering help to pregnant women; Evangelical Adoption and Family Service Organization, 201 S. Main Street, North Syracuse, NY 13212; and Bethany Christian Services, 901 Eastern Avenue NE, Grand Rapids, MI 49503.

Pornography

The same immorality that fosters the spread of AIDS, warehouses the elderly, and sucks babies down the drain also incubates the vast American pornography infection. Pornography is not just poor literature: It is the fuel for almost unlimited sexual exploitation, sexism, homosexuality, and the rape and molestation of thousands of children.

One of the most visible forms of exploitation today is the eight billion dollar a year industry called "adult entertainment" by its purveyors, and pornography or perversion by its opponents. But pornography is worse than perversion. It is anti-life.

Pornography exploits women. It demeans not only the women portrayed, but in fact exploits all women by turning them into mere objects for man's lust. Pornography presents women in such a way that its consumers come to believe that: (1) a woman's value is primarily sexual and once enjoyed or consumed may be discarded as an overused plaything; and (2) that women basically share this depiction of their sexuality.

When husbands begin to look at their wives through this perspective, marriages dissolve. When young men pursue women with this mindset, healthy relationships are impossible. Indeed, pornography's influence on supposedly healthy marriages is as dangerous as it is subtle.

As the Child and Family Protection Institute of Washington, D.C., reported in their excellent study of *Pornography and Its Effects on Family, Community and Culture*:

> New, unpublished studies by Zillman and University of Houston colleague, psychologist Jennings Bryant, show that massive exposure to nonviolent, non-coercive, consensual, heterosexual [i.e., "soft core"] pornography leads to sexual dissatisfaction in both men and women, particularly in men. Both men and women, in comparing their intimate partner's responses to the sexual behavior portrayed in pornographic materials, became dissatisfied with the sexual performance, and even physical appearance, of their intimate partners, coming to see them as less attractive, even less worthy, individuals. Moreover, they began to devalue their intimate partners in the same way that they had the victims of rape in the laboratory.[25]

> One reason, Zillman noted, is that the females portrayed in pornography are shown engaging in sexual behaviors that the women who are the intimate partners of the men who consume this pornography do not want to, or will not engage in. This leads to reports of sexual dissatisfaction from both males and females.[26]

> These same studies show that massive exposure to these materials leads to a devaluation and depreciation of the importance of monogamy, and to a lack of confidence in marriage as either

a viable or lasting institution. Moreover, mature adults as well as college students exposed to these materials came to view non-monogamous relationships as normal and natural behavior.[27]

Pornography has other consequences as well. Numerous news stories and scholarly studies have linked pornography to violent/sexual crimes against women and children. While logic dictates that repeated exposure to pornography would lead to sex crimes — thoughts lead to emotions which must be released by action — the Child and Family Protection Institute's study has done a considerable public service in summing up some of the major research now available:

> Pornography desensitizes. Exposure to these materials, whether violent or nonviolent, coercive or non-coercive, experimentally increases male aggressive behavior against women, and decreases both male and female sensitivity to rape and the plight of the rape victim. Both males and females, after viewing this material, judge the female rape victim to be less injured, less worthy, and more responsible for her own plight.[28]

> Following even brief exposure to this material, particularly to violent materials, *two-thirds* of a group of normal college students studied by Malamuth reported an increased willingness to say that they would force a woman into sex acts if they were assured they would not be caught or punished. *One-third* reported an increased willingness to actually commit rape under the same circumstances.[29]

Does pornography lead to violence? The Institute presents some disturbing statistics:

> A recent study of thirty-six serial-killers revealed that twenty-nine were attracted to pornography, and incorporated it into their sexual activity, which included serial rape-murder.[30]

> In his most recent study, Marshall found that almost half of the rapists he interviewed used so-called "soft-core," consenting sex pornography to arouse themselves in preparation for seeking out a victim. He found "that nineteen percent of the rapists used forced-sex sadistic-bondage pornography to incite them to rape, while thirty-eight percent used consenting sex pornogra-

phy immediately prior to committing an offense. Even more strikingly, he found that fifty-five percent of the homosexual child molesters he studied used child pornography to instigate their crimes.[31]

The President's Commission on Pornography, headed by U.S. Attorney General Edwin Meese, contained additional revelations that shocked many Americans.

Increasingly, the most *prevalent* forms of pornography involve sado-masochistic themes, including whips, chains, devices of torture and so on. Another theme involves the recurrent theme of a man making some sort of sexual advance to a woman, being rebuffed and then raping the woman or in some other way *violently forcing himself* on the woman. In almost all of this material, whether in magazine or motion picture form, the woman eventually becomes aroused and ecstatic about the initially forced sexual activity, and usually is portrayed *as begging for more.*[32] (italics added)

This means that the *eight billion dollar* pornography market is increasingly glamorizing violent sex — convincing men and boys that women really want to be raped — the more violent, the better! And *they are being convinced*, the President's Commission reported:

Evidence strongly supports the conclusion that substantial exposure to violent, sexually explicit material leads to a greater acceptance of the "rape myth" — that *women enjoy being physically hurt* in a *sexual context*, and that as a result, a man who forces himself on a woman sexually is in fact merely acceding to the "real" wishes of the woman, regardless of the extent to which she seems to be resisting. In both clinical and experimental settings, exposure to sexually violent materials has indicated an increase in the likelihood of aggression.[33]

Pornography, whether sold as "men's magazines" at the local convenience store or as X-rated videos from the local video store or in America's eighteen thousand "adult bookstores," can and should be outlawed. But it takes concerned citizens to work hard to elect representatives who will pass such laws and to elect judges and district attorneys who will aggressively enforce them.

Pornography Is a "Winnable War"

We can actively work for the recommendations of President Reagan's National Commission on Pornography, which called for *a national assault* on the pornography industry through a combination of more vigorous law enforcement and *increased vigilance by citizens' groups*. We can help *citizens band together* into "watch groups" to file complaints, put pressure on local prosecutors, monitor judges and, if necessary, boycott merchants selling pornographic material.

We can honor our local law enforcement officers when they take action. A recent example occurred in Santa Rosa, California, when a few concerned Christians decided to sponsor a public appreciation luncheon for the local district attorneys who had fought a long, hard, and expensive battle to close down several X-rated pornography shops, which my wife and I had personally picketed. Their reaction to being appreciated in this way was overwhelming. No one had ever bothered to thank them or encourage them. No wonder most law enforcement agencies find it easier to avoid battling the American Civil Liberties Union (ACLU) and the high paid lawyers who protect the pornography industry.

The district attorney honored at the luncheon stated he hadn't been officially honored in this way in fifteen years of service to his city; the assistant district attorney pointed out she could make a higher salary in private practice but chose the DA's office because of her concern for victims of child abuse and molestation. At the luncheon our county sheriff made this extremely important observation:

> Pornography is against the law, but there are three things that must happen for that law [as well as many others] to be adequately enforced: (a) an officer of the law must be willing to arrest and "bring in" the accused, (b) a district attorney must prosecute the accused, (c) citizens must support these officials. He explained that it was up to the citizens of a community to make sure the officials enforce the law. Our law enforcement officials need community support to motivate them to enforce pornography laws.[34]

The luncheon also honored Kay Wendt, a private citizen who was responsible for helping to set the entire chain of events into motion that led to the victory being celebrated. Kay was a concerned citizen who was outraged at the degradation local pornographic bookstores brought to her neighborhood. She particularly became incensed when she realized that the bookstore and its customers were disturbing the many elderly people who lived in a nearby mobile home trailer park. She really began her work in answer to *their* cries. Kay took her complaint to her local county supervisor who then appointed a citizen's committee to study the town's pornography problem and appointed Kay Wendt to the committee. From her position on the committee, Kay was able to motivate other citizens to request action from the responsible county authorities.

Of course, there are literally hundreds of stories from coast to coast of local citizens successfully closing down local pornographers or convincing local merchants to stop carrying *Penthouse, Playboy,* and the like. These campaigns usually start with only a dozen committed volunteers and usually mushroom to several hundred participants.

Richard Enrico lived in a Virginia suburb of Washington, D.C. He also lived among major supermarkets and drugstores that proffered a wide variety of offensive men's magazines. Joining forces with a local activist pastor, Jay Ahleman, and his growing Church, Richard formed "Citizens Against Pornography" (CAP). Within a short time CAP had enlisted three hundred other churches and succeeded in pressing large chain stores like Dart Drug to stop selling the offending material.

In North Carolina, citizens led by Joseph Chambers, mobilized enough citizens to pass a major state law (which was substantiated on appeal by the North Carolina Supreme Court) which resulted in the closing down of over five hundred "adult bookstores."

Jerry Kirk, a Presbyterian minister, organized a few parishioners and cleaned pornography out of Cincinnati, Ohio. Now he has launched an extremely professional campaign nationwide called STOP, "Stand Together Opposing Pornography." As *Christianity Today* reported:

> The pilot STOP campaign is taking place in Kansas City, Missouri, where N-CAP estimates two hundred retail outlets are

selling illegal obscenity. N-CAP President Jerry Kirk calls the STOP effort "a mass-media blitz," including a television special, TV and radio spots, billboards, bumper stickers, buttons, direct-mail efforts, and a petition drive. Said Kirk: "It's a total market blitz to get across one message: Pornography destroys. It destroys children, young people, women, marriages, and families."

N-CAP's goal with STOP is to cover the entire nation with city-by-city campaigns. The group will train denominational leaders, civic leaders, and concerned citizens from fifty cities to conduct STOP campaigns.[35]

Pornography expert, March Bell, recommends a number of excellent citizen action steps, some of which follow:

1. Take responsibility for your own neighborhood and city by forming a group in your Church or civic organization to work and study together.

2. If you purchase a major item such as an automobile or stereo, send a copy of the receipt to the manufacturer and explain that you disapprove of advertising in *Playboy, Penthouse, Cosmopolitan,* and the like. The post-purchase technique is most effective for major purchases.

3. Ask your group to save purchase receipts from your local grocery or drugstore for two months. Arrange a meeting with the manager and politely present the receipts to him and request that the offensive material be removed. Explain that young cashiers should not be required to sell such magazines over the counter.

4. Find out if local pornography establishments (bookstores, massage parlors, etc.) accept major credit cards. Arrange a meeting between representatives of your group and the bank that handles the credit card account. Remind the bank official of the numbers of your group that have accounts with the bank. Ask that the bank cancel the credit cards that support pornography.

5. Contact your city councilman and request that he sponsor a zoning/land use study on the effects of adult business on the crime rate, real-estate values, and local businesses. Meet with the real-estate developers who operate in the area surrounding adult businesses and enlist their support.

6. Insist that the local prosecutor prosecute adult businesses as a public nuisance. (Atlanta, Georgia, has removed forty adult businesses under this strategy.)

7. Lobby the city council and mayor's offices not to accept cable programming contracts that include pornographic movies.

8. Publicize a list of local stores that refuse to sell pornography. Have members of your group reinforce the manager's decision by communicating why you chose that particular store. Develop a similar list of businesses that have withdrawn from selling *Playboy.*[36]

There are several excellent national organizations that you can contact to assist you in removing pornography from your community, whether it's on Cable TV, in an "adult" bookstore, or on a corner store's magazine rack.

Perhaps the flagship of the anti-pornography movement is the National Federation for Decency founded by my friend Don Wildmon, a United Methodist minister. Over the last ten years, the NFD has enlisted tens of thousands of churches and Christian leaders in its fight to clean up sex and violence on television, as well as in the corner store. The NFD led the much publicized and successful campaign to force the huge 7-Eleven convenience store chain to stop selling their highly profitable men's magazines. The NFD sends an excellent monthly magazine to its members monitoring TV programs and involving members in various action strategies. Write the NFD at P.O. Drawer 2240, Tupelo, MS 38803.

I've already mentioned Jerry Kirk's STOP campaign. You may write them for information on how to bring a STOP campaign to your community. Write STOP, 800 Compton Road, Suite 9248, Cincinnati, OH 45231.

Morality in Media, another anti-pornography movement, may be contacted at 475 Riverside Dr., New York, NY 10115, (212) 870-3222. MIM has recently held a series of excellent national conferences on pornography and have produced a large quantity of excellent materials. Their *Handbook on the Prosecution of Obscenity Cases* is a must for lawyers and law enforcement officials. Other groups include: Chicago Statement Foundation,

P.O. Box 40945, Washington, D.C. 20016; and Citizens for Decency Through Law, 2331 W. Royal Palm Road, #105, Phoenix, AZ 85021.

In the last two chapters we have seen the vital necessity of our involvement as Christians to combat the problems of poverty, AIDS, the elderly, abortion, and pornography. In each of these areas we need to be servants with vision — servants who will sacrifice to extend the righteousness and mercy of God into our communities.

However, our involvement doesn't end there, in our own communities. Some have referred to our contemporary earth as a "global village" — with all world citizens our "neighbors." In this respect the Bible agrees — *all* men are our neighbors, and *all* need the positive, life-changing impact of God's Word. In the next chapter we will look at this broader perspective: God's compassion and justice exercised in the midst of war and oppression.

ELEVEN

DEFENDING OUR NATION

As we have already shown, God is not apathetic about justice and righteousness. He expects it of all nations. He demands it of His own people! But God is not just interested in justice and righteousness. He is Justice and Righteousness. He is the source of all justice and righteousness. As Christians we are called to demonstrate these attributes of God to others as He expresses them through us, as the Body of Christ.

As God's children we are to bear fruit. The fruit we bear should spring forth from God's Spirit within us, reflecting His heart. We have seen that God is much more interested in our securing justice for the helpless and oppressed than He is in "lip-service" Christianity (see Isaiah 58), empty religious acts, and faith without deeds (see James 2:17ff).

In Isaiah, chapter 1, God clearly tells us that our "sacrifices" (verse 13), our endless Church meetings and assemblies (verses 13-14), are detestable to Him (so much so that He will not ever hear our many prayers [verse 15]) if we fail to wash our hands of blood (verse 15), and unless we begin to seek justice for the oppressed and the exploited (verses 16-17).

We have already discussed our responsibility toward the victims of self-centered economics as opposed to Biblical economics in the chapter on poverty. In the last chapter we argued for Christian responsibility to champion the causes of the victims of self-centered exploitation: the fifty-four million babies killed annually worldwide; those dying from AIDS, alone and without Christ; and those, most of whom are women and children who are exploited by pornography.

In this chapter we will explore our obligation to bring God's justice and righteousness to bear on the twin ravages of war and oppression.

War

Are there just wars and unjust wars? Are there also just and unjust ways of fighting wars? The nations of the world are spending hundreds of billions of dollars preparing for war or trying to avoid war, so our leaders must at least suspect its possibility. What can Christians living in America do?

First, we should familiarize ourselves with the two basic approaches to our national defense policy.

The Right or conservative element of Republicans, Democrats, and Evangelicals, believes that the Soviets can be trusted only to carry out their oft-stated goal of "liberating" the entire world from Capitalism and repressive religion to the "freedom" of Marxism/Leninism, despite Gorbachev's winning smile and formidable public relations skills. Conservatives believe that this Soviet agenda will be accomplished through strategic military maneuvers that cut us off from our sources of raw materials like chrome (for stainless steel), uranium, and oil; or by nuclear blackmail; or even by a pre-emptive nuclear strike designed to disable our retaliatory abilities; or by a combination of the three. The Right's answer, as demonstrated by the Reagan administration, is to keep the U.S. defenses equal to or greater than the Soviet's, subscribing to the theory that the Soviets won't "pick a fight they can't win."

> U.S. deterrence policy has specific objectives vis-à-vis the Soviet Union—that is, there are specific acts the United States hopes to deter the Soviet Union from ever undertaking. The United States attempts to deter the Soviet Union from:
>
> 1. Highly provocative or coercive behavior that might erupt into war;
>
> 2. Nuclear or conventional attacks on U.S. allies and friends around the world;
>
> 3. Nuclear or conventional attacks on the America people and homeland.
>
> These goals have remained the constant objective of U.S. deterrence policy. This is important because the United States possesses nuclear weapons to support these deterrence policy goals. But it is essential to understand that U.S. policy is built

on the view that nuclear weapons are useful as a deterrent primarily if they remain an unused threat, not if they are launched.

If force must be used in response to the unwanted action, deterrence has largely failed. Similarly, if the Soviet Union takes the unwanted actions above, despite the best U.S. deterrent efforts, then the deterrent role for nuclear weapons largely would have failed. Ironic as it may seem, it is absolutely accurate to describe U.S. deterrence policy as possessing nuclear weapons as a deterrent so that they will never have to be launched.[1]

In Evangelical circles this theory is often referred to as a "moral defense deterrent," also popular with conservative Christians is the just war theory as summed up by Payne:

Human government has been established by God and given the responsibility to exercise necessary force for keeping order, rewarding good, and punishing evil (Romans 13:1-7; 1 Peter 2:13-17). God has not only condoned war in the past, He has also participated in it and promises to do so in the future. Since we know God is perfect, holy, and good, we cannot say that all wars are inherently evil (Exodus 15:1-18 and 17:8-15; Numbers 10:35 and 31:1-3; Deuteronomy 2:26-31, 3:1-7, and 20:1-4; Joshua 5:13-6:27; and Revelation 6:1-2, 19:11-21, and 20:7-10).

The sixth commandment condemns murder but not all taking of human life. There must be a distinction made between murder, which Scripture clearly condemns, and some forms of killing—such as war, self-defense, and capital punishment—that Scripture has commanded (Exodus 20:13, 21:12-19, and 21:29). Both the Old and New Testaments condemn taking personal revenge but demand that authorized civil servants exercise just retribution against injustice and evildoers (Genesis 9:6; Exodus 21:23-25; Matthew 5:38-39; Romans 12:17-13:17).[2]

The Left or liberal view, popular with our media and educational elites and some Evangelicals, is that this "arms race" will eventually lead to war: that the Soviets aren't really trying to do us in; and even if they were, "it's better to be red than dead"! If we discontinue the arms race on our own—through a unilateral nuclear weapons freeze—they argue it will demonstrate to the Soviets our good intention; and they will then let us live happily ever after. The Evangelical version of this view is usually called "moral disarmament," or "radical pacifism."

While the implications of these two positions are far more complex than we can deal with here, you need to familiarize yourself with them and determine exactly where the politicians you vote for stand. The position you choose will be the position on which you stake your life and your family's life. Both positions and a number of other variants are described fairly, clearly, and briefly in the National Association of Evangelical's *The High Cost of Indifference* and in *A Just Defense*, by Keith and Karl Payne.

Before we can intelligently or effectively work for world peace, we must understand the nature of our adversaries in control of the Soviet Union—not the people of the U.S.S.R.—but the un-elected elite in charge of the Soviet people's massive resources. Are the Communist leaders really "nice guys—just like us," only misunderstood, as liberal idealists would have us believe? Or are they fanatically zealous believers in the inevitable world domination of Marxism/Leninism (as they profess to be, and as most right-wingers believe them to be)? I believe neither explanation to be totally adequate. Each is too simple, too pat, too easily conformed to our own biases and ways of interpreting others' actions.

For instance, the "they're-just-like-us" argument fits too easily into our wanting to wish away any problems: "We have no enemies, they're really our friends, therefore we can be happy, and live our lives without any interruptions or sacrifices." This same form of escapist fantasy allowed the allies to ignore Hitler's pre-World War II military buildup—with devastating consequences.

Russian dissident, intellectual, scientist, and author Vladimir Bukovsky provides us with his authoritative insight:

> Normally we try to understand an opponent by taking his place, getting into his shoes, so to speak. That is why most people try to explain Soviet behavior in terms of "normal human motive," that is, by motives familiar to them. And that is exactly why they constantly pile one mistake upon another. For it is extremely difficult for a "normal" human being to put himself inside the skin of a mentally ill one.[3]

He further explains our psychological imperative compelling us to cling to this misconception even in the face of massive contradictory evidence:

Once again, the universal craving for peace right now, this very moment, and at any price, has rendered people utterly illogical and irrational, and left them simply unable to think calmly.[4]

Deep in their hearts most of these terrified people have a very simple answer to all these "whys." They know that the only real source of danger is to the Soviet Union and that anything which might make the Soviets angry is dangerous for that very reason. But fear is a paralyzing and deranging force, so deranging as to lead some people to advocate the abolition of the police because the criminals are becoming too aggressive.[5]

To understand this adversary that has the military power to kill every American ten times over and brags that one day they will liberate the world from decadent Capitalism, we must ask, what really is their goal?

Many liberals argue that the Soviet posture is purely defensive. They are afraid of the West. I ask, why?

In World War II we stopped Hitler from destroying Russia, which he was fully capable of doing. We gave the Soviets billions of dollars of armaments — much of which found their way to the North Korean forces during the Korean War. When the U.S. conquered Germany, we waited until the Soviets arrived in Berlin to give them an equal share of the spoils. We gave them total control of Eastern Europe, which had been non-Communist before World War II.

We have given them tens of billions of dollars worth of loans, and fed their armies with billions of dollars of our wheat (all on credit) for years. We didn't lift a finger to help two of their Eastern European colonies, Hungary and Czechoslovakia, when they tried to break away from Soviet military domination. Other than tough rhetoric, we offer them only token resistance wherever they display their massive military power, whether it's Angola or Afghanistan.

What do they have to be afraid of? With their massive intelligence system do they seriously think our weak-willed, divided, fearful society is going to risk all we have to attack a nation we want nothing from? Such a scenario is unlikely at best.

On the other hand, arch right-wingers insist that there is an international Communist conspiracy committed to turning every human into a truly committed Marxist automaton. This theory, which I believed for many years, seems somewhat reasonable in the light of constant Soviet aggressionism. But it, too, is oversimplified. To understand what really makes the Soviet system tick, we need only to read the many great Soviet intellectuals or highly placed Soviet defectors who offer us insight that only members of the inner circle possess.

Bukovsky, currently a neuroscientific researcher at Stanford University, provides us with what I believe, after observing the Soviet system for two decades and talking to numerous defectors, is a highly accurate assessment of Soviet motivations.

> The Soviet rulers are a totally cynical lot, much more preoccupied with their own privileges and pleasures than with Marxist ideas. They probably hate Communist dogma more than any Western capitalist. Moreover, the majority of the Soviet people are as cynical as their leaders. There are many more sincere Communists to be found in the West than the U.S.S.R.[6]

> The two sides of the Soviet regime—internal oppression and external aggression—are inseparably interlocked, creating a sort of vicious circle. The more the regime becomes rotten inside, the more pains are taken by its leaders to present a formidable facade to the outside world. They need international tension as a thief needs the darkness of the night. In the political climate of latent civil war, given the enormous and senseless sacrifices of the last fifty years, the constant economic difficulties, and the lack of basic rights—not to mention, again, the extraordinary privileges enjoyed by the ruling clique—the only hope for stability lies in the need to cope with an external threat:

> In this artificially created state of war, the worker's demand for a better deal, or a captive nation's demand for its independence, can then be treated as an act of subversion, "playing into the hands of the enemy."[7]

What Bukovsky describes is George Orwell's nightmare novel *1984* come true—a brutally and effectively totalitarian state that keeps its population subdued by daily raising the specter of a fearfully menacing enemy (that, in fact, does not exist).

But how do we explain the Soviet Union's unrelenting and extremely draining military adventurism around the globe? Bukovsky offers a credible explanation:

Nor is it enough to create a devil in order to maintain one's religious zeal. This imaginary enemy must be defeated over and over again or there will be the risk that he will seduce you. American "imperialism" must be defeated at any cost, and the liberation of proletarians in the capitalist countries must be promoted by all means. The failure to support a "friendly government," to establish Communist rule in a new country, will immediately be perceived as a weakening of Soviet power, and therefore an encouragement to the sullen and embittered population at home. Any failure of the Soviet international adventure may thus trigger a chain reaction leading to the ultimate collapse of the Soviet ruler. This is why they cannot allow a popular uprising in Hungary, a "Prague Spring" in Czechoslovakia, an anti-Communist "Holy War" in Afghanistan, or an independent alternative center of power in Poland.[8]

So, like it or not, it appears we have a very powerful adversary in the world. What will our response be?

If you think you can escape this unpleasant reality by simply ignoring it, you are mistaken. Such an attitude only ensures that weak-willed and opportunistic politicians will have a free hand in deciding the issue for you. It means you are willing to trust your life to the wisdom, common sense, and integrity of our political leaders. I, for one, want to understand life or death issues that will affect my family and not blindly trust some legislator, about whom I know nothing, to automatically do the right thing.

Working for Peace

How can we work effectively for true lasting peace? Not everyone can get elected commander-in-chief of our armed forces, but elections do play a vital role. Congress has a great deal to say about our defense policy and particularly how much funding it will receive—witness Ronald Reagan's struggle with Congress over funding for his Strategic Defense Initiative—his proposed shield in outer space against incoming enemy missiles— or for aid to the Nicaraguan resistance.

If you're willing to devote a little time and energy every two years to help elect a Congressman who reflects your beliefs on national defense, you can play a real role in establishing our nation's national defense policies.

I also recommend that you read *A Just Defense: The Use of Force, Nuclear Weapons and Our Conscience* by Keith and Karl Payne. One of America's top-ranked scholars, Michael Novak, in *Moral Clarity in the Nuclear Age*, offers a brilliant analysis of the pro's and con's of nuclear disarmament in the real world in which we live. *Who Is For Peace* provides a Christian overview of the "nuclear freeze-peace movement" and underlying issues. The book consists of three major essays. Francis Schaeffer examines the secular humanist worldview and the need for military defense; Russian dissident and author Vladimir Bukovsky defines the Soviet view of peace; and Catholic scholar James Hitchcock analyzes the U.S. Catholic bishops' position on nuclear disarmament. *Who Are the Peacemakers?* by Jerram Barrs examines the misapplication of Scripture by some pacifist groups and presents a clear and easy to understand Biblical position on war and peace (Crossway Books).

The Oppressed

We affirm that God is both the Creator and the Judge of all men. We therefore should share His concern for justice and reconciliation throughout human society and for the liberation of men from every kind of oppression.[9]

War is a moral issue because it obviously involves the issues of life and death, peace and security, justice and righteousness — all things that God is deeply concerned about. War is also a violent and very visible form of oppression, of denying freedom and fair treatment to the innocent. But there is another, almost invisible side to oppression — the oppression that is internal, whether hidden behind the Iron Curtain of the Soviet Union or the palace walls of a Third World dictator. As Bukovsky points out, in Marxist nations "internal oppression and external aggression are inseparably interlocked."[10]

If we read the newspaper or news magazines, we are familiar with the external part of the equation. But what about the invisible part of oppression?

Well, you say, here's at least one issue I don't have to worry about. Nobody is oppressed in America, or at least no significant portion of the population is systematically oppressed by government design.

But Jesus didn't tell us that our duty to help the oppressed stops within our own borders. In fact, he told us just the opposite. He instructed us to go to all the nations of the world (Matthew 28:18-20) and do as He taught us: share the Gospel, and assist the oppressed and the poor. Jesus, in announcing the beginning of His public ministry, stated:

> The Spirit of the Lord is on Me, because He has anointed Me to preach good news to the poor. He has sent Me to proclaim freedom for the prisoners and recovery of sight of the blind, to release the oppressed, to proclaim the year for the Lord's favor. (Luke 4:18-19)

God's desire is to extend justice to the oppressed (Psalm 103:6) and as Christians we can be His instruments for doing so.

God detests oppression (read Isaiah 58) and He opposes nations that oppress their own people or other people (read Amos chapters 1 and 2). His instructions to us are clear:

> Defend the cause of the weak and fatherless; maintain the rights of the poor and oppressed. Rescue the weak and needy; deliver them from the hand of the wicked.[11]

So what about oppression in our world today? Oppression occurs when a government deprives its people of the basic human rights of freedom of religion, speech, choice of profession, the right to emigrate, and the right to impartial justice. The people in the Soviet Union, China, Vietnam, Cambodia, and Eastern Europe do not enjoy these basic freedoms. The same is true in our own backyard, most notably in Cuba and Nicaragua, and in many other nations around the world. If you think I'm picking on Communist nations, you're absolutely correct. The plain fact is that since Hitler's failure to impose his will on the world, the only political and economic philosophy irrevocably committed to the denial of basic freedoms and human rights is Marxist/Leninist Communism.

There are also a few anti-Communist, authoritarian dictatorships or "one-party governments" like those in Chile or Taiwan. These regimes are authoritarian rather than totalitarian. They do not allow political freedom, or freedom of political speech, which would threaten to replace or challenge their authority. But unlike the totalitarian regime of the Left, they do allow most other basic freedoms such as freedom of movement, emigration, choice of profession, and of religious expression; and private property and personal income are protected rather than confiscated.

Oppression manifests itself differently in every country. Here are a few brief examples I have selected from hundreds of documented cases of outrageous oppression just within two nations.

Nicaraguan Oppression

By the end of 1987 an estimated 400,000 to 500,000 Nicaraguans had fled "the workers' paradise" established there for them by the Marxist Sandinista regime led by Daniel Ortega. Since Nicaragua's entire population is only 3.3 million, this means that well over ten percent of the population has fled the homeland. This would be roughly the equivalent of every single citizen in California, Washington, and Oregon leaving the United States. Most of them walked miles and miles through jungles to live in prison-like refugee camps or to barely survive like animals in inhospitable territory.

As chairman of an international relief organization, I dispatched one of our directors on a sixty-day trek to verify the many horror stories we had heard or read. Not only did he substantiate the sub-human living conditions of those who had escaped Nicaragua, but he shed light on the causes of the brutality and suppression currently taking place in Nicaragua. While Mr. Ortega lectures the United Nations and Congressional leadership on the finer points of the democratic process, the scenario at home is somewhat different.

Jimmy Hassan is a young man whom our relief fund has helped to sponsor. Here is his story:

> "You are a dog, and your life has no value to us. Any of us could kill you with pleasure. You are an enemy of the revolution." These are the words of Sandinista State Security agents to a Protestant pastor, the Rev. Jimmy Hassan, when he underwent two days of harrowing intimidation in Managua. "The problem is that you teach the young people about Jesus Christ. And because of that they separate themselves from Marxism,

and this we will never permit in Nicaragua," one of his interrogators said.

Hassan was arrested October 31. He is co-pastor of La Primera Iglesia Centro Americana de Managua [First Central American Church of Managua], one of the largest Pentecostal congregations in Nicaragua. He also worked for Campus Crusade for Christ International, which State Security closed down October 30, seizing its files and other property. When Hassan was arrested, he was taken to the Interior Ministry, where a captain warned him that if anyone ever found out what had happened he would be sorry. A pistol was put to his head to emphasize the point.

At 4 P.M. he was released, but at 11 P.M. an Interior Ministry official knocked at his door and told him to appear at the ministry at 8 A.M. the following morning. When he reported, he was asked how much the CIA paid him and why he did not make statements in favor of the Sandinista revolution. Hassan insisted that his work was wholly religious.

Next an official entered the room and held a gun to Hassan's head, pulling the trigger. The gun was empty. Hassan was taken to a State Security jail. Because he refused to cooperate, he was told his wife would be arrested.

Several Campus Crusade staff members and leaders of various Protestant churches were shown to Hassan, some naked, all in closet-like rooms, two feet by two feet. Hassan was questioned again. He heard a woman sobbing and was told it was his wife. Later he was released. From what others who had been detained told him, "he was treated better than the rest," he says.[12]

Omar Rubio's story is distressingly similar:

I was working for the Banco Nicaraguensa when the Sandinistas came to power. But the new government fired me because I would not participate in their ideology or their cause. I looked for a job for a while and couldn't find one, but I got by because I can do a little of everything—painting, electrical work.

In 1980 I started doing community work with Cepad, a Christian Evangelical group. But the small churches began to report persecution from the government. The Sandinistas would throw out the congregation and use the Church as military headquarters. Some of the churches reported members disappearing. I started reporting these instances to human rights organizations and to journalists, and this was why the Sandinistas came and captured me. This was in June 1981. They took me to Ocotal, a coffee plantation which they had confiscated. At times there were three men, at times five. First they beat me over my whole body with fists and rifle butts, breaking three ribs and damaging my liver and testicles. They burnt my buttocks and stuffed an M-16 down my throat. They pulled the trigger six times but it did not fire.

I confided in God, and each time they hit me I would just say "glory to God." It went on for fifteen days, and I had almost no sleep. On the last day they tied my hands behind my back and pulled them up over my head and pulled my arms out of the sockets. I thought I was going to die, and I called on God. And then they stopped torturing me. After being like beasts they became like lambs. After they released me they tried to make me become one of their spies among the Churches, but I refused. I continued my work with the Church, but in 1982 I finally had to come to Honduras. I think the Lord has put me in this camp [at Jacaleapa] for a special reason. I am not the one to decide when I will leave.[13]

Religious suppression and the brutality to keep the suppression effective have long been features of those nations who find their savior in Marx and Lenin rather than in Christ. This should come as no surprise, given the voluminous anti-Christian statements of both Marx and Lenin:

The religion of the workers has no God, because it seeks to restore the divinity of Man.[14]

Every religious idea, every idea of a god, even flirting with the idea of a god, is unutterable vileness of the most dangerous kind, "contagion" of the most abominable kind. Millions of sins, filthy deeds, acts of violence, and physical contagions are far less dangerous than the subtle spiritual idea of a god.[15]

European Oppression

While the Soviet Union tells the world press how free and enlightened it's becoming, its vassal states continue to actually increase the level of repression against any religion other than Marxism.

Romania serves as an excellent example.

The U.S. media devoted extensive coverage to Billy Graham's speaking to a few small and very carefully selected audiences in the Eastern Bloc and Romania. What they overlooked reporting was the aftermath of Dr. Graham's trip:

> Ioan Popescu, the Director in the Department of Religious Affairs who approved the tour and accompanied Dr. Graham, was fired from his job. Harsh sentences were passed in the trials of Christians who were arrested for distributing Bibles and Christian literature. Constantin Sfatcu was sentenced to 4.5 years in prison and denied all visitation rights: Elisei Rusu, Cornel Mich, Levi Nicula, and Ilie Dociu Ilie were sentenced to work one year labor without pay.[16]

In addition, the Romanian Missionary Society reported:

> Baptists in the town of Blaj saw their Church building demolished on October 10, after it was half built. The local authorities considered that some building rules had been violated and on that pretext they bulldozed the entire building down.
>
> The Bristrita Baptists are still waiting for approval to rebuild their sanctuary, which was demolished a year ago. So are the Pentecostals in Tirgu Mures, and Medias, and Cimpia Turzii — their sanctuaries were also torn down.[17]

The case of the Guilesti Baptist Church, located in the suburbs of the capitol city of Bucharest, is instructive. The Church was half demolished by government bulldozers on June 4, 1985.

> Church leaders explained that they had attempted for several years to get a proper building permit to enlarge their facility, but their requests had fallen on deaf ears. Out of frustration the Church began building without a permit. The government's response was to level the rest of the building and then to torture the architect and deacon and order the pastor, Rev. Buni Cocar, out of town.[18]

It is a sad commentary on the moral bankruptcy of America's State Department, Congress, and foreign policy that

Romania still enjoys the massive economic benefits from America with most-favored-nation status.

More than sixty percent of all Christians live in countries where they are restricted in the practice of their Christian faith. They face discrimination, torture, imprisonment, and even martyrdom. They look to the Church in the Free World for help.[19]

What Should We Do?

Should we give humanitarian assistance to those who resist oppressive governments? Should we also try to influence our own government's policies toward these nations, insisting that our government do everything in its power to promote justice throughout the world? Or should we just shut our eyes tight as innocent people are slaughtered? Should we limit our interest in justice just to those few fortunate enough to have been born American? Will no one speak up for the oppressed who are unable to speak up for themselves? Who will defend those who cannot defend themselves (see Proverbs 31:8)?

Do we have an obligation to speak out? The delegates to the International Congress on World Evangelism, representing leaders of the Evangelical Church declared:

> The message of salvation implies also a message of judgment upon every form of alienation, oppression and discrimination, and we should not be afraid to denounce evil and injustice wherever they exist.[20]

What can we do to carry out God's instruction to "encourage the oppressed" (Isaiah 1:17)? The answer is much the same as that for influencing our military posture. Helping or hindering the oppressed in foreign lands is greatly influenced by American foreign policy and our State Department. Whom we elect as our president and as members of Congress will be the ones who mold American foreign policy.

As Carl Henry reminds us:

> All human beings are duty bound to advance justice and to protest injustice. Whether others do so or not, Christians should identify themselves with the whole body of humanity and speak up in the name of transcendent right and justice.

They should do so not simply when Christians suffer discrimination or oppression but also when any people so suffer.[21]

Let us take the Word of God seriously. Let us begin to restore justice and righteousness to our nation and to all nations.

Then Jesus came to them and said, "All authority in heaven and on earth has been given to me. Therefore go and make disciples of all nations, baptizing them in the name of the Father and of the Son and of the Holy Spirit, and *teaching them to obey everything I have commanded you*. And surely I am with you always, to the very end of the age." (Matthew 28:18-20, italics added)

The oppressed require more than our sympathy. They require our active participation on their behalf.

We also express our deep concern for all who have been unjustly imprisoned, and especially for our brethren who are suffering for their testimony to the Lord Jesus. We promise to pray and work for their freedom.[22]

T W E L V E

A NEW VISION
DEMANDS NEW LEADERS

Exploitation, poverty, AIDS, the elderly, abortion, alienation, war, oppression, justice, righteousness—these are the
issues of the nineties. But who has the wisdom, the integrity, the
compassion to provide the leadership required to successfully
confront such a staggering array of problems? Problems that if
not now at a crisis stage, will be very shortly?

America is an empty, drifting nation. Americans are
alienated from themselves, from God, from their leaders. We are
starving for vision. America is suffering an unprecedented crisis
of confidence in its leaders and its institutions. Over sixty percent of our population feels alienated from those who govern
them. People feel that no one, leaders in particular, really cares
about them. A global vacuum is being created as God continues
with His plan to draw all nations to Himself, and as man's best
efforts are revealed as increasingly futile.

Robert Nisbet, in the epilogue of his *History of the Idea of Progress*, states:

> By every serious reckoning the spell of politics and the political,
> strong since at least the seventeenth century, is fading. It is not
> simply a matter of growing disillusionment with government
> and bureaucracy; fundamentally it is declining faith in politics
> as a way of mind and life. If such apparent decline be real and
> lasting, the case is all the stronger for a recrudescence of religion.[1]

Everywhere people are asking, where are our leaders? More
and more people are concentrating on our obvious lack of heroes.
Pollster Lou Harris's in-depth study summarized: "It is fair to
conclude from these results that the country somehow does not
any longer produce leaders of heroic stature."[2]

In reviewing George Roche's scholarly book *A World Without Heroes* Allan Brownfeld writes:

> Never before in history, Mr. Roche declares, have the best-educated classes of society rejected a religious basis for life and have less-educated men been so deprived of moral leadership. The results are clear for all to see — more abortions than live births, widespread addiction to drugs, growing numbers of teen-age pregnancies, a mounting rate of homicide, rape, and the kidnaping of children.[3]

Even the rekindling of national hope that Ronald Reagan briefly provided is fast fading. Reagan's mystique and political success was to a large degree dependent upon his ability to recall the good old days to our minds, not as a thing of the past, but as the future within reach. Ronald Reagan's "personal goodness," charming sincerity, and superb communication skills convinced our nation that it could return to its original heritage. Everything would be pleasant, safe, and wholesome again.

Because Ronald Reagan actually believed these dreams, so did we. Unfortunately, as Reagan lost his energy and his administration lost its focus, people lost their confidence that the America of old was back. With the spell of the Reagan legacy broken, we were forced to face the real world around us. It more resembled Jimmy Carter's national malaise than it did Reagan's "city on a hill." In fact, our world is deteriorating morally and economically at a greater speed than before Ronald Reagan took the helm.

Our Current Bankrupt Leadership

The question now is, to whom shall we turn for leadership? Who will provide answers for the pressing problems and dramatically worsening human needs discussed in the last several chapters? Who will solve all of the other problems we didn't even mention? Who will provide the strength for us to face that fear of the unknown, the increasingly turbulent and frightening twenty-first century? Who has the ability to call Americans together again? To provide them with a common vision and purpose?

I can tell you who the vision will not come from. It will not come from those who normally provide the direction for our society. The fact is, our leadership establishment is intellectually and morally bankrupt. The university intellectuals and their mimics in the media, the professional politicians and their financiers, the captains of Wall Street, all are burnt out, depleted, finished.

Managing our government are technocrats, men who are adept at the amoral manipulation of government policy or public administration rather than heroes or statesmen. Our elected leaders are nothing more than political opportunists who have replaced morality and courage with popular consensus. They worship at the feet of the almighty opinion poll waiting to sense the direction of public opinion. Then they jump out in front to "lead." They are followers rather than leaders. Writing in *Newsweek* magazine on why Congress could not agree on much needed federal budget cuts, Robert Samuelson astutely commented:

> Government can't run on public-opinion polls. . . . There's a bipartisan conspiracy of silence. No one wants to talk about clear-cut choices. The only consensus in Washington today is to delay making the toughest choices. But all the solicitude for public opinion ultimately backfires. It generates public cynicism, because government can't govern.[4]

The entrepreneur is a vanishing breed on Wall Street and among the Fortune 500, America's largest corporations. The innovator has been replaced by the administrator, the creative by the mundane and bureaucratic. Business ethics have been replaced by a "let's-get-away-with-it-if-we-can," get-rich-quick attitude. Polls reveal that a majority of Americans now believe greed is a proper motivator for business and that breaking the rules is acceptable if you're not caught.

The Federal bureaucracy is now totally out of control, eating up hundreds of billions of dollars and responsible to no one — certainly not to the president or Congress. Meanwhile, these public servants have become detached and insensitive rulers of those whom they supposedly serve — the American people.

America is bankrupt because our intellectuals, our philosophers, our cultural trendsetters, are disillusioned with America — with themselves. Those who tell us what to think about, when, and how to think about it — who mold our culture through our universities and the media, who run think tanks founded by giant tax-exempt foundations, who provide the bureaucracy its intellectual capital — they are all tired and bewildered.

Believing this country's values are too corrupted to serve as a model for the world, they have nothing left to export to other nations. All that is left is the despair, hopelessness, cynicism, and escapism now rampant in all forms of the arts and unmistakenly symbolized by our sexual, materialistic, and drug-frenzied society. Their humanistic theories of the perfectibility of man have been buried by the collapse of the new frontier, the great society, and the appalling failure of literally all of their major welfare or social schemes, including public education.

But let us not just blame others for our nation's current leadership crisis. America is also bankrupt because much of our religious establishment is old and tired. Too many of our leaders are still locked into the escapist, apathetic, and disorganized Church described in Chapter 4. As one of America's leading Evangelical theologians, Carl Henry states:

> Can we turn the tide? Have we the resources to transpose the secular society's current plight into a program of spiritual aspiration and moral earnestness?
>
> One disturbing possibility, of course, is that Evangelical agencies with ready funding may have too little depth and vision to cope with the current conflict. God's kingdom is built not on perpetual motion, one liners, and flashbulbs, but on Christ, His sure Word. What counts is not how many enterprises we create, but why we create them and how worthily and effectively we maintain them. I come therefore to maneuver three: We need to get on with more effective Evangelical engagement in the public arena.[5]

The Bible tells us that the religious leaders of Jesus' day were like "old wineskins" that could not receive the new power of Christ and His message, the "new wine." The new wine is too powerful, too vibrant for the rigidity of the old wineskin. The potency of the new wine will burst the seams of its old and rigid container.

New Leaders Required

And so it is with new vision. A dramatic, even revolutionary new vision cannot be implemented by those still bound to visions whose time has come and gone, or worse, are still wedded to a visionless pragmatism. To quote Carl Henry again:

> Must we not implore Almighty God for new vision? Traditional Evangelical hand-me-downs are inadequate for this turning-time in history. Easily vocalized pieties and hurried sermonic clichés may continue to attract those whose dream bubbles have popped and who welcome some convenient escape hatch while they try to flee this planet.[6]

A burning determination to energetically restore justice, mercy, and morality to our nation, flowing from a Christ-like compassion for others, requires a new generation of leaders. As none other than Dr. Billy Graham recently remarked:

> As this century draws to a close, a new generation of leaders must be willing to step out boldly and chart a course for the future.[7]

The truth is that our leaders have lost their credibility. Even if the establishment did offer vision, it would fall on deaf ears. As Harris observed in *Inside America*:

> The plain truth seems to be that solutions bearing the imprimatur of the establishment are for the most part likely to fall flat on the public. The price of cynicism and disillusionment has been so great that endorsement by those running major institutions is no longer a strong testimonial at all.[8]

Our political establishment can offer us very little. Most of their most articulate spokesmen are men with dubious personal ethics. As Robert Beckel, national campaign manager for Walter Mondale in 1984, observed during the myriad political scandals of 1987-1988:

> You can't subject the process to this much bad news and not have substantial fallout in the country. If there was cynicism in America before this, I don't think we've seen anything yet.[9]

And our religious establishment is in need of reform as well. From the beginning revelations of Jim Bakker's disgusting performance in March of 1987 to Jerry Falwell's resignation from the PTL Board in November of 1987 to Jimmy Swaggart's humiliation in March of 1988, it took just twelve months to convince many people, including Christians, that certain religious leaders shared some of the same goals and values as the crooks on Wall Street, as well as the same modus operandi—lawsuits, takeover fights, bitter recriminations, and obviously self-serving denials. As Richard Foster succinctly states in *Money, Sex & Power,*

> In recent decades true [spiritual] power has been stifled by entrenched bureaucracies and a system of pastoral training that produces scribes rather than prophets. In order to have more freedom, many para-church organizations have sprung up, but these seldom have any mechanisms for accountability and usually end up being dominated by a single individual. As a result, we have, in the main, timidity in the churches and egotism in the para-church movements. . . .

> What is needed is a new renaissance of leadership within the Church.[10]

Obviously, America is ready for new leadership. As Lou Harris summed up in 1987:

> The American people are ready for competent and inspirational leadership in nearly all fields.[10]

> What appears to be needed is . . . some reassurance that those at the helm of major institutions really care about the lot of ordinary people.[11]

What America is crying out for is leaders in the Church, the volunteer sector, and in business and government who have integrity and compassion, who truly care about average people. As Americans lose faith in the establishment, they will seek new solutions, even radical solutions. Will they be Christian solutions? Or those of some new anti-Christian demagogue?

The Chance for Recovery

Clearly this is our opportunity to show forth God's love and compassion, share His answers for people's problems, through a Christian worldview and demonstrate our integrity through our selfless efforts to help people solve their problems.

As economic, military, and personal safety fears continue to tighten their grasp on our neighbors, those operating in God's strength and courage must be looked to as examples of courage in an increasingly fearful society.

What characteristics will we have to master in order to effectively serve our community? After twenty-five years of seeking political power and training others to achieve it and exercise it, I only recently learned some very basic lessons as God led me step-by-step through His leadership training course.

Leadership That Works

One invaluable lesson I learned was that leadership is earned through the hard work of serving those in our community. It is not won by one political combatant out-maneuvering the other. In short, leaders are not elected, they are made (of course, there are exceptions to this rule, but they are just that—exceptions—and most of them do not stay in office unless they very quickly learn to serve).

Earning our right to lead will not be easy. We must unlearn the defeatist habits and mentality that are so deeply ingrained in us. A new vision not only takes new leaders, it also demands new methods of leadership. We must learn to earn our right to lead by first serving those whom we ask to follow us.

We must etch deeply into our minds that true, lasting leadership is earned, not sought as a prize. We in the Christian Right made the mistake of trying to "win" leadership electorally before earning it among the electorate. We were too busy trying to pose as leaders to serve our communities' real needs. Our attitude was perceived to be—drug abuse, crime, poverty, who cares? We have our agenda—we're concerned with national defense, abortion, and prayer in schools!

While these issues are excellent concerns, they are not on the top of most people's priority lists. We shouldn't have been surprised when our community didn't follow our lead when we asked them to help with our agenda, but didn't offer to help with theirs. Human nature being what it is, each generation's memory is limited to its own time and experiences. This requires Christians to *prove anew* why we should be awarded the mantle of leadership at a time when civilization itself is threatened with total destruction as never before. After all, what have we done for *this* generation? Or the last one for that matter?

The reason the humanists are running our society today is because they are the ones ministering most effectively to human needs in the twentieth century, as the Church did in the eighteenth and nineteenth centuries. And our citizens wisely pick their leaders from those who serve and educate them.

When today's unsaved person hears a humanist on TV or radio, the humanist is usually addressing his concern for humanity across a wide spectrum of rights: civil rights, women's rights, children's rights, disabled rights, and gay rights; or of dangers: pollution, land abuse, nuclear war, extremist groups, violence, and drug abuse; or of needs: the poor in America and the world, the homeless, the under-educated, the underpaid, the undernourished, the underloved, the persecuted, the under-privileged, the oppressed, the exploited, the abused, battered wives, and the like. All in all, the secularists appear to most Americans to be legitimately concerned with problems faced by real people.

By contrast, when the average "unsaved" person sees or hears a Christian on TV/radio, he all too often hears extended money pitches to build this or that monument interrupted by short, not-so-subtle, messages on how the listener can get more out of God for his own personal blessing and well-being. Little or no attention is given to pressing family or global problems on all too many programs, and the attention remains centered on a gospel of self.

If you were an average non-Christian, which group would you choose to run your government's national policy?

How Humanists Fill the Christian Vacuum

When our common, unsuspecting citizen, who doesn't know he's supposed to automatically recognize us as the good guys, chooses between us in the local marketplace, he will usually use the exact measurement prescribed by Christ (ironically enough). That is, he will look for unity, love, and concern, or "know them by their fruits" (John 15:38, 17:21-23). The *NIV Study Bible* footnote of John 17:22 observes,

> Believers are to be characterized by humility and service, just as Christ was, and it is on them that God's glory rests. The

Lord emphasized the importance of unity among His followers, and again the standard is the unity of the Father and the Son.[13]

As humanists are fond of gleefully pointing out, if you're looking for love, compassion, service, and unity, don't look to the local Church, which only seems to offer judgment, unconcern, apathy, or laziness and which expends more energy disagreeing with other churches or denominations than in serving others.

On the other hand, the humanists at least appear to offer love and compassion (if a little weak on unity) and they do serve!

The average American notices the humanists offering every service conceivable under the sun: abortion counseling, family planning, sex education, AIDS education, all forms of psychiatric and family counseling, drug/alcohol abuse centers, day care for gifted children, handicapped children, normal children, meals-on-wheels for shut-ins, shelters for the homeless, soup kitchens, food banks, battered women's shelters, child abuse programs, and all kinds of self-improvement programs.

And then there are the causes! You can actually sign up with a real *live/action* local volunteer group to *actively serve* for civil rights, gay rights, women's rights, workers' rights, underprivileged rights, environmental protection, animal protection, nuclear freeze, abortion rights, apartheid, peace in El Salvador, and Hands off Nicaragua.

In contrast, the average citizen will be hard-pressed to find his local churches sponsoring any services to the community at-large, except for perhaps a few pregnancy counseling centers and the rare food bank, and even harder pressed to find any truly viable volunteer groups committed to making his city a better place to live, with the occasional exception of some terribly undermanned anti-porn/pro-life groups (in many cases existing in spite of, rather than because of, local Churches).

Judging by their fruits, who would you choose as the most concerned with your community, and therefore the most qualified for school board and other leadership positions? Who would you think of as *really wanting* to help you, your family, and your community? How devastating our lack of service has been! How negatively it has impacted our ability to affect society as salt and light, to restore justice and righteousness, or even to effectively evangelize, all three of which demand winning the hearts of the unsaved!

When will we ever learn? *Actions speak louder than words*. The average citizen won't read a tract, but he will observe your actions in sacrificing your time and energy for others! *We* are the witnesses, not the literature we may distribute. Our lives are to be a living witness to the reality and glory of God operating through us by loving others. As Brian O'Connell, a public affairs officer for the National Association of Evangelicals, observes:

> Unfortunately, some Evangelical notions of evangelism have not always included social concern. . . . Historically, however, most missionary societies before the twentieth century did not regard evangelism as exclusively verbal proclamation. For them it included ministering to the social needs of individuals. It emphasized the transformation not only of individuals but also of the unGodly aspects of their cultures. The Evangelical Church in our day needs to recapture this heritage of linking evangelism and social concern.
>
> In 1982, Evangelical leaders from around the globe met to study this relationship between evangelism and social action. They concluded that there were three relationships between the two, all equally valid: Christian social concern is a consequence of evangelism, can be a bridge to evangelism, and should be a partner of evangelism.[14]

Why should Christians be chosen to mold our nation's destiny? Just because we realize that things are bad, and we want back into the nation's driver's seat vacated by our parents and grandparents? Because, all of a sudden, the Church feels threatened? Because we now want to reclaim our Christian historical tradition of providing salt and light to our culture, our government, our neighborhood?

It is not enough for us to protest "we must lead," because in the eighteenth and nineteenth centuries "we" built the colleges, hospitals, and every other mercy project conceivable. Our generation has the right to ask, *what have you done for me lately?*

I believe the public regarded the Christian Right as Johnny-come-latelys to their problems. One day we showed up in town demanding they rally around our agenda for their families, for their town, their state. While our agenda may have made some sense, we did not. Who were we? What were our credentials to be telling them what to do? What had we been doing the last few years? Had we been building a credible record of community service to the poor, the elderly, the unloved, the homeless, the jobless, the drug dependent?

Or had we been sitting safely and smugly in our Churches? Our only public service being that of occasionally warning the community they were all destined to hell. Then one day, we "see the light." We move out of our self-imposed "Christian ghetto." We propose ourselves as leaders for our community. We don't know who they are or what their needs are, but we will lead them anyway. Our claim to fame is that we are active in a Church that is deeply committed to noninvolvement and has no interest in the community and its problems. How ludicrous we must have appeared. How presumptuous we were. It is little wonder we failed to enlist America in our holy crusade.

Having no training in serving, no record of service, we simply did not understand the requirements of leadership. So, how then, if we are to provide the leadership that our generation requires, are we to learn to serve?

Learning to Serve

We have seen in Chapters 6 and 7 that if we are to be used by God to restore justice and righteousness, we must learn to express God's compassion for those in need of our aid. As Hudson Armerding, the late president of Wheaton College, states in his book *Leadership*, "to be moved by injustice [is] a reaction requisite to leadership."[15]

If our compassion and faith are sincere, they must lead to action. They will cause us to burn with a Godly anger at evil and injustice. As John Stott says, we will no longer be willing to "accept the unacceptable,"[16] or, to put it into the words of Richard Foster, "religious piety is bankrupt without justice."[17]

Too many of our current leaders have made peace with injustice, oppression, and exploitation. They have accepted the unacceptable in order to avoid conflicts that might hurt Church growth. In pursuing ecclesiastical peace and stability, they have sacrificed our culture, our families, and even our churches to the ravages of the diabolic.

But it is not too late for our generation to set its own course. Our symbol is the Good Samaritan. Our formula is: Christ's compassion plus Spirit-led involvement equals restoration.

Our compassion must flow from God's love. Our involvement must be in obedience to God's command to action. Our nation will be healed as God works through us to restore justice, mercy, and righteousness to our people.

Compassion means that we must commit ourselves to discovering, then thinking about, and then finally feeling others' hurts and needs, whether it be for food or freedom, for housing or hospitalization, for spiritual or emotional help, or for fiscal or physical aid. Only when our thoughts create in us an emotional response will we, like Jesus, be moved to compassion "by our guts."

As the great Christian writer A. W. Tozer said,

> We must not forget that a state of emotion always comes between the knowledge and the act. A feeling of pity would never arise in the human heart unless aroused by a mental picture of others' distress, and without mercy. That is the way we are constituted. Whether the emotion aroused by a mental picture be pity, love, fear, desire, grief, there can be no act of the will without it. What I am saying is nothing new. Every mother, every statesman, every leader of men, every preacher of the Word of God knows that a mental picture must be presented to the listener before he can be moved to act, even though it be for his own advantage.[18]

To have compassion we must open our eyes and ears to the world around us. We must stop blocking out the cries of anguish and pain of the homeless, the aborted, the lonely, the abused, the hungry, the oppressed. They are everywhere, reaching out for help, if only we will slow down a moment to notice them. To effectively lead we must be humble enough to empathize with the needs and problems of those whom we would serve through our leadership.

Our leadership must be a partnership in problem solving—helping those we serve as leaders to solve their own problems. If we are going to lead in our homes, our Churches, our communities, and our nation, we must listen very carefully to determine the problems of those around us who need help. Then we must be willing to take responsibility for carrying out Christ's commandment to love and care for all people.

Author R. E. McMaster succinctly summed up the interaction of three vital leadership characteristics:

> Men who have humility have the ability to listen, learn, change, grow, adapt, and respond to their environment, in other words, to be successful. Personal humility followed by a willingness to accept responsibility leads to leadership, power, freedom, and prosperity. Power is given inescapably [for helping meet needs]. Empathy towards our fellow man allows us to meet those needs, and to eventually anticipate what those needs will be. Empathy leads to success.[19]

Think about it this way—to lead, a leader must possess a measure of power or authority. Power or authority is earned by those who accept and faithfully execute responsibility since responsibility, to be effectively administered, demands authority. Responsibility is awarded to those who have empathized with people's problems and have played a role in solving them. This is how servant-leaders—true leaders—are made.

This should be good news to Christians who may be short on knowledge and experience but long on integrity and strength. Knowledge will come with experience and experience will come when we are humble enough to serve. In the 1990s, anyone willing to take responsibility with integrity and compassion will quickly be elevated to leadership, whether of the local PTA, assistance league, or to the U.S. Congress. When people see that we truly empathize with their needs out of God's compassion and not our personal agenda, when they understand that we are committed to the unchanging standard of God's justice and righteousness for everyone, then they will respect our integrity.

Today, more than ever before, Americans are searching for local, state, and federal leaders with integrity that has been consistently and perseveringly demonstrated through self sacrifice and service.

As the Harris poll devastatingly demonstrated, Americans are alienated from their leaders primarily because they don't trust their integrity. A leader's command of issues, his smoothness, or his appearance are secondary to how the public perceives his honesty and trustworthiness. Democratic campaign strategists attributed Ronald Reagan's defeating Jimmy Carter in his native South to the integrity issue:

> "It has less to do with issues," explains Democratic campaign consultant David Doak, "than with the image of the candidate that flows from them: weakness versus strength, character versus lack of character, family values versus nontraditional ones."[20]

I believe Christian Right leaders are making a crucial strategic error in urging newly recruited activists to concentrate solely on political issues. We will never ever have enough political volunteers to convince voters to accept an agenda from people who have never served them.

Instead, we need to urge Christian activists to volunteer their time in the community, meeting its real needs. In ten years, by the beginning of the twenty-first century, it will be Christians who are looked to in the local community for leadership and guidance. Then, when Christians who have served their community ask their neighbors to join with them in an effort to restore justice and righteousness, people will follow.

Of course, this is an unattractive option for those who find stardom more glamorous than service, who are too impatient to wait a few years to reap the harvest, and who value the momentary thrill of expressing one's political views over the obtainment of concrete results.

The Samaritan Strategy is the only method that will lead us to the results we desire. The simple truth is, we cannot restore this nation without the active participation of the American people. And they will not follow us unless we first serve them.

I am afraid that if we continue on our present course of trying to build ill-fitted alliances with strange bedfellows for the purpose of trying to impose our agenda on an unreceptive public, all we will reap is one giagantic and well-deserved backlash.

We do not need to drain ourselves to mobilize America on behalf of some moralistic crusade. Is it not plain to see God Himself is bringing judgment to our land? As judgment—

AIDS, economic collapse, war, alienation, and the like—comes, many will repent. They will be looking for servant-leaders with answers. We need to be ready.

What else will God require of those servants who now want to step forward to lead our generation through the challenges and perils of the 1990s? In the next chapter we shall explore some answers.

THIRTEEN

HOW DO WE BEGIN?

The 1980s are over.

> Decades are not a function of calendar time. They are trends, values and associations, bundled up and tied together in the national memory.

> One more thing about decades: they are never exactly ten years long. The peculiar amalgam that we now think of as the eighties lasted six years, eleven months and fifteen days, finally collapsing with the Dow on October 19, 1987.[1]

U.S. News & World Report announced:

> The United States no longer controls its destiny, confidently dictating the rules of engagement to friends and foes alike. It would be pretentious to assume that thoughtful leaders and even ordinary folk do not sense this seismic change in the affairs of nations — evidence of it plays across the front page every morning and the network news every night. But our heads won't acknowledge what our hearts know: The American century is over. America's children — our dependencies of the postwar era — have reached adulthood. The struggle against this reality is not just an American phenomenon. Our allies seem paralyzed, too. Both pay lip service to the new "interdependent" world and the need to pull together, but no one can quite figure out how to go about it, much less what the trade-offs are. Welcome to 1988 and the burden-sharing blues.

> But the game is nearly up. We are simply overextended, and tougher times seem inevitable — if not next year, then in 1989.[2]

As our nation faces new crises, and as a corresponding national anxiety develops, old alliances — political, social, even religious —

are breaking apart. People are searching for new answers — and new vision that our current leaders have failed to provide.

For the next several years, we as the Body of Christ have a unique "window of opportunity" to re-establish ourselves as servant-leaders to our neighbors. If we will allow God's wisdom, love, and compassion to flow through us to meet the needs of our community, a new America can emerge.

Christians will be called upon to lead America, not back to former good times, but beyond, to new standards of justice and righteousness. America can indeed become a city on a hill, a light to all the world. But how do we start, where do we go from here?

To Review

Let's review just what it is that we are to begin and why.

We know that we are to serve others as part of God's divine plan for our lives. We are set aside for service (see Ephesians 2:10). We are being equipped by God for service (see Ephesians 4:12). We are commanded by Christ in His second great commandment to serve and care for each other.

We learned that service is nonoptional, and that the Bible is very clear that service means helping the poor, the elderly, the innocent, the orphaned, and all those oppressed or in need (Isaiah 58).

In a complex world where we acknowledge our spiritual immaturity — our Biblical, doctrinal, and theological ignorance, and we admit our confusion over what we are to do with our lives — it is reassuring to discover that Jesus repeatedly tells us it is very simple. We are to help those in need, to mature spiritually, and we are to proclaim by teaching and example the Gospel — that God loves His creatures and offers redemption through a new King, Jesus Christ, and His Kingdom.

Our service to others may lead us into the arena of government as we search for solutions to long-term problems. At the very least, our exercise of good stewardship and obedience to our Lord's command to be "salt and light" demands that we be active citizens and informed voters.

The early Church was not afraid to challenge the authority of the Roman government with its proclamation of a new King, a new Kingdom, and a new Gospel that directly challenges the existing order (read Acts 17:7). Persecuted as "atheists and traitors" by the Roman church/state authorities, Christians gladly sacrificed their lives.

We have verified that America is a highly alienated society, in desperate need of healing. Our generation is looking for answers. But they want more than just answers. They're looking for leaders with compassion, empathy, and integrity. They're looking for average people like you and me to help them, on a one-to-one basis.

Citizens choose their leaders from those who serve them best. We cannot expect to lead our nation, city, Church, or block until we learn to serve others. The reason that humanists are running our society is that, for the most part, they are the ones serving our community. We have discussed the need for new vision inspired by Godly compassion. Without vision our nation or our Church loses its cohesiveness, unity, direction, and discipline — and so it will perish. As theologian Carl Henry wrote one year before I was born (1948),

> Evangelicalism must offer a formula for a new world mind with spiritual ends, involving Evangelical affirmation in political, economic, sociological and educational realms. . . .[3]

We have rediscovered God's vision for our land — justice and righteousness — based on our obedience to God and implemented through our service to our neighbors as Christ commanded.

One reason the Christian Right failed to mobilize the Church was that it tried to substitute reason for compassion, urgency for love, an agenda for service. Cold logic or social agendas without God's expression of love and compassion will always be regarded as threatening or uninviting. The average citizens do not want Christians to be responsible for their community, because they do not trust us to administer justice or maintain righteousness with any sense of compassion. They expect us to be legalistic, unreasoning, uncompassionate. They are correctly suspicious of those who want to order their lives for them yet have never been willing to serve them. People instinctively recognize such an authoritarian spirit.

On the other hand, when we empathize with people and serve them, we are gladly accepted into leadership. I'm sure Mother Teresa could win any office she ran for!

We noted that throughout the New Testament Jesus was moved with deep compassion by the needs of those He saw. He expects us, as He illustrated in the parable of the Good Samaritan, to "go and do likewise."

And finally, we suggested an agenda for meeting the needs of our generation as we enter the last decade of the twentieth century. We are surrounded by those who need our help, young and old, men and women, locally and globally. Only the hardest heart, the most self-centered of persons, could refuse service to those mired in poverty and illiteracy, to those exploited by pornography or abortion, to those oppressed by governments, to those who are helpless—our elderly, our orphans, or our AIDS victims.

Getting on Track

How will you, in obedience to God, help in establishing justice, mercy, freedom, and moral sanity? Will you choose to disobey or obey? The decision will be yours as you finish this chapter. Will you rise to the challenge of standing in the gap to help others? Not everyone is called to be a leader, but we are all called to serve. As Wheaton's Armerding pointed out,

> What we may not realize, however, is that God sovereignly calls us not only to salvation, but to vocation. This is not understood by some Christians. They apparently feel that only a segment of the Christian Church is called of God into specific areas of service. Thus, believers are classified as clergy and laity—dividing us into those called to serve god and those who decide for themselves what they will do in life. Such a distinction is not Biblical. Scripture teaches that every Christian has a God-given ministry to perform in the place of the Lord's choosing.[4]

In discussing what constitutes true conversion to the Christian faith, he asserts,

> The second characteristic of conversion is "to serve the true and living God."[5]

> If a conversion does not produce the ongoing evidence of serving the living and true God, such conversion cannot be real.[6]

The Bible teaches that true conversion demands commitment, obedience, fruit, action, and service. We cannot rest on being born again and forget the rest.

Gaining knowledge of the needs around us through first-hand observation, discussions with others, or by reading must precede any serious thinking about problems and remedies. You need to read widely about some of the areas we've discussed in this book to get a better understanding of the various areas of need. You don't need to become an expert, but it is helpful the more you learn about an area.

Don't worry about becoming a leader right away. As you spend several years volunteering and gaining more confidence, God may move you into a position of greater authority or leadership. You don't need to wait until you become perfect spiritually, fully mature, or totally clean before you're ready to serve. God does not tell us to wait until we've become totally pure and self-satisfied spiritually to serve! In Proverbs 21:31 we are reminded that we must step out in faith to enter the battle, to be trained to fight.

As you become more familiar and concerned with particular needs, use your common sense to see what areas of service you feel you could provide — assess your gifts and resources — or what areas of need you are most drawn to. Recheck the various areas of need listed in our agenda chapters. Talk to some of your friends who are concerned and involved with important issues in the community or are helping people in some way. Begin a discussion group with some of your friends, even as few as two or three. Meet weekly for coffee or breakfast and discuss what issues touch you, or what you would like to see your Church do, or how you could get additional friends involved in an area of service.

Before you do any of the above, spend time each day for as long as it takes — days, weeks, or even months — seeking God's direction. Pray for God to direct you to an area of service where your light can shine. Ask Him to direct you to others who are knowledgeable about a need or service area in which you are interested.

Keeping on Track

Getting on track is the easy part. Our big challenge is how to stay on God's track and not deviate onto our own. We must not

repeat the mistakes of the Christian Right. We cannot implement our own agenda in our own power, motivated by our own
interests, no matter how worthy they may be.

We will lose everything, and the purpose of this book will be
totally perverted, if tomorrow we rush out to accomplish God's
agenda on our own power apart from Christ. Apart from Christ
our Vine, we can accomplish nothing that is considered good by
God. As Francis Schaeffer warned,

> There is nothing that will kill things as quickly as thinking that
> a strategy as a strategy is sufficient in itself without looking to
> God daily for wisdom and for strength, and surrounding the
> thing with serious prayer.
>
> Evangelicals tend to have many weaknesses because we too are
> part of the fallen world, but one is certainly a great triumphal-
> ism. We love to grab a strategy. We love to grab an idea. And
> building up a great triumphalism, built on strategies, built on
> the optimistic news we hear, we just rest on the strategy. If we
> do that, this dream that we have, this longing that we have, is
> dead. It must not be that. It must be the understanding that it
> must be in the power of God, it must be looking to Him daily,
> there must be leadership of the Lord in it. There must be a liv-
> ing prayer that surrounds it. There must be a willingness to
> really be under His leadership and not merely caught up in the
> mechanical framework of even a good strategy.[7]

One of the major errors of the Christian Right was in the
way we represented (or misrepresented) our positions. As
Schaeffer observes in *True Spirituality*,

> The Christian is not called to present merely another message
> in the same way as all the other messages are presented. We
> must understand that it is not only important what we do, but
> how we do it.
>
> In the area of "Christian activities" or "Christian service," how
> we are doing it is at least as important as what we are doing.
> Whatever is not an exhibition that God exists, misses the whole
> purpose of the Christian's life now on this earth.[8]

How are we to allow God to express His love through us? As
Schaeffer points out, Romans 7:6 makes it clear that we are to be

empowered in our service by the Holy Spirit. Only by relying on Him moment-by-moment can we show forth God's strength, love, peace, and wisdom. We must learn through constant trial and error to call upon the Holy Spirit within us to aid us at our exact moment of need, a dozen times, a hundred times a day.

The Bible teaches that Christ will bring forth His fruit through us. But we must let Him. We hinder Him by adopting either of two extremes — by refusing to do anything at all, or by automatically doing everything with our own direction through our own strength.

As Bible teacher Bob Mumford points out in his book *In the Face of Temptation,*

> A work is something which a man produces for himself; a fruit is something which is produced by a power which he does not possess. Man cannot make fruit.[9]

> Taking another promise of Jesus, we note: "I am the vine, you are the branches; he who abides in Me, and I in him, he bears much fruit" (John 15:5). The promise is that we shall produce fruit, provided we live in Him and allow HIm to live in us. Jesus goes on to explain why this is so. "For apart from Me you can do nothing. If anyone does not abide in Me, he is thrown away as a branch, and dries up; and they gather them, and cast them into the fire, and they are burned" (vv. 5, 6).[10]

Jesus' disciples had the same question any novice activists have: how are we to do this? It sounds so mystical. Mumford explains,

> One day the disciples asked Jesus, "What are we to do that we may [habitually] be working the works of God? [What are we to do to carry out what God requires?] Jesus replied, "This is the work (service) that God asks of you: that you believe in the One whom he has sent" [that you cleave to, trust, rely on, and have faith in His Messenger] (John 6:28, 29, Amplified).

Jesus said that when we stop trying to do things in our own strength and recognize our own insufficiency, then we can let Him work through us.

It is only when we come to a position of total reliance on Jesus —
total trust, obedience and rest from our own labors — that we
will see Jesus bring salvation to others through us; see Him heal
and comfort others and set them free through us. Always it is His
doing through our willingness and obedience to His command.[11]

How does this principal actually work in our harried daily
lives?

This is something that I had to learn the hard way from
years of trying too hard in my own strength, which left me feeling drained, exhausted, and burnt out emotionally, physically,
and spiritually.

In 1984, my self-made job description included serving as
chairman of the Reagan/Bush re-election campaign Christian
mobilization task force; developing and implementing strategies
to bring together thirty major religious leaders to conduct a voter
registration drive through one hundred thousand Churches;
hosting a daily radio program broadcast in twenty-five states;
producing a major national TV special; producing anti-
Mondale TV commercials and flying to the national Democratic
convention site to unveil them in a press conference; writing,
directing, and producing a series of anti-Ferraro TV commercials and flying to Washington, D.C., to unveil them in a press
conference; funding and co-publishing five million *Presidential
Biblical Scoreboard* magazines; writing, directing, and producing
the obligatory promotional TV spots and flying to the convention in Dallas to unveil them at a press conference; overseeing
our Texas five-man field office in distribution of 2.5 million individual report cards to churches, which resulted in the surprise
defeat of four "safe" Congressmen; overseeing a ten-member
staff in my Washington, D.C., and California offices; and editing and publishing a book on political strategy. I also had the responsibility for raising the millions of dollars required to fund
these activities.

It's early 1988 as I write, and I'm still recovering.

Now why in the world would I undertake such an insane
schedule? For the very same reasons most activists or volunteers
overload themselves: I saw a job that needed to be done; I saw
that no one else was going to do it; and I knew I had the abilities

to perform each task separately but I didn't have the wisdom or energy to perform them all well, collectively, and simultaneously.

Naturally I assumed I was the man for the job! This is what most of us do. God wants this problem cleared up! I had the will, time, energy, and talent; I was in the right spot at the right time, so I did it! But I forgot that proceeding at full power without God's leading and empowering was doomed to failure.

In God's Strength

Seeing the need, we must be careful that we don't attempt to fill it on our own strength. On whose strength are we going to rely? If it's our own, we will surely fail or "burn out." But how will we know the difference between relying on our strength or on God's?

The key is not what task we undertake, but where do we place our confidence for the successful completion of that task. If we place our confidence in our own ability to make things happen, we will inevitably overextend ourselves. We will not be satisfied until we have followed up every little detail, checked and rechecked everyone's performance, and anticipated every possible problem. Multiply this process by several projects, and you are already on the road to overdoing it. Add in the fact that since you are relying on your own efforts and those of others whom you know are fallible — or even incompetent — and you will be too stressed out, too intense, or too anxious to enjoy any personal peace.

On the other hand, if we rely on God to give us the victory, we can do our part and then we can rest in Him. We can be confident that He has used us, and we are able to leave the rest up to Him. An example of relying on God occurred in 1987 when I decided that no one was effectively mobilizing the Christian community behind the nomination of Justice Robert Bork to the Supreme Court.

So I wrote a ten-page newsletter, complete with a sample enclosure for Church bulletins and sent it to twenty-five thousand activist Churches. I also couriered the same package to several dozen major religious leaders and TV ministers who had constituencies numbering in the millions. So far so good. I did what I could do comfortably without straining, without overextending myself.

Then came the temptation. Shouldn't I do the job "right"? Do it all the way? Shouldn't I take a week that I didn't have to follow up on the phone with all those key leaders to make sure things happened as I wanted them to? But by then, in mid-1987, I had learned some lessons. The answer was a resounding no! I had worked hard and diligently. I had done my best. I would rely on God for the results, not my own self-effort. If I had relied on my abilities to make it happen, Bork would still have lost, and I would have been exhausted because I would have expended time and energy that I simply did not possess.

The principle is that as we serve at God's pace, we are to work at a comfortable level of exertion. Christ said His yoke is an easy one. It is not one that we should be straining to pull. Exerting ourselves, yes, straining no.

The lesson that the Christian Right forgot was that it is God who gives us the victories, not our own self-effort. As Isaiah 49:25-26 states, the glory of victory is to be the Lord's, not ours:

> But this is what the Lord says: "Yes, captives will be taken from warriors, and plunder retrieved from the fierce; *I* will contend with those who contend with you, and your children *I* will save. *I* will make your oppressors eat their own flesh; they will be drunk on their own blood, as with wine. Then all mankind will know that I, the Lord, am your Savior, your Redeemer, the Mighty One of Jacob." (italics added)

On January 1 of each year, my wife, Miriam, and I make it a practice to wait on the Lord for a sense of His direction. As we spent the day quietly before the Lord, studying the Bible, praying, waiting upon Him, the Lord gave me the following verse as a guideline for the next several years as I learn to balance my activity with His learning and empowering:

> Trust in the Lord and do good; dwell in the land and enjoy safe pasture. Delight yourself in the Lord and He will give you the desires of your heart. Commit your way to the Lord; trust in Him and He will do this: He will make your righteousness shine like the dawn, the justice of your cause like the noonday sun. (Psalm 37:3-6)

In this psalm God makes us a promise. He will use us in a mighty way to bring justice and righteousness to our nation *if* we will place our delight, our trust, our commitment in Him. This means that we really, truly, actually rely on Him. That we perform our daily tasks with an active faith that God is aware, concerned, and in control of events every moment of every day. We must enter the battle, but He gives victory. We set ourselves in motion, but He gives the direction. 2 Chronicles 20:1-30 provides us with a detailed portrait of this balance, and it is worth your careful study. We're ready for battle by equipping ourselves and training. But God gives us the victory if we have been obedient.

Our alternative is to practice what I call Christian atheism or Christian humanism. We affirm our belief in God's sovereignty, but we act as if He is dead. Or, we act as if God once having set our world in motion has abandoned us to our own devices as He has moved onto more pressing business elsewhere in the universe.

The other verse that I felt God impressing upon me that day was Proverbs 3:5-6:

> Trust in the Lord with all your heart and lean not on your own understanding; in all your ways acknowledge Him, and He will make your paths straight.

Here God promises us that if we are willing to trust Him and not ourselves, if we will acknowledge Him (meaning to serve and obey Him), then He will clear the obstacles from our path; because then it won't be our path, it will be God's path for our lives.

God commands that we actively serve Him and others. But He wants us to rely on Him for the wisdom, perseverance, and strength to "press on toward the goal," as Paul instructed us in Philippians 3:13-14.

The Power of Prayer

If we are to be led by God, we must learn to communicate with Him in an effective way. We see many areas of need. We feel moved to help in a hundred causes. How can we know which cause God is calling us to? Once there, how can we be sensitive to His constant guidance and redirection of our course?

The perfunctory prayer for guidance so common in today's Evangelical circles will not suffice. If we continue to pray trite little formula-like prayers and then go on relying on our own strength, that's exactly where God will leave us — in our own strength.

And, as we have seen, in our own strength there is only defeat, exhaustion, burnout, and disillusionment ahead. We must remember that God knows our hearts and our motivations. Is our purpose to offer Him fanciful words, even asking for His approval or blessing, all the while intending to rely on our own resources? If we want big results, miraculous answers, even a reversal of our nation's nonstop drive toward self-destruction, we must learn to pray so that God will not only hear us, but answer us as well.

There is no doubt that when God's people collectively get serious about prayer, seemingly insurmountable odds are easily beaten. If we are to succeed in restoring righteousness and justice to our nation, we must realize that we are in a spiritual battle and therefore, as Paul tells us in Ephesians 6, we must pray unceasingly. Only spiritual weapons can win spiritual wars, and prayer is our greatest spiritual weapon. Ronald Reagan's "Star Wars" space defense will not save us. Neither will tripling the defense budget. God is our answer and serious prayer is the avenue. We are to be God's instruments of implementation.

Have you ever wondered why the Old Testament has so many stories of battles won and lost? What possible meaning do such obscure battles in a small area of the world thousands of years ago have for us today? Why would God waste His time, or ours, with all these "irrelevant" stories, which is precisely how the average Christian views the Old Testament?

The answer is that within each story, each battle, is a lesson for us to learn (much like the parables of Jesus). If we wish to fight and win spiritual battles, we need to study how and why God led His people to either defeat or deliverance. What does God require of us to receive His power, His intervention in battle? While the Bible is full of such examples, I will mention just two.

In 2 Chronicles 20:1-30, we read that God's people of Judah were about to be conquered by an overwhelmingly superior invasion force. King Jehoshaphat called his entire nation to serious prayer and fasting, petitioning God to deliver them. He did so in spectacular fashion, causing the invading armies to turn on each other and to destroy themselves.

In another instance women initiated prayer and fasting to save the entire Jewish nation from destruction. The book of Esther tells us that the emperor of Persia had decided to annihilate the Jewish nation—every man, woman, and child. "Esther and her maidens" went into action. Fasting and praying seventy-two straight hours, and joined by the residents of the capitol, Esther's efforts were well rewarded! She was elevated to great heights of political influence, and the emperor's chief adviser and his family were destroyed.

The Old Testament, including the Psalms, is replete with such examples, if only we will learn from them! No wonder Paul tells us to pray without ceasing!

Humbling Ourselves

The favorite verse of the Christian Right—Ronald Reagan had the Bible turned to the page when he placed his hand on it to be sworn in as president of the United States)—2 Chronicles 7:14, gives us the key:

> If My people, who are called by My name, will humble themselves and pray and seek My face and turn from their wicked ways, then I will hear from heaven and will forgive their sin and will heal their land.

Unfortunately, it was our favorite verse to quote, but not to follow. Much of the problem is that neither the Christian Right nor the Church can seem to get past the first requirement to "humble ourselves." As God tells us in James 4:10, we must humble ourselves before Him before He will "lift us up."

How do we humble ourselves? Through repentance (*metanoia* —from the Greek) which means a "change of mind." We must be willing to change our natural direction from being self-centered to God-centered, from focusing exclusively on our concerns to obedience to His concerns, from serving ourselves to serving others.

Repentance will lead to spiritual illumination that in turn gives us freedom from bondage and sin. This increased spiritual freedom leads to greater maturity and closer communion with God. Then we are truly ready to serve others in a manner ultimately pleasing to God.

So, how do we show God that we're truly serious and repentant? Fasting is an important key. Fasting (going without food for several meals or even days while praying, reading the Word and waiting upon God) is so unfamiliar to our modern Evangelical thinking that one would think Christ ordered us to discontinue the practice.

Yet quite the opposite is true. In fact, in the Sermon on the Mount He gave us instructions on how to honor God in the conduct of our fasting (see Matthew 6:16-18).

As I pointed out in Chapter 7, God does not accept prayer and fasting in place of service. Likewise, without our service being empowered by prayer and fasting, we will never bear lasting fruit. We will produce our own works not those of Christ. This was God's message to His people through Isaiah. In Isaiah 58, we are told that God will not honor prayer and fasting that is in "form only," and not balanced with works of service:

> Is not this the kind of fasting I have chosen: to loose the chains of injustice and untie the cords of the yoke, to set the oppressed free and break every yoke? Is it not to share your food with the hungry and to provide the poor wanderer with shelter—when you see the naked, to clothe him, and not to turn away from your own flesh and blood? (Isaiah 58:6-7)

God is telling us two things. First, He weighs our motivations. If we are serious in humbling ourselves in repentance and seeking His forgiveness, then obviously we must be serious enough to carry out His will in caring for others. Second, He is telling us that true fasting, true humbling, followed by our obedience in service, will result in the fulfillment of His promises to us as His people:

> Then your light will break forth like the dawn and your healing will quickly appear; then your righteousness will go before you, and the glory of the Lord will be your rear guard. . . . The Lord will guide you always; he will satisfy your needs in a sun-scorched land and will strengthen your frame. You will be like a well-watered garden, like a spring whose waters never fail. Your people will rebuild the ancient ruins and will raise up the age-old foundations; you will be called the Repairer of Broken Walls, Restorer of Streets with Dwellings. (Isaiah 58:8-12)

What a wonderful promise of total restoration! It is the enactment of God's promise from 2 Chronicles 7:14 to heal our land. And all it takes is our obedience in humbling ourselves through fasting and repentance, and in restoring justice and righteousness for the poor, the oppressed, the exploited.

God has provided for us the promise of both a blessing for obedience and a curse for disobedience:

> If at any time I announce that a nation or kingdom is to be up-rooted, torn down and destroyed, and if that nation I warned repents of its evil, then I will relent and not inflict on it the disaster I had planned. And if at another time I announce that a nation or kingdom is to be built up and planted, and if it does not obey Me, then I will reconsider the good I had intended to do for it. (Jeremiah 18:7-10)

Which route will we choose?

While fasting is a foreign word to both our Church and our culture, it was not always so. In fact, following the Old Testament's example, our founding fathers consistently called our entire nation to prayer and fasting whenever disaster threatened.

Fasting in American History

When the British, in May 1774, threatened to blockade American ports, the Virginia Assembly set aside June 1, 1774, as "a Day of Fasting, Humiliation, and Prayer, devoutly to implore the Divine Interposition, for averting the heavy Calamity which threatens Destruction to our civil Rights, and the Evils of civil War."[12]

The fact that such proclamations were taken seriously by citizens and leaders alike is borne by a notation in George Washington's diary for the first of June, "went to Church and fasted all day."[13]

A few years later, when our infant republic was on the verge of war with a very powerful France, President John Adams set aside a day in May 1798:

> . . . as a day of solemn Humiliation, Fasting and Prayer: That the citizens of these states, abstaining on that day from their customary worldly occupations, offer their devout addresses to

the Father of Mercies, agreeably to those forms or methods which they have severally adopted as the most suitable and becoming: That all Religious Congregations do, with the deepest humility, acknowledge before God the manifold sins and transgressions with which we are justly chargeable as individuals and as a nation, beseeching Him at the same time of His infinite grace through the Redeemer of the World, freely to remit all our offenses, and to incline us, by His Holy Spirit, to that sincere Repentance and Reformation, which may afford us reason to hope for His inestimable favor and Heavenly Benediction: That it be made the subject of particular and earnest supplication, that our country may be protected from all the dangers which threaten it: That our civil and religious privileges may be preserved inviolate, and perpetuated to the latest generations. . . .[14]

As we know, a potentially devastating war was avoided.

When war finally did erupt again with Britain, President James Madison knew exactly what to do. After meeting with both houses of Congress, he set aside January 12, 1815, as a national day of "repentance, humility, prayer, and fasting. . . ."[15] British forces ended all hostilities shortly afterward. But Madison was not the last of the American leaders who were wise enough to follow the Biblical formula for calling upon God's help in crisis. Abraham Lincoln decreed on three different occasions such appeals for God's intervention and protection. Perhaps the most famous of these was his proclamation of a day of national prayer and humiliation for April 30, 1863, which read in part:

And, insomuch as we know that, by His divine law, nations, like individuals, are subjected to punishments and chastisement in this world, may we not justly fear that the awful calamity of civil war, which now desolates the land, may be but a punishment inflicted upon us for our presumptuous sins, to the needful end of our national reformation as a whole People? We have been preserved, these many years, in peace and prosperity. We have grown in numbers, wealth, and power as no other nation has ever grown. But we have forgotten God. We have forgotten the gracious hand which preserved us in peace, and multiplied and enriched and strengthened us; and we have vainly imagined, in the deceitfulness of our hearts, that all these blessing were produced by some superior wisdom and virtue of our own. Intoxicated with unbroken success, we have become too self-sufficient to feel the necessity of redeeming and preserving grace, too proud to pray for decency and forgiveness. Now, therefore, in compliance with the request, and fully concurring in the views of the Senate, I do, by this my proclamation, designate and set apart Thursday the 30th day of April, 1863, as a day of national humiliation, fasting, and prayer. And I do hereby request all the People to abstain on that day from their ordinary secular pursuits, and to unite, at their several places of public worship and their respective homes, in keeping the day holy to the Lord, and devoted to the humble discharge of the religious duties proper to that solemn occasion.[16]

Lincoln was obviously mindful of God's warnings of national blessings and cursings outlined in Deuteronomy 28 and 29. Lincoln recognized that we had fallen into precisely the same trap that God's people had on an earlier occasion. We had progressed. We had forgotten God.

Lincoln's proclamation, along with its foundation in Deuteronomy, deserves our special attention, for it is at a similar juncture that we find ourselves today. Except today, 125 years after Lincoln's proclamation, things are worse. Lincoln's proclamation was the last time that the nation's leaders called all citizens to national prayer and fasting.

It is interesting to note that with the end of the era of presidents who, like Lincoln, knew how to call the nation together to effectively seek God's aid, our nation's spirit has progressively worsened. In fact, the period following Lincoln marked the beginning of the Church's withdrawal from the social arena and the simultaneous growth of secular and anti-Christian groups.

Can there be any wonder why, when we refuse to follow God's instructions for obtaining His help, we don't receive it? To our modern sophisticated, proud, and lazy minds such things as consistent intercessory prayer, fasting, repentance, and humbling seem remote and old-fashioned. And so they are. They do not fit into our vocabulary, our lifestyles. And until they do, certain other attributes will continue to be absent from our modern age and our busy lives: namely, peace, justice, righteousness and compassion for our generation.

To successfully seek God's direction, we must make time for Him in our overly busy schedules. We must set aside a quiet time, if only for a few minutes each day. We must take a "Sabbath" day each week. We must use this time to study, pray, reflect, consider, seek, and receive God's Word, mind, and direction.

As John Stott comments:

> The final mark of a Christian leader is discipline, not only self-discipline in general [in the mastery of his passions, his time, and his energies], but in particular the discipline with which he waits on God. He knows his weakness. He knows the greatness of his task and the strength of the opposition. But he also knows the inexhaustible riches of God's grace.
>
> But our supreme exemplar is our Lord Jesus Himself. It is often said that He was always available to people. This is not true. He was not. There were times when He sent the crowds away. He refused to allow the urgent to displace the important. Regularly He withdrew from the pressures and the glare of His public ministry, in order to seek His Father in solitude and replenish His reserves of strength.
>
> It is only God who "gives strength to the weary and increases the power of the weak." For "even youths grow tired and weary, and young men stumble and fall; but those who hope in the Lord," and wait patiently for Him, "will renew their strength. They will soar on wings like eagles; they will run and not grow weary, they will walk and not be faint" (Isaiah 40:29-31). Only those who discipline themselves to seek God's face, keep their vision bright. It is only those who live before Christ's cross whose inner fires are constantly rekindled and never go out. Those leaders who think they are strong in their own strength are the most pathetically weak of all people; only those who know and acknowledge their weakness can become strong with the strength of Christ.[17]

If we are to obey Christ in serving others, we must ask God daily to show us how to serve others in His power, not ours! We must not make the mistake of those in the past who emphasized good works by their own power. Just as faith without works is dead, works apart from faith are useless.

If service is for service's sake only, we will soon burn out. If it is for ourselves, we will soon sense a terrible hollowness. We will not bear any true or lasting fruit because we are cut off from Christ the Vine, the source of all fruitfulness (see John 15:3-5).

The entire purpose of this book will be terribly twisted if you try to go off and produce fruit on your own. Christ promises us we will produce lasting fruit only if we stay in Him. This means we must not rely upon our self-sufficiency and frantic self-effort. We must depend on Him to work through us, to obtain victory, to remove obstacles. We must set ourselves in motion, but He must guide us. We must enter the arena on our own, but He must give us the victory. We must work diligently, but we must rely on Him for the outcome. This attitude of dependence upon God does not come naturally. Relying on our own efforts does come naturally. If we are to be victorious, we must not repeat the mistakes of the Christian Right. We must not "lean on our own understanding." Rather, we must "trust God with all or our heart and mind." In our own efforts, guided by our own wisdom, or empowered by our own talents and resources, we are only capable of producing projects, programs, and movements, which in a few years' time utterly fail or fade away. Lasting fruit is produced through us by a power over which we have no control— God's power. But for God to use us, we must be willing to submit to His direction. We must not allow our own good plans and ambitions to block out our sensitivity to God's leading and enabling, or all will be lost.

If we understand that God expects our involvement, we can rely on Him to give us wisdom, direction, courage, and strength. Our involvement will be successful.

It is God who has planned for us a life of service. The *NIV Study Bible* commentary on John 17:15 says, "The world is where Jesus' disciples are to do their work; Jesus does not wish them to be taken from it until that work is done." And Ephesians 2:10 (TLB) tells us: It is God himself who has made us what we are and given us new lives from Christ Jesus; and long ages ago He planned that we should spend these in helping others.

It is also God who will empower us to carry out His will:

Now, glory be to God who by His mighty power at work within us is able to do far more than we would ever dare to ask or even dream of, infinitely beyond our highest prayers, desires, thoughts, or hopes. (Ephesians 3:20 TLB)

We can make our plans, but the final outcome is in God's hands. (Proverbs 16:1)

Commit your work to the Lord, then it will succeed. (Proverbs 16:3 TLB)

We toss the coin, but it is the Lord who controls its decision. (Proverbs 16:33 TLB)

We must pray that our motivation in wanting to serve God will be pure. We must be led and empowered by the Holy Spirit. We must develop a spirit of service so that people see Jesus, not us—not our "big sacrifice" or our "great deed." This is true evangelism! And true servant-leadership!

END NOTES

Chapter 1—The Rise of the Christian Right

1. Dave Palermo, "Religious Right: The Impact on Election '80," *Herald Examiner*, 7 November 1980.
2. Evangelical Press News Service, 2 April 1983.
3. "The Connecticut Mutual Life Report on American Values in the '80s: The Impact of Belief," Connecticut Mutual Survey Report.
4. Richard J. Neuhaus, *The Naked Public Square: Religion and Democracy in America* (Grand Rapids, Michigan: William B. Eerdmans Publishing Company, 1984), p. 7.
5. Neuhaus, p. 5.
6. Evangelical Press News Service, 3 January 1981, p. 3.
7. Erling Jorstad, *The Politics of Moralism* (Minneapolis: Augsburg Publishing House, 1981), p. 6.
8. Neuhaus, p. 5.
9. Kenneth A. Briggs, "Evangelicals Turning to Politics Fear Moral Slide Imperils Nation," *New York Times*, 19 February 1980.
10. Jorstad, p. 17.
11. Louis Harris, *Inside America* (New York: Vintage Books, 1987), p. 262.

Chapter 2—Changing History

1. Harris, p. 252.
2. "How the 'Moral Majority' Voted," *Evening Sentinel*, 28 November 1980.
3. John Lofton, *Human Events*, 22 November 1980.
4. Evangelical Press News Service, 6 June 1981.
5. Morrie Rykskire, *Human Events*, 22 November 1980.
6. *U.S. News & World Report*, 17 November 1980.
7. Connecticut Mutual Life Report, p. 10.
8. John Buchanan, "Alliance with Religious Extremists Threatens Integrity of GOP" *The Hartford Courant*, 4 February 1985.
9. *Newsweek*, 9 July 1984.
10. *Newsweek*, 24 November 1984, p. 27.
11. *San Francisco Chronicle*, 15 September 1984.
12. Marshall Ingerson, "Christian Right Drawing Agenda for Political Challenges in 1986," *The Dallas Times Herald*, 1 June 1985.
13. Thomas B. Edsall, "Onward, GOP Christians, Marching to '88," *The Washington Post*, 4 August 1987.
14. Neuhaus, p. 40.
15. The Connecticut Mutual Survey.

16. John Whitehead, "Activism: Has the Light Gone Out?" *The Rutherford Institute Report*, March-June 1987, p. 3.
17. Harris, pp. 267-268.
18. *Los Angeles Herald Examiner*, 7 November 1980.

Chapter 3—Why the Christian Right Failed

1. Harris, pp. 267-268.
2. Connecticut Mutual Survey, p. 10.
3. Neuhaus, pp. 52-53.
4. Ibid., pp. 108-109.
5. Francis Schaeffer, *The Church at the End of the Twentieth Century* (Downers Grove, Illinois: InterVarsity Press, 1970), pp. 29-30, 35.
6. A. James Reichley, *Religion in American Public Life* (Washington, D.C.: The Brookings Institute, 1985), p. 201.
7. Ibid., p. 202.
8. John Stott, *Involvement: Social and Sexual Relationships in the Modern World*, Volume 2 (Old Tappan, New Jersey: Fleming H. Revell Company, 1985), pp. 249-250.
9. From a personal conversation with Wil Pilcher.

Chapter 4—The Failure of Our Churches

1. C. C. Goen, *Broken Churches, Broken Nation* (Macon, Georgia: University Press, 1985), p. 181.
2. Ibid., pp. 146-147.
3. Ibid., p. 189.
4. Ibid., p. 147.
5. The Lausanne Covenant, Resolution No. 11, International Congress on World Evangelization.
6. Richard F. Lovelace, *Renewal as a Way of Life* (Downers Grove, Illinois: InterVarsity Press, 1985), p. 52.
7. Ibid., p. 56.
8. Goen, p. 164.
9. Stott, p. 27.
10. Lovelace, p. 57.
11. Ibid.
12. Stott, p. 27.
13. *Christianity Today*, 6 November 1987, p. 42.
14. Stott, p. 35.
15. Francis A. Schaeffer, *The Complete Works of Francis A. Schaeffer, A Christian Worldview*, Volume 3 (Westchester, Illinois: Crossway Books, 1982), pp. 200-201.
16. Kenneth Barker, ed., *NIV Study Bible: New International Version* (Grand Rapids, Michigan: The Zondervan Corporation, 1985), p. 1806.
17. Stott, p. 46.
18. Neuhaus, p. 14.
19. The Lausanne Covenant, Resolution No. 11, International Congress on World Evangelization.

Chapter 5—Failing to Meet the Needs of Our Time

1. Harris, p. 33.
2. Ibid.

3. Stott, p. 95.
4. Harris, p. 36.
5. Ibid., p. 35.
6. Ibid., p. 258.
7. Ibid., p. 259.
8. Ibid., p. 260.
9. Reichley, p. 317.
10. Harris, p. 8.
11. Ibid., p. 60.
12. Ibid., p. 75.
13. Eva Schindler-Rainman and Ronald Lippit, *The Volunteer Community* (Fairfax, Virginia: NTL Learning Resources Corporation, 1971, 1975), pp. 22-23.
14. Harris, p. 38.
15. Connecticut Mutual Survey, p. 10.
16. Donald P. McNeill, Douglas A. Morrison, Henri J. M. Nouwen, *Compassion: A Reflection on the Christian Life* (Garden City, New York: Doubleday & Company, Inc., 1982), p. 25.
17. "Darker U.S. Mood, Poll Says," *New York Times*, 22 February 1988, p. 10.

Chapter 6 — Vision

1. C. C. Goen, p. 44.
2. Ibid., p. 27.
3. Paul Johnson, *Modern Times: The World from the Twenties to the Eighties* (New York: Harper & Row, 1983), pp. 271-272.
4. Ibid., pp. 447, 548.
5. Armando Valladares, *Against All Hope* (New York: Ballentine Books, 1986), pp. xv, xvii.
6. Barker, p. 859.
7. Stott, p. 38.
8. *San Francisco Chronicle*, 14 November 1987.
9. Ibid.
10. Ibid.
11. *Human Events*, 23 January 1988, p. 23.
12. Barker, p. 1805.
13. McNeill, et al, p. 52.
14. Ibid., pp. 53-54.
15. Rollo May, *Love and Will* (New York: Dell Publishing Company, 1969), p. 137.

Chapter 7 — What Does God Want Us to Do?

1. Richard F. Lovelace, *Renewal as a Way of Life* (Downers Grove, Illinois: Inter-Varsity Press, 1985), p. 39.
2. Cited in DeVern Fromke, *Unto Full Stature* (Cloverdale, Indiana: Sure Foundation, 1964), p. 150.
3. Barker, p. 1899.
4. Cited in Larry Richards, *Dictionary of Bible Truths* (Grand Rapids, Michigan: Zondervan Publishing House, 1987), p. 160.
5. Stott, pp. 36-37.
6. Lovelace, p. 117.
7. Carl F. H. Henry, *The Christian Mindset in a Secular Society* (Portland, Oregon: Multnomah Press, 1984) p. 100.

8. Ralph Earle, *Word Meanings in the New Testament* (Grand Rapids, Michigan: Baker Book House, 1982), p. 183.
9. Wilhelm Niesel (translated by Harold Knight), *The Theology of Calvin* (Grand Rapids, Michigan: Baker Book House, 1980), p. 142.
10. Stott, p. 42.
11. The Lausanne Covenant, Resolution No. 12, International Congress on World Evangelization.
12. Lovelace, p. 18.

Chapter 8 — Reasons for Political Involvement

1. Charles Colson, *Kingdoms in Conflict* (New York and Grand Rapids: William Morrow/Zondervan Publishing House, 1987).
2. Monte E. Wilson, *The Reformer*, July/August 1986, p. 1.
3. Ibid.
4. Ibid.
5. Ibid.
6. Henry, pp. 126-127.
7. Abraham Kuyper, *Lectures on Calvinism* (Grand Rapids, Michigan: Wm. B. Eerdmans Publishing Company, 1931), p. 81.
8. Ibid., pp. 82-83.
9. The Lausanne Covenant, Resolution No. 13, International Congress on World Evangelization.
10. Richard Cizik, ed., *The High Cost of Indifference* (Ventura, California: Regal Books, 1984), pp. 10-11.
11. Barker, p. 1725.
12. Richard J. Foster, *Money, Sex & Power* (San Francisco, California: Harper & Row, 1985), p. 225.
13. *Moody Monthly*, October 1987.
14. *Charisma*, December 1987, p. 32.
15. Lovelace, p. 125.
16. Stott, p. 32.
17. Mark Noll, *Chronicles of Culture*, September 1987, p. 40.
18. Goen, p. 48.
19. Ibid., pp. 30-31.
20. Rus Walton, *Biblical Principles Concerning Issues of Importance to Godly Christians* (Plymouth, Massachusetts: Plymouth Rock Foundation, 1984), pp. 338-339.
21. First Amendment.
22. Cizik, p. 5.
23. *Christianity Today*, 4 January 1980.
24. Taken from the back cover of Vern McLellan's, *Christians in the Political Arena*, (Charlotte, North Carolina: Associated Press).
25. The Lausanne Covenant, Resolution No. 5, International Congress on World Evangelization.

Chapter 9 — An Agenda for the 1990s

1. Cindy Rocker, "The Kingsburg California Community Assistance Program," *Chalcedon Report*, May, 1986.
2. Francis A. Schaeffer, speech given to STEP Foundation (Strategies to Elevate People) at Dallas, Texas, 24 September 1982.

3. "Poverty," *FAC-Sheet* #49, Plymouth Rock Foundation, p. 1.
4. From Charles Murray, *Losing Ground: American Social Policy 1950-1980* (New York: Basic Books, 1984), p. 15.
5. Ibid., p. 32-33.
6. Ibid., p. 40.
7. Jack E. White, "Re-examining America's Underclass," *Time*, 11 May 1987, p. 28.
8. Murray, p. 14.
9. *FAC-Sheet*, #49.
10. Murray, pp. 126-127.
11. Ibid., p. 73.
12. Ibid., pp. 75-76.
13. Ibid., pp. 77-78.
14. Ibid., p. 133.
15. Ibid., p. 9.
16. Ibid., p. 146.
17. Ibid.
18. Ibid., p. 160.
19. Julis Lester, "Integration Rethought: Debunking the Myths," *Washington Times Magazine*, 27 July 1987, p. 4.
20. *Time*, 28 December 1987, p. 44.
21. Murray, p. 9.
22. *FAC-Sheet*, #49, p. 2.
23. Murray, pp. 227-228.
24. Ibid., pp. 228-229.
25. Ibid., p. 229.
26. *Time*, 11 May 1987, p. 28.
27. Lester, p. 5.
28. *FAC-Sheet*, #49.
29. Rocker.
30. *FAC-Sheet*, #49, p. 4.
31. Ibid.
32. *World Vision*, February/March 1988, p. 19.
33. *People* magazine.
34. "The Children of the Homeless," *U.S. News & World Report*, 3 August 1987, p. 20.
35. "Professional Journals Urge U.S. Doctors and Lawyers to Help the Poor More," *San Francisco Chronicle*, 4 December 1987.

Chapter 10 — Restoring Righteousness

1. Terry Muck, "AIDS in Your Church," *Christianity Today*, 5 February 1988, p. 12.
2. *The Press Democrat*, 3 June 1987.
3. *Newsweek*, 24 November 1986.
4. Ibid.
5. *San Jose Mercury News*, 13 June 1986.
6. *Newsweek*, 12 August 1985.
7. "AIDS: At the Dawn of Fear," *U.S. News & World Report*, 12 January 1987.
8. Ibid.
9. *Newsweek*, 24 November 1986.
10. *U.S. News & World Report*, 12 January 1987.
11. *New York Times*, 7 June 1987.

12. *Christianity Today*, p. 13.
13. *The Press Democrat*, 7 November 1987.
14. Robin Meuller, "AIDS: New Frontier for Christian Ministry," *Lutheran Witness*, April 1986.
15. *Christianity Today*, p. 12.
16. *Christianity Today*, p. 12.
17. *Orange County Register*, 28 December 1987.
18. Cizik, p. 17.
19. Cizik, p. 65.
20. Harold O. J. Brown, *Death Before Birth* (Nashville: Thomas Nelson Publishers, 1977), pp. 99-100.
21. Cizik, 57.
22. Ibid., p. 56.
23. Herbert Schlossberg and Marvin Olasky, *Turning Point* (Westchester, Illinois: Crossway Books, 1987), pp. 128-129.
24. Brown, 104.
25. "Pornography and It's Effects on Family, Community, and Culture," Child and Family Protection Institute, 4:2, March 1985, p. 10.
26. Ibid.
27. Ibid.
28. Ibid., p. 9.
29. Ibid.
30. Ibid., p. 13.
31. Ibid., p. 14.
32. President's Commission on Pornography
33. Ibid.
34. From a telephone conversation with the Sonoma County Sheriff's Office.
35. *Christianity Today*, 6 November 1987, p. 46.
36. Cizik, pp. 137-138.

Chapter 11—Defending Our Nation

1. From Keith B. Payne and Karl I. Payne, *A Just Defense* (Portland, Oregon: Multnomah Press, 1987) pp. 32-33.
2. Ibid., pp. 45-46.
3. Francis Schaeffer, Vladimir Bukovsky, James Hitchcock, *Who Is for Peace?* (Nashville: Thomas Nelson Publishers, 1983), p. 71.
4. Ibid., p. 48.
5. Ibid., p. 50.
6. Ibid., pp. 75-76.
7. Ibid., pp. 78-79.
8. Ibid., p. 79.
9. The Lausanne Covenant, Resolution No. 5, International Congress on World Evangelization.
10. Schaeffer, p. 78.
11. Ibid., pp. 873-874.
12. "Religion Under the Sandinista Gun," *Insight*, 13 January 1986, p. 30.
13. "Brutality Leads Latinos to Rebuild Lives Elsewhere," *Insight*, 28 April 1986, p. 6.
14. "Persecution of Christian Groups in Nicaragua," *White House Digest*, a service of the White House Office of Media Relations and Planning, 29 February 1984.
15. Ibid.

16. "Cold Winter Ahead for Christians in Romania," *The Voice of Trust*, The Romanian Missionary Society, November/December 1985, p. 1.
17. Ibid., p. 2.
18. "Most Urgent Religious Rights Violation in the Socialist Republic of Romania," *Response*, Christian Response International, 13 February 1986, p. 2.
19. "Called to Declare Liberty," *Response*, Christian Response International, September/October 1985, p. 4.
20. The Lausanne Covenant, Resolution No. 13, International Congress on World Evangelization.
21. Henry, p. 101.
22. The Lausanne Covenant, Resolution No. 13, International Congress on World Evangelization.

Chapter 12 — New Vision Demands New Leaders

1. Robert A. Nisbet, *The History of the Ideas of Progress*.
2. Louis Harris, p. 260.
3. Allan Brownfeld, "They Just Don't Make Heroes Like They Used To," *The Washington Times*, 13 October 1987, p. F3.
4. Robert J. Samuelson, "The Politics of Obscurity," *Newsweek*, 30 November 1987, p. 56.
5. Henry, pp. 20-21.
6. Ibid., p. 18.
7. From an endorsement statement for Leadership '88 Conference in Washington, D.C.
8. Harris, p. 270.
9. *The Press Democrat*, 4 October 1987, p. 11.
10. Harris, pp. 260-261.
11. Ibid., p. 38.
12. Barker, p. 1630.
13. *Discipleship Journal*, Issue 41, 1987, p. 20.
14. Hudson Armerding, *Leadership* (Wheaton, Illinois: Tyndale House Publishers, 1978), p. 102.
15. Stott, p. 250.
16. Foster, pp. 224-225.
17. Fromke, p. 143.
18. *Lifechangers Newsletter*, July, 1987, p. 3.
19. Tamar Jacoby, *Newsweek*, 14 September 1987, p. 40.

Chapter 13 — How Do We Begin?

1. Bill Barol, "The Eighties Are Over," *Newsweek*, 4 January 1988, pp. 40-41.
2. "It's Time for Nations to Behave Like Adults," *U.S. News & World Report*, 28 December 1987/4 January 1988, p. 22.
3. Carl F. H. Henry, *The Uneasy Conscience of Modern Fundamentalism* (1947).
4. Armerding, p. 30.
5. Ibid., p. 42.
6. Ibid., p. 43.
7. Francis A. Schaeffer, speech given to STEP Foundation (Strategies to Elevate People) at Dallas, Texas, 24 September 1982, pp. 9-10.

8. Francis A. Schaeffer, *True Spirituality* (Wheaton, Illinois: Tyndale House Publishers, 1971), pp. 71-72.
9. Bob Mumford, *In the Face of Temptation* (Altamonte Springs, Florida: Creation House, 1987), p. 112.
10. Ibid., pp. 24-25.
11. Ibid., p. 26.
12. Derek Prince, *Shaping History Through Prayer and Fasting* (Old Tappan, New Jersey: Fleming H. Revell, 1973), p. 139.
13. Ibid.
14. Ibid., pp. 141-142.
15. Ibid., p. 142.
16. Ibid., pp. 6-7.
17. Stott, pp. 262-263.

SELECTED BIBLIOGRAPHY

Barron, John. *The KGB Today: The Hidden Hand*. New York: Readers Digest Press, 1983.

Barrs, Jerram. *Who Are the Peacemakers?* Westchester, Illinois: Crossway Books, 1984.

Belli, Humberto. *Breaking Faith*. Westchester, Illinois: Crossway Books, 1985.

Brennan, William. *The Abortion Holocaust: Today's Final Solution*. St. Louis: Landmark Press, 1983.

Brookes, Warren T. *The Economy in Mind*. New York: Universe Books, 1982.

Brown, Harold O. J. *Death Before Birth*. Nashville, TN: Thomas Nelson Publishers, 1977.

Cizik, Richard., ed. *The High Cost of Indifference*. Ventura, CA: Regal Books, 1984.

Davis, John Jefferson. *Evangelical Ethics: Issues Facing the Church Today*. Phillipsburg, New Jersey: Presbyterian and Reformed Publishing Company, 1985.

d'Encausee, Helen. *Confiscated Power: How the Soviet Union Really Works*. New York: Harper & Row.

Eidsmoe, John. *God & Caesar*. Westchester, Illinois: Crossway Books, 1984.

Grant, George. *Bringing in the Sheaves*. Atlanta, Georgia: American Vision Press, 1985.

_____. *Grand Illusions: The Legacy of Planned Parenthood*. Brentwood, Tennessee: Wolgemuth & Hyatt, 1988.

_____. *The Dispossessed: Homelessness in America*. Westchester, Illinois: Crossway Books, 1986.

Henry, Carl F. H. *Christian Countermoves in a Decadent Culture*. Portland, Oregon: Multnomah Press, 1986.

——————. *Christian Mindset in a Secular Society*. Portland, Oregon: Multnomah Press, 1984.

Hoffecker, W. Andrew, ed. *Building a Christian Workview*. Phillipsburg, New Jersey: Presbyterian & Reformed Publishing Company, 1986.

Koop, C. Everett and Francis A. Schaeffer. *Whatever Happened to the Human Race*. Westchester, Illinois: Crossway Books, 1979, 1983.

LaHaye, Tim. *Faith of Our Founding Fathers*. Brentwood, Tennessee: Wolgemuth & Hyatt, 1987.

Mother Teresa, Francis A. Schaeffer, Malcolm Muggeridge, John R. W. Stott. *Who Is for Life?* Westchester, Illinois: Crossway Books, 1985.

Murray, Charles. *Losing Ground*. New York: Basic Books, 1984.

Novak, Michael. *Moral Clarity in the Nuclear Age*. Nashville: Thomas Nelson Publishers, 1983.

——————. *The Spirit of Democratic Capitalism*. New York: Simon & Schuster, 1982.

Packer, J. I. *Christianity: the True Humanism*. Waco, Texas: Word Books, 1985.

Payne, Karl and Keith Payne. *A Just Defense: The Use of Force, Nuclear Weapons and Our Conscience*. Portland: Multnomah Press, 1987.

Payne, Leanne. *The Healing of the Homosexual*. Westchester, Illinois: Crossway Books.

Peacocke, Dennis T. *Winning the Battle for the Minds of Men*. Santa Rosa, California: Alive & Free, 1987.

Perkins, John. *Let Justice Roll Down*. Ventura, California: Regal Books, 1976.

——————. *With Justice for All*. Ventura, California: Regal Books, 1980.

Schaeffer, Francis A. *The Great Evangelical Disaster*. Westchester, Illinois: Crossway Books, 1984.

——————. *A Christian Manifesto*. Westchester, Illinois: Crossway Books, 1981.

——————. *How Should We Then Live?* Old Tappan, New Jersey: Fleming H. Revell, 1976.

Schaeffer, Francis; Bukovsky, Vladimir; Hitchcock, James. *Who Is for Peace?* Nashville: Thomas Nelson Publishers, 1983.

Schaeffer, Franky. *Bad News for Modern Man.* Westchester, Illinois: Crossway Books, 1984.

Scheidler, Joseph. *Closed: 99 Ways to Stop Abortion.* Westchester, Illinois: Crossway Books, 1985.

Schlossberg, Herbert. *Idols for Destruction.* Nashville: Thomas Nelson Publishers, 1983.

Shevchenko, A. N. *Breaking with Moscow.* New York: Ballantine Books, 1985.

Shifrin, Avraham. *The First Guidebook to Prisons and Concentration Camps of the Soviet Union.* New York: Bantam Books, 1980.

Simons, Julian. *The Ultimate Resource.* Princeton: Princeton University Press.

Solzhenitsyn, Aleksandr I. *The Gulag Archipelago.* New York: Harper & Row, 1973.

Sproul, R. C. *Ethics and the Christian.* Wheaton, Illinois: Tyndale House, 1986.

_____. *Lifeviews.* (Old Tappan, New Jersey: Fleming H. Revell, 1985).

Valladares, Armando. *Against All Hope.* New York: Ballantine Books, 1986.

Walton, Rus. *Biblical Solutions to Contemporary Problems: A Handbook.* Brentwood, TN: Wolgemuth & Hyatt, Publishers, 1988.

Whitehead, John W., ed. *Arresting Abortion: Practical Ways to Save Unborn Children.* Westchester, Illinois: Crossway Books, 1985.

Whitehead, John W. *The End of Man.* Westchester, Illinois: Crossway Books, 1986.

_____. *The Second American Revolution.* Elgin, Illinois: David C. Cook Publishing Co., 1982.

_____. *The Stealing of America.* Westchester, Illinois: Crossway Books, 1983.

COLOPHON

The typeface for the text of this book is *Baskerville*. Its creator, John Baskerville (1706-1775), broke with tradition to reflect in his type the rounder, yet more sharply cut lettering of eighteenth-century stone inscriptions and copy books. The type foreshadows modern design in such novel characteristics as the increase in contrast between thick and thin strokes and the shifting of stress from the diagonal to the vertical strokes. Realizing that this new style of letter would be most effective if cleanly printed on smooth paper with genuinely black ink, he built his own presses, developed a method of hot-pressing the printed sheet to a smooth, glossy finish, and experimented with special inks. However, Baskerville did not enter into general commercial use in England until 1923.

Substantive editing by George Grant
Copy editing by Steve Hines
Cover design by Kent Puckett Associates, Atlanta, Georgia
Typography by Thoburn Press, Tyler, Texas
Printed and bound by Maple-Vail Book Manufacturing Group
Manchester, Pennsylvania
Cover Printing by Weber Graphics, Chicago, Illinois